The Complete Leader's Guide to Christian Retreats

RACHEL GILMORE

VALLEY FORGE, PA

Library of Congress Cataloging-in-Publication Data
Gilmore, Rachel.
The complete leader's guide to Christian retreats / Rachel Gilmore.—1st ed.
p. cm.
ISBN 978-0-8170-1546-6 (pbk. : alk. paper) 1. Spiritual retreats. 2. Church work. I. Title.
BV5068.R4G55 2009
269'.6—dc22

2008038477

Printed on recycled paper in the U.S.A.

First Edition, 2009.

Contents

Foreword

Do you long for more community in your life, in your church, in your—well, community? You hold in your hands the only book of its kind I've ever seen: everything you need to pull people out of their same-old, same-old ruts and move them into exciting new relationships. With themselves, one another, and God. Get ready for an adventure.

I came to this manuscript with a history of retreats. Before I began speaking at retreats professionally over the last decade, I remember being isolated in a small church in rural Illinois and hungering for opportunities to be with women in a deeply spiritual setting. I remember the loneliness, longing to grow in my relationship with God and praying for community.

But I also remember feeling overwhelmed with my life, with logistics in my own life, and with not having the faintest idea how to pull together a retreat myself.

Holding the manuscript in my hands for Rachel's book, *The Complete Leader's Guide to Christian Retreats,* I wanted to jump up and down. Here is the tool I longed for as a young pastor's wife, as a fledging in ministry, as someone who wanted to help create community and opportunities for spiritual growth, but without the expertise or time or energy or resources to build it from scratch.

The Complete Leader's Guide gets a huge "welcome!" from me. It contains every single item necessary to start from the ground up and build your own retreat, whether for a group or for your own personal getaway. I've never seen a resource more complete and more versatile, with the basic building blocks to begin right where you are today.

Rachel's own life-changing experiences at retreats, her continued commitment to creating retreat opportunities for a variety of groups, and her depth of reading and learning provide the undergirding for this book. The pullout tips are excellent eye-catchers. The resources and people cited are solid and helpful, and the entire second half of the book devoted to sample retreats made my heart pound. What a treasure, with samples for women, men, family, youth, and older adults' retreats, yet allowing plenty of room for creativity and personality within the template of each retreat. There you'll find everything you need, from the first "Hello!" to the "Ah-ha!" moments that you pray will happen.

But just wait—if it's possible to improve on excellent, you'll find it in the appendices. As a nonadministrative person who loathes coming up with all those informative pieces, I wanted to cheer when I discovered the pages and pages of reproducible forms—everything from specific handouts for each sample retreat, to the letters to retreatants, and even a form to fill out for the caregivers keeping the home fires burning. And that's just Appendix A.

Appendix B contains a state-by-state listing of retreats centers and getaways, and the specific appeals and uniquenesses of each listing. I wanted to get out my calendar and pencil in reservations. And, as someone for whom personal retreats has become a lifesaving venue—I'm convinced I'd be dead without that discovery—I am deeply grateful for Rachel's words about personal retreats.

The majority of American churches have one hundred or fewer people—people who hunger for community, for special opportunities to go deeper, though without the paid staff (or time) to create it. A savvy volunteer would be smart enough to avoid committing to coordinating a retreat, unless—unless!—that volunteer had a copy of *The Complete Leader's Guide to Christian Retreats* in hand.

Regardless of your church's size or the number of people on staff, this is a book for the masses, for individuals, volunteers, and leaders. It will be a vital investment in your commitment to community and spiritual growth, both personally and in your church.

The Complete Leader's Guide to Christian Retreats is a generous offering of creativity, experience, help, and possibility to our churches and groups today. It is a must-have for every library and every leader in our churches.

Expect connection. Expect transformation. Expect to meet God, yourself, and others in new ways.

Jane Rubietta
Speaker and author of *Resting Place: A Personal Guide to Spiritual Retreats*
www.JaneRubietta.com

Acknowledgments

Here's to a little R & R! Thank you to Presbyterian Camps at Saugatuck where I learned to retreat, to my First Pres Homewood family whose retreats planted the seed for this book twenty-five years ago, to my fellow MomsLINKers who saw those seeds take root, to my New Life Church family who walked with me through the final growth of this book, to Jane Rubietta who believed in *The Complete Leader's Guide to Christian Retreats* from its beginning, and to my family—Dave, Alex, Kai, Max, Mom, Dad, Bonnie, John, Erik, and Kate. Without your support, I never would have been able to share this book with others. God is good, all the time!

INTRODUCTION

In the Beginning . . .

The human mind plans the way, but the Lord *directs the steps.*
—Proverbs 16:9

Soon after I received word in April 2008 that Judson Press was going to publish this retreat planning guide, I attended a Highlights Foundation writing workshop in northeastern Pennsylvania. I was hesitant to travel, since I knew that I had a rapidly approaching editorial deadline and much work needed to be done. However, my plans had been set—and paid for—for several months, so I decided to go. Now, I'd never been to northeastern Pennsylvania, and I'd never not driven myself to a conference. I could feel the panic rising as our driver took us deeper and deeper into the hills along winding country roads. I'm a map person, and there was no map to be had. By the time we got to the farm where our workshop would be held, I was not a happy camper, the idyllic surroundings a sharp contrast to my anxious mood.

Our driver showed us the farmhouse where we'd have our meals and sessions and then deposited us at the back of the property where we hiked up a little gravel road to our individual cabins. "And by the way," she called as she drove away, "there's no cell phone or Internet service here. We're too far out. There is a landline phone at the house, but you have to use a calling card."

A what? I thought to myself, the tears welling up in my eyes. *I haven't had a calling card since the early '90s, and I didn't call home yet because I wanted to get where I was going. Now I'm out here in the middle of nowhere. I can't call my family, and I don't even know where here is. I want to go home!*

And then it hit me: I was days away from diving in wholeheartedly to what would be an incredibly demanding project—delivering *The Complete Leader's Guide to Christian Retreats* on time. What had God just given me? Four days away from the world to renew and refresh, to rest, to reconnect with God and give thanks for this gift of writing he's blessed me with. Once I remembered who was in control, my attitude did a 180, and those four days were some of the most productive, most spiritually connected days of my life.

That retreat gave me the strength and the courage and renewed faithfulness to bring *The Complete Leader's Guide to Christian Retreats* to you. It is truly a labor of love that has been in the works for many years, with God adding time and space for more life experiences to bring the book to its full potential. Very exciting to me are the "Need to Know" tips from retreat and camp professionals around the country that evolved in this final draft. Being able to talk with these people and share their wisdom is an incredible blessing, and I thank them for their time. Equally exciting to me are the book's companion website and blog, www.completeretreat-guide.com, where readers can ask questions, post personal recommendations for locations and themes, find additional resources, and more.

This book is designed to encourage you to embrace the retreat experience, which has meant so much to me in my faith journey. That said, please use this guide to plan a retreat that will best meet the needs of your group. If you don't think a particular activity will work, substitute your own. If my idea gives birth to one of your own, all the better. Please ask God to guide your planning process as he has guided mine.

Do not be conformed to this world, but be transformed by the renewing of your minds, so that you may discern what is the will of God—what is good and acceptable and perfect. (Romans 12:2)

PART 1

Planning for Spiritual R & R

CHAPTER 1

It's Time to Get Away

What Is a Retreat?

During high school my youth group would go every fall to a camp that sat high on a dune above Lake Michigan. By October the air was crisp and full of the scent of burning leaves; the lake choppy and layered in shades of blue and gray, heralding the change of seasons. The weekend held the promise of all-night girl gab sessions, midnight hikes up the dunes, and intense small group discussions. I couldn't get my sleeping bag in the van fast enough.

Yet aside from being with all my friends and spending a weekend away from "the parents," Presbyterian Camps at Saugatuck was where I first learned what it meant to retreat. I learned about looking inside myself, about taking time away from the drama of my daily high school life to get to know more about me and my place in God's world. I learned about friendships, including how to build them and what destroys them. I learned how to see others' gifts and talents and help them understand what they had to share. Yet as much as these retreats were about growth and exploration of relationships, earthly and divine, retreat was mostly about coming home, about getting comfortable with the self God created me to be.

So the first step in planning a retreat is to make sure everyone involved understands the purpose. A retreat is a going-away time, an opportunity to take a little time for yourself. It's a time to renew and refresh your mind, body, and spirit. More specifically, a retreat is designed to model God's concept of Sabbath. God created the world and included time to rest, but the busyness in our lives has pushed us far away from that divine gift of R & R. The added bonus of a group retreat, however, is that it strengthens the sense of Christian community. Friendships formed on retreat can carry people through the bumpy parts of life when they return home. A well-planned retreat allows opportunities for personal growth, as well as person-to-person growth, in one's faith journey.

A well-planned retreat also takes into account the different ages and stages of retreat-goers. It allows for all participants to express themselves and share opinions in an emotionally safe setting, and it provides reassurance to those who only wish to listen and observe. A well-planned retreat does not pressure people into doing something or discussing something that they are not comfortable with. A gentle nudge to encourage risk-taking is fine; a shove over the edge is not. When people return home, they should feel hopeful, encouraged, rejuvenated, energized, joy-filled, and purposeful. Above all, they should feel reconciled to God, having given to God all of the burdens they have been hauling around and having given themselves time to be renewed and refreshed to continue their faith journeys.

Who Goes on Retreat?

Anyone can go on retreat. There are no special qualifications, no absolute prerequisites. The simple truth is, women tend to be joiners, so they may be the most common small group to be involved. However, women are not the only ones who can benefit from a retreat. Typically, a church is home to many small groups, and these flow quite naturally into a retreat experience. Men's groups, youth groups, family groups, whole church intergenerational groups, older adult groups—all can enjoy a little R & R on retreat.

Nor are participants limited by age. Mixed age groups provide opportunities for mentoring and sharing of life experience, which can be a real blessing for younger retreat-goers and affirming for older ones. However, heterogeneous age groups can broaden individual horizons and lead to new or deeper peer friendships.

The same is true for common interests. Small groups wanting to plan a retreat will most likely have at least one thing in common by virtue of being in that particular small group. However, one of the most rewarding things about a retreat is finding out what you have in common with people you perhaps only knew on a surface level. I remember one women's retreat I participated in where I learned that lesson well. Throughout the weekend discussions, I discovered that a woman whom I had always found to be pushy, abrasive, and difficult to like actually had many of the same personality traits as me. What a revelation that was, and it certainly made me rethink my opinions of her! Equally intriguing is seeing different sides to people when they are out of their comfort zones and put in a retreat setting. A well-planned retreat opens up possibilities for personal growth and person-to-person growth as participants move closer to the Lord.

A word about personal retreats: While this book mainly focuses on group retreats, personal retreats are an option for those who need quiet time away to individually reconnect with God more than they need to connect with others. The how-to planning information that follows can be utilized for personal retreats but will need to be greatly scaled back. For more specific suggestions on how to plan a personal retreat, see chapter 18.

Need to Know Tip

"The key component in a personal retreat is rest. It's not about doing things in the right way; it's about unwinding and decompressing and catching our breath. God often whispers."

Brenda Jank, Director of Personal Retreat Ministries, Camp Lutherhaven, Albion, Indiana

---

Where Can You Have a Retreat?

The plans in this book are for retreats held outside your church setting. These plans can, however, be adapted to your church setting. Appendix B provides a list of camp and conference centers that are open to do-it-yourself retreats. Recommendations from your own group members are also great places to start. Hotels, spas, and bed and breakfasts are options to explore, too. Finding your perfect location will depend mainly on how far you want to travel, how much you want to pay, and how large or small your group is. A little phone work and a site visit or two will ensure that your group's accommodations meet your needs for the weekend.

Need to Know Tip

"Your personal retreat location should match your personality and spirituality. If you're not the rustic type, don't be afraid to book a room in your favorite hotel. If you need to get back to nature, then by all means look for a retreat center in the woods. Think about where the best setting is for you to connect with God."

Jane Rubietta, author and veteran retreat speaker

When Do You Go on Retreat?

Because of work and family schedules, it is generally easiest to plan a retreat for a weekend, leaving on Friday evening and returning Sunday. For groups new to the retreat experience, however, a Saturday–Sunday overnight may work well the first time around. Some retreats are as short as a few hours, while others may take place over an entire week.

Groups will also need to take into account the seasonal nature of camp and conference centers. Many run a residential camp program, making a summer reservation next to impossible. Fall and spring are also popular times for church and school groups to book retreats, so you might have trouble finding availability. The more flexible your group can be in picking a date and the sooner you start this process, the more options you'll have.

Interestingly, winter is often a good time for a retreat. Not only does it provide for a much-needed recharging after the holidays, but it is often a slow time for camp and conference centers, depending on geographic location. Your group may even be able to take advantage of lower rates during off-season times. Often because of the financial and time commitments required, a retreat is simply an annual event. If your group can go more than once a year, praise God!

Why Do God's People Need a Retreat?

Quite frankly, God's people need to go on retreat because we're over the edge most of the time—overscheduled, overcommitted, overtired, overworked, overworried, overemotional, over budget—over and over and over again. A retreat helps break that pattern of routinely going over the edge. It inserts a time-out, a Sabbath rest, in the middle of our fast-paced, sensory overloaded, modern lives.

I've often thought that pioneer folk, although their work was hard and sometimes unpleasant, had it easy with their well-defined roles and limits. Contemporary society, however, has encouraged us all to multitask with no end in sight. Regardless of gender or age, we are expected to do it all and be it all. Not that multitasking is all that bad. Certainly, it's a way to cope with our twenty-first-century lifestyles. Yet a retreat is designed to help individuals let go of the expectations and the pressures of everyday life and take a step back. For forty-eight hours, someone else will cook and clean for you. The only person you have to worry about is yourself. The only schedule you have is the prearranged retreat schedule, and if you don't make it to a session, you won't lose your job or be locked up for child abandonment or be sent to the principal's office (although youth leaders usually do require session attendance for their youth, and with good reason). A retreat is a little blip in the time-space continuum that helps you get right and stay right with God.

How Can My Group Hold Its Own Retreat?

Holding a retreat for your group is easy when you follow the step-by-step planning instructions in this guide. Your group will form a Retreat Leadership Team (RLT) to organize your event. You will work together on one task at a time to create a transformational weekend for you and your group. With user-friendly directions, you can harness the creative abilities of your group members and write your own discussion questions and activities. However, sample retreat plans are included if you get to feeling overwhelmed or just need a jumpstart. And don't worry, if your group would like to try something new or just doesn't feel comfortable taking on facilitation/speaker roles, there are many wonderful, experienced Christian speakers who would love to come and share their stories with your group (see chapter 3, page 16).

God's people have developed an incredible tolerance for the "overs" previously mentioned. With a change in perspective, you can channel that tolerance into productive energy for planning a retreat. No doubt your group will quickly learn the postretreat chant that starts as soon as you pull out of the retreat center parking lot: "Only 364 days to go! Only 364 days to go!"

CHAPTER 2

The Master R & R Plan

Forming a Retreat Leadership Team (RLT)

The first year I organized a retreat for my moms group, MomsLINK, I did a lot of delegating. No one attending had ever been on a retreat before and therefore had no idea what to expect. The RLT consisted of the current group president, another officer, and an interested group member, in addition to me. I did a lot of explaining and showing examples of activities from other retreats I'd led. Together we did a lot of brainstorming. Then the women took on tasks they felt comfortable organizing. One woman planned a mixer. Another created discussion questions for a film clip. The third planned our group craft. I handled the rest of the overall organization and session planning. The result was a wonderful retreat that left women renewed and refreshed.

In forming your RLT, you should keep a few things in mind. First, your team size will vary depending on your group size and needs. In general, use a minimum of three for a small (eight- to twelve-person) retreat and eight to ten for larger (fifty-person and up) retreats, and be sure to include youth on your planning team if you are organizing a youth or intergenerational retreat. Second, your planners should also be committed to attending the retreat because they will have some on-site responsibilities. In addition, these leaders need positive attitudes and a willingness to cooperate and work together, especially during the first year's planning process. (Note: You may need to pull in additional volunteers to handle specific tasks, such as facilitating a discussion group, storytelling, or leading worship. Do what makes sense for your group.)

Need to Know Tip

"You need an army of guys who all have a role: emcee, work with the facility staff, plan recreation, lead music. The more ownership people have the better. It is not possible to do this on your own. You have a much better chance of making a real impact if you have a strong core team."

Rod Handley, Founder and President, Character That Counts

In general, your planning will begin eight to twelve months before the event, and the RLT should anticipate meeting three to four times during the first few months to secure the site reservation and begin initial planning. Depending on how far in advance you have started, your RLT will likely have a break for several months when no action is needed. Then approximately six months before your retreat, the RLT will need to meet fairly regularly for several weeks to finalize the theme, prepare the registration brochure, decide on publicity, and brainstorm session activities.

Once the registration brochure (see this book's companion blog www.completeretreatguide.com for samples) is out, the RLT will probably meet once a month to continue planning and to organize the registrations. Approximately two weeks prior to departure, the RLT will meet to finalize numbers, give a final count to the conference center (unless required before this date), prepare a master retreat to-do list, assign carpools and housing, and divide up any remaining tasks and/or decide on the on-site responsibilities for RLT members.

Finally, your RLT should have a built-in mentoring mechanism so that the team never starts over with all brand-new members. Think about creating two- and three-year positions that will always allow for experienced RLT members to show the ropes to newcomers. To help you gather potential planners, include a question about serving on the RLT on your evaluation form (see Appendix A, p. 110).

Need to Know Tip

"It starts with leadership. It's paramount to create a spirit of unity on the leadership team so that it's not about one person's agendas or ideas or self-esteem. The question leadership needs to be asking is 'What does the Lord want for and from our group?'"

Jane Rubietta, author and veteran retreat speaker

Choosing a Site and Securing Your Reservation

Site selection is key to a well-planned retreat. With your team, make a list of the priorities you have for your housing and meeting space (see chapter 4 and Appendix B). One other important factor is the physical surroundings of the retreat center. Most camp and conference centers make full use of their natural surroundings, which enhance a participant's experience. Some centers have densely wooded grounds. Others are on a lake or have a stream or river running through them. Still others may be set in rural farmland or in the mountains. And some will be in urban or suburban neighborhoods.

Your RLT will need to take into account whether your group will want to or be able to take advantage of outdoor recreation opportunities. Maybe your retreat will be in January in Ohio, so being outside is only a priority if you're counting on snow. Or maybe your small group is your church quilting group, and all free time will be spent indoors working on projects, so weather and surroundings aren't as important. Plan accordingly.

The terrain may be a factor for your group, as well. One camp I have used extensively in Michigan is built on a gorgeous sand dune. While there are boardwalks in place throughout most of the camp, it is not totally handicapped accessible and would be challenging for someone with impaired mobility (although the camp continues to make accessibility improvements). If your group has anyone with special needs, your RLT should be sure to discuss those needs with the conference center manager to make sure every member of the group will be reasonably accommodated by the facilities. If not, you may need to consider another site.

After making a list of your priorities, your RLT should begin the site search process. You can start with the centers listed in this guide (see Appendix B). Or use the personal recommendations of group members who are familiar with camp and conference centers in your area. Make a list of sites that sound appealing and assign a team member the task of calling to see if your chosen date is available. You may want to have an alternate weekend or two just in case. If no one in your group has used your chosen facility, your RLT should designate at least two people to do a site visit before you make a nonrefundable deposit, which will most likely be the next step in your reservation process.

Pricing Your Retreat

When your RLT confirms a date with your chosen retreat center, the center should send out a contract confirming the date, specifying any special rules or policies, and listing the price for the weekend, including all meals, lodging, and special services. This should be broken down per person by the facility. The contract will also state the deposit required to hold your reservation. The amount will vary from center to center, so make sure you understand what is required of your group up front. To cover this amount, your group could do several things:

- If your group has a budget and money available, vote to approve that the deposit funds come from group money. You can then either reimburse the account when all retreat registrations are paid, or your group can subsidize the retreat cost by covering the initial deposit.

- Hold a special fund-raiser to cover the deposit cost or designate funds raised from an upcoming fund-raiser as reimbursement to the group account for the retreat deposit.
- If you're working six to twelve months ahead of time, ask all those who think they might be interested in attending the retreat to help secure the reservation by sending in a deposit. These initial personal deposits will guarantee them a space at the retreat. Most likely you will be able to refund the deposit if someone is unable to attend later on. (However, this will depend on the guaranteed minimum rules of the conference center you choose. Read your contract thoroughly!) The amount you require up front should be deducted from the total retreat cost once the registration brochure comes out.

Unless your group has a budget that is subsidizing your retreat, your RLT will need to use the camp costs as the minimum price. The RLT may also want to add in money to be distributed to those who drive the carpools, money to be spent on craft or session supplies, and money to be spent on hospitality kits (see chapter 5). Your RLT may decide, too, to set a price that specifies optional items, such as a craft or meals on the road. If you are hiring an outside speaker, you will need to factor in that additional expense, as well, which could be anywhere from $300 to $3,000. Keep in mind that for some individuals $100 or more for a weekend away is not a big expense; for others this amount can be overwhelming. To keep costs reasonable, google the word fund-raiser and you will get more prepackaged options than you can imagine. For those entrepreneurial spirits, your group might try a mass garage sale at a single location to which everyone contributes items and all profits go toward retreat costs, or try a rent-a-hand day during which members go out and do yard work or other household projects for a donation to the retreat fund. When I was a youth, our youth group held an annual Super Bowl sub sandwich sale in January to pay for our spring retreat (a tradition that is still in place today!).

Need to Know Tip

"If there's a financial circumstance that prevents men from coming, everyone's invited to contribute what they can, and we scholarship the rest. Men who are blessed and are able to contribute to the scholarship fund do that."

Dale Garwood, servant, Granger Community Church, Granger, Indiana

Publicizing Your Retreat

Your group size will determine the amount of publicity you need to do. If you are a single small group that has already been discussing going on retreat, simply distributing a preliminary interest flyer and requesting initial personal deposits before finalizing a reservation should be sufficient. However, if your group is larger or if you will be opening up the retreat to nonmembers, you will want to put publicity items in your church bulletin or newsletter and/or get the information on your website as soon as you have a date and location. The retreat brochure should be distributed three months prior to the event. If you have a web team that can set up online registration for you, even better!

Above all, your RLT needs to set the example in being inclusive. Host a sign-up table at church and encourage both people whose names you know and those you don't to sign up for the retreat. This invitation demonstrates the spiritual gift of hospitality and will let everyone know that all are welcome, not just a select few. Making a personal phone call to all potential retreat participants is another great outreach tool to make individuals feel included.

Need to Know Tip #6

"Having your senior leader be an active promoter, supporter, encourager of the retreat, that's key. Maybe the pastor is only there for a portion of the retreat, not necessarily on the platform, just being in jeans, hanging out. It can further help the event to be successful."

Dale Garwood, servant, Granger Community Church, Granger, Indiana

Retreat Planning Timeline

Your RLT should use the following timeline as a guide for your group. If you're starting with less than a year to plan, adjust accordingly.

Twelve months ahead

- Assemble a Retreat Leadership Team.
- Recruit a prayer team to pray for the RLT and the retreat and its participants.
- Determine priorities for retreat center amenities.
- Select preferred date and one or two alternates.
- Assign an RLT member the task of contacting retreat centers to check availability and offerings.
- Get price quotes and availability.
- Schedule site visit.
- Determine how your group will cover the initial deposit required by the center.
- Create a list of fund-raiser ideas if needed.
- Create initial publicity flyer with retreat date, approximate cost, and other basic information; request personal deposits if needed.
- Collect initial personal deposits if needed.
- Sign a contract and return it to the retreat center with deposit funds.
- Assign the RLT the task of thinking about possible retreat themes, activities, crafts, and service projects.
- If using an outside speaker, verify that she or he has your weekend available. Then review and sign the speaker's contract and return with a deposit.

Six months ahead

- Hold an RLT meeting to brainstorm retreat themes. (See chapter 3)
- Select a theme.
- Begin brainstorming session activities and crafts.
- Prepare a tentative retreat schedule (see sample retreats, chapters 8–17).
- Set the inclusive price and know what your optional additional costs may be.
- Assign one RLT member to create the retreat brochure.
- Assign other RLT members particular pieces to work on (specific sessions, the craft, mailing labels, etc.).
- Hold fund-raiser if still needed.
- Assign one RLT member as the registrar.

Five months ahead

- Have the RLT meet to proofread the brochure copy.
- Double-check that the brochure includes the date, the price, any possible optional costs, the retreat center contact info, the actual registration form, the deposit amount and due date, the final payment amount and due date, and where to turn in the form. It is also helpful to include your theme, a tentative schedule, general information about the purpose of the retreat and/or your chosen location, along with a request for carpool drivers. Now is the time to make potential participants aware of any aspects they may find upsetting, such as bunk beds or shared bathrooms.
- Assign one RLT member the task of copying the brochure and distributing it by a set date.
- Discuss the progress team members have made with their assigned tasks, such as session development or craft planning.
- Check the contract to see if any additional deposit money is required before the final payment.

Three months ahead

- Distribute registration brochure.
- The registrar should keep a record of who turned in a form, how much money was given, and whether it was a check or cash.
- Turn in monies to treasurer if applicable.
- Create a potential participants list and divide it among RLT members so that they can issue personal invitations.

Two months ahead

- Finalize session plans, including discussion questions and supplies needed.
- Assign one RLT member to lead each session or activity on retreat—this person should also collect the materials necessary to do the session.
- Assign one RLT member to call the retreat center to confirm arrangements for any audio-visual equipment or meeting supplies, such as white boards or flipcharts and to confirm the meeting space specifics (size, number of tables and chairs, working fireplace, AV equipment in place, etc.).
- Continue collecting registrations and money.
- Assign one RLT member to call any individuals who gave initial deposits but have not yet turned in a registration form.
- Begin looking at transportation—who will drive, whether you will caravan or leave at various times, how riders will connect with their drivers.

- Brainstorm ideas for hospitality kits. Will each RLT member donate from his or her household stash a gift bag, a roll of paper towel, liquid soap, and sample-size bathroom products, or do you need to assign one RLT member to purchase these things with group funds?
- Finalize any plans for retreat souvenirs and assign one RLT member to purchase any needed items.
- Assign one RLT member to create the Final Details Letter (see Appendix A, p. 109) and retreat schedule for participants. Leave blanks for carpool information to be inserted later by hand or plan to do a separate carpool information sheet. To make the participants' departuture smoother, include a copy of the kids' Daily Schedule (see Appendix A, p. 107–108).

Six weeks ahead

- Have the RLT meet to proofread the Final Details Letter and retreat schedule.
- Publicize final payment due date if needed.
- Review all session plans and activities.
- Create RLT master to-do list and supply list.
- Assign one RLT member to create the Retreat Evaluation Form (see Appendix A, p. 110).

Four weeks ahead

- Meet to proofread evaluation form.
- Assign one RLT member to copy and bring the evaluation forms and pens.
- Assign one RLT member to call any remaining participants who still have not sent in registration forms but did send in initial deposits.
- Refund any initial deposits, if you are able, to those no longer going.
- Finalize the hospitality kit contents.
- Review master retreat to-do list and supply list. Put individual RLT member names by each task or supply and make a copy for each team member.
- Close the registration process. Review registrations to identify carpool drivers and roommate preferences.
- Arrange carpools.
- Assign roommates if needed. (It generally works best not to share this information until participants arrive at the retreat center in case last-minute adjustments are needed.)
- If using an outside speaker, touch base to confirm numbers of participants, travel arrangements, special equipment needs, etc.

Three weeks ahead

- Assign one RLT member to insert the carpool information in the Final Details Letter; copy and distribute the letter.

Two weeks ahead

- Call retreat center to confirm meal and lodging counts for billing (unless your contract specified that you call before this time).
- Begin gathering and boxing any supplies you will need to take.

Four to seven days ahead

- Have the RLT meet to confirm that all supplies have been gathered and all copies made.
- Double-check master retreat to-do list and supply list, matching them against session activities and the schedule.
- Rest and relax—the fun is about to begin!

CHAPTER 3

Ready for Renewal

How to Pick Your Theme

You've decided you want to plan a retreat, and you have your Retreat Leadership Team in place. Now what? Now you hold a brainstorming session to get your theme. Set a meeting date for the RLT when you will have a solid, uninterrupted chunk of time, at least two hours. Provide some refreshments to get the creative juices flowing, and set to work. Assign one RLT member the task of writing down all ideas as they pop out. Here are some categories to consider to get you started:

- Chick flicks, macho movies, or family film favorites, old or new, that would relate to your group's interests
- TV shows, old or new, that would relate to your group's interests
- Songs (song titles and/or lyrics)
- Novels, popular nonfiction works, or possibly even children's books with themes that would relate to your group's interest
- Faith-based books or a book of the Bible that would relate to your group's interests
- Anything from popular culture (reality shows, tech-related issues, fitness/nutrition, etc.) that you could tie in to your group and its faith journey
- Life stages (single adulthood, married with children, parents of teens, empty nesters, professionals with no kids or grown kids, teens, tweens, multitasking moms who work inside and outside the home, grandparents raising grandchildren, etc.)
- Personal growth topics: faith, hope, love, peace, joy, patience, balance, wisdom
- Hobbies/interests: triathlons, gardening, ethnic cooking, mountain biking, bird-watching, journaling, scrapbooking, detective novels, the Olympics

Once you get a list of specific themes from general categories (try for five or six at a minimum), choose your top three favorites and begin playing around with them. As a group, think of possible discussion questions or activities that might naturally flow from the overall theme. The group reporter should start a new list with the themes as headings and the session/activity ideas being recorded under each one. If you can't flesh out more than one session or activity per theme, you probably want to put that one on the back burner and focus on the ones generating multiple ideas. If needed, replace it with one of your other choices or just focus on your remaining top two.

For example, let's say your group consists of forty- to sixty-year-old women who play bridge after Bible study each week. The RLT comes up with these possible themes:

- Bridge Builders (using the card game of bridge as a metaphor for a more purposeful life)
- Patience (how to be a more patient person at work and at home)
- *Terms of Endearment* and *The Evening Star* (using the relationships in the movies to talk about their own family and friend relationships)
- "Turn, Turn, Turn" ("To Everything There Is a Season") written by Pete Seeger and made famous by The Byrds (looking at the "seasons" of our lives and how we handle change)
- Gardening (from nurturing seeds to nurturing ourselves)

After some discussion, the RLT decides to throw out "Patience" and *"Terms of Endearment."* The reporter starts a new list with "Bridge Builders," "Turn, Turn, Turn," and "Gardening" as headings. The RLT begins to brainstorm session and activity ideas that might fit with these themes. They come up with the following:

Bridge Builders

- *Card Game Match-up Mixer.* This game involves two lists, one of card game names from the 1800s to modern day, the other a brief list of descriptions. Participants have to match up the name with the description. Set a time limit for answering. Then share results. The person with the most correct matches wins a small bridge favor.
- *Luck of the Draw or a Game of Skill?* Session questions focus on how participants deal with life. Do they react to everything life deals them, or do they play the game of life proactively, using experience and faith-based strategies for happiness? How does one's faith in God affect the outcome of the game?
- *Bidding to Win.* Session questions focus on things women can do to improve their mental, emotional, physical, and spiritual health.
- *Playing the Trump Card.* The session activity might be a "what if" discussion. If you won the lottery, what three things would you do with your money right away? If God blesses your life in an unexpected way, what is your response? What form might some of these victories come in?
- *Am I Vulnerable or Invulnerable?* Session questions focus on weaknesses and strengths, making an action plan for turning weaknesses into strengths, and determining how both weaknesses and strengths can be used to serve God.
- Find bridge strategy books that focus on skill development; use some of the techniques as metaphors for real-life personal growth applications.

Turn, Turn, Turn

- *Name That Tune Mixer.* Play song clips from the 1950s and '60s and have teams compete to list the most number of right answers.
- *Where Were You? Mixer.* Go around the group and have everyone share one or two things that were going on in her life in 1962 the year "Turn, Turn, Turn" came out.
- Plan sessions based on nature's seasons as a metaphor for life's seasons—questions would relate to spring (childhood), summer (young adulthood/adulthood), fall (midlife, grown kids period), winter (the "golden years"/retirement).
- Plan sessions that stem from the biblical passage in Ecclesiastes 3, from which the song lyrics are taken.
- Use movie clips that show different "seasons" or "turning points" in a woman's life (maybe bring in a clip or two here from *Terms of Endearment).*

Gardening

- *Seed Packet Mixer.* Gather a variety of seed packets and have each woman choose one that in some way represents herself and explain why.
- *A Scentimental Self Mixer.* Use Kate Greenaway's *The Language of Flowers* book to create a list of flowers with their meanings that identify personality traits. Distribute the list along with paper flower cutouts. Have women pick out traits they feel represent themselves and write them on the paper flower cutouts. Each woman can share one or two flowers from her bouquet with the group.
- Plan sessions that relate to phases of growing plants (seed, young plant, blooming plant, a dormant perennial in winter) as metaphors for our relationships with God and others.

- Plan sessions that relate to tending a garden (prepare the soil, plant the seeds, water the seeds, add fertilizer, harvest the crops) as a metaphor for our relationships with God and others.
- Find quotes, poems, or Scriptures on gardening, nature, flowers, etc., that could be used for reflection, journaling, or discussion.

You will need to keep three guidelines in mind when picking your theme and planning the sessions:

1. Unless you have one ultra-creative person on your RLT who has a passion for creating discussion sessions and activities, and the group *delegates* this task to that person, team work is the key here. Allow each person on the team to share ideas. They might not all be terrific, but new variations and expansions will flow from each contribution. The purpose of brainstorming is to get many possibilities out into the open. Don't be shy. Let everything come out. You can elaborate or toss out an idea later on in the process.
2. Theme creation is also easier when you let your mind travel back to your old language arts homework on metaphors. A metaphor, simply put, is a comparison. Your RLT will be looking for comparisons from external people, places, and things that can become models for understanding our internal spiritual lives and how they both relate to our walk with God. Another way to ask that is: How does this IMAX-size issue out in God's world relate to my small-screen TV life? The goal of the retreat sessions will be to connect a general concept or theme to your participants' personal faith journeys. The metaphor just gives you a more creative way to talk about the topic. Need help with stories and illustrations? Check out www.bible.org/illus.php for access to more than forty thousand sermon and speech illustrations.
3. Don't get uptight about "getting it right." Focus on what your group likes to do. Think about the kinds of conversations your group has when you get together. What kind of topics do you gravitate to? Do you focus on heavy issues or family stories? Let your group be your guide.

Need to Know Tip

"In a family or intergenerational retreat, there needs to be time for adults to do adult sessions apart from kids. The greater need of kids is to get out and run around and not be in a focused group setting for too long. Adult sessions can be on the retreat theme, parenting topics, or strictly adult stuff. And you need the best possible leadership for those discussions."

Karen Maurer, veteran Christian educator and family camp planner

Key Retreat Components

Now that you have a theme and a few session ideas, you will want to make sure you get the most out of your discussions. A really effective retreat includes both small group time and large group time, as well as time alone. It will provide for personal growth, as well as person-to-person growth, with the goal of helping individuals build Christian community and move closer toward God in their faith journeys.

In general, retreats should open with a large group session providing a welcome and an overview of the schedule and then moving into a large group mixer to help people relax and start interacting with one another. From there, the next session or two can start in large group format, which is less threatening for most people, with a whole group activity, maybe another mixer or game. From there the entire group might watch a movie clip or a skit or listen to a team member read and reflect on a poem or passage from the Bible or other book. After this large group time, participants might divide into groups of two to eight people for small group discussion of the general topic. To wrap up the session, participants might regroup and share discussion findings or come back to answer one more question in large group. In addition, you will want to find natural places to open and close your times together with worship and prayer. It's okay if this piece is different each day/session. Do what works best for your group.

Depending on how many total sessions your retreat will have, another option would be to end the second or third session with time for individual journaling. Or, you may choose to have an entire session devoted to journal time. The RLT can make simple journals ahead of time from 8½ by 11 paper folded in half like a book with reflective quotes and/or questions printed on the bottom of each page. The journal can be completely private or can be used as a springboard for group discussion.

When creating your sessions, the RLT should also keep in mind the overall faith-centered goals of personal growth and person-to-person growth. To achieve these, retreat sessions should also include time for **self-affirmation**—looking at oneself and thinking about one's strengths, gifts, and talents—asking, "What do I like about myself?" or "What's good about me?" or "How has God enabled me to serve?" RLT members should encourage participants to be positive and should offer suggestions if needed.

Another goal is that of **self-discovery.** Here participants will look at their lives and be asked to think about what they would like to change. The focus becomes: Where can I improve and make myself more like Christ? What can I do to bring peace, joy, and love to myself and others? What one action could I take that would transform my spiritual life? These are all questions to consider when planning your discussions as they relate to your overall theme.

Need to Know Tip

"Church cannot compete with school and the larger wow factor that's out there. The Christian sector has to figure out what they can do. The next generation is about relationships rather than 'wow me, thrill me.' Kids still hunger for relationships. Church [retreats] have to fill the need for going the distance, to make those relationships be a life choice."

Laura Vroom, Executive Director of Manitoqua Ministries, Frankfort, Illinois

---

Last of all, a well-planned retreat should encourage **risk-taking**—not in the sense of bungee jumping or betting one's 401(k) on the stock market, but in its most personal form. It involves asking participants to open up their minds enough to see their strengths and weaknesses, their positives and negatives as a person. It involves giving Christians permission to be imperfect in God's eyes and the eyes of their brothers and sisters in Christ. It's hard to be humble. It's hard to be vulnerable. But a well-planned retreat will provide opportunities to take this risk, to take that quiet time to explore God's dreams and desires for us without the noise of the world crowding in. For many people, learning to let go and dig deeper in their faith is a risk they're not comfortable taking in everyday life. A retreat should give these individuals that "what if" time, that R & R time.

Promoting the Cycle of Share-Grow-Learn

Once you have incorporated the goals of self-affirmation, self-discovery, and risk-taking into your retreat, your RLT will want to make sure your discussions follow the share-grow-learn pattern. At retreat, your RLT members will serve as facilitators of the discussion groups, to start the question and answer period and to keep the conversation flowing. As group leaders you need to keep in mind that you should be willing to share first; it makes others less nervous if they know they won't be put on the spot immediately. By sharing details about yourself, your relationship with the Lord, and how the Lord is at work in your life, you will grow a little in your knowledge of self. Also, as others in your group share, you will learn more about them, about what you have in common, about other life experiences and faith stories. The more you share, the more you grow and learn, strengthening the sense of Christian community and moving forward in your walk with God. Note that the group leader should encourage participants with gentleness and compassion to share as much as they are comfortable so that they can stretch their individual and corporate spiritual growth.

Need to Know Tip

"Initially, women are much more likely to jump into personal things. Unless someone in the group puts their toe in the water and discloses personal information, men will be slower to respond. The very opening questions should be surface level–'What's one thing that struck you in that talk?' Once guys answer that, they're willing to go deeper."

Rod Handley, President and Founder, Character That Counts

Achieving Closure

Another important dynamic in retreat is closure. Throughout your discussion sessions and activities, a crescendo of emotions, thoughts, and feelings has been building. People have been sharing bits of their lives they had tucked away in a corner of their brains or maybe never talked about before. They are making new friends or reconnecting with old ones. They are remembering what it means to take time for oneself, to have a little alone time, to renew and refresh their spirits and reconnect with God. Whether you recognize it or not, all of your sessions are leading up to the final good-bye when participants will have to return to the real world. A well-planned retreat will have an "ah ha moment" that brings closure to the weekend, something that affirms in the participants the discoveries they have made about themselves, their peers, and their faith and encourages them to keep making God-honoring choices back home. For a sense of the possibilities, browse through the Session 3 ideas and Closing Activities listed in the sample retreats in part 2.

Need to Know Tip

"One of the things I've tried to share is that camp is like a greenhouse. Conditions at camp are ideal to grow, but this is not where you are to be planted. You're intended to be planted out in the world. Conditions there are not ideal, but God wants you out there."

Calvin VerMulm, Director of Ministries, Inspiration Hills, Inwood, Iowa

Accommodating Different Learning Styles

As if you didn't think your job was big enough, another thing the RLT needs to keep in mind is that different people learn differently. What this really means for you as planners is that you want to combine a variety of techniques into your sessions and activities. Some people learn best by moving and doing, so incorporating some physical activities is helpful for them, probably even more so for youth or men's retreats. Others learn best by seeing or reading, so using handouts with directions or movie clips or skits for the basis of discussions works well. Still others learn better when they hear things, so giving directions orally is a help even when they are printed on a page. Obviously, you may not be able to integrate each strategy into every activity, and that's okay. Just keep in mind that different people learn differently and try to be as flexible as possible.

Tips for Facilitating Group Discussion

Do-it-yourself retreats are very different from speaker-led retreats in that your RLT members carry a lot more of the responsibility for programming. However, RLT members should think of themselves as facilitators who understand the retreat purpose and will do their best to help people move closer to God during the weekend.

Part of this involves being willing to read the questions and be the first to respond. Group leaders can certainly ask and encourage others to share first, but if no one volunteers, they are up to bat. It also means that they need to be fantastic listeners, restating what the speaker is saying from time to time, asking for clarification when needed, or thanking someone for sharing a difficult thought. In addition, they need to be sensitive to those who are reluctant to share. Certainly, they can encourage these individuals to speak, but they also need to patiently reassure them that it's okay if they don't want to add anything at the moment. Finally, group leaders need to be aware of the speakers who will monopolize the discussions with their stories of self or others or completely random topics. As the facilitators, they need to listen carefully and be willing to jump in with a redirection or gentle "Thank you for sharing" as needed in order to let everyone converse.

Above all else, effective group leaders will remind participants of the ground rules ahead of time—that everything said at retreat stays at retreat. They'll also review the time limits set for group discussion and periodically mention that people need to monitor themselves and not talk too long so that each group member has a chance to speak. Opening and closing each session with prayer is an easy way to set the tone for your sessions and remind people that God's presence is being intentionally recognized, honored, and appreciated. In all that you do, RLT members need to be upbeat, welcoming, encouraging, grace-filled, and God-honoring.

Need to Know Tip

"Guys need to be encouraged. Sometimes they need a kick in the back end. But it's okay. You can do that with guys. They need to be challenged."

Dale Garwood, servant, Granger Community Church, Granger, Indiana

Inviting a Speaker

Sometimes bringing in a speaker may be just the ticket for your group. This decision needs to be made at the beginning of the process, as your speaker's availability may determine your date. Fees for speakers vary widely, and your RLT will need to be aware of all costs specified in the contract, as well as all deposit and cancellation clauses. Also know that speakers may or may not be able to customize their talks to your theme. You will need to be very clear about your expectations and make sure you understand what your speaker is able to offer. However, having a speaker lead your sessions gives the RLT a bit of a breather and may be the best option for your group.

The following websites may help you jumpstart your speaker search:

Christian Speakers Services,
www.christianspeakerservices.com
American Speakers Bureau,
www.speakersbureau.com

Need to Know Tip

"Be realistic about how many times and how long you want the speaker to speak (how long can your group really sit and hear one person?). Be sensitive of the speaker's need for downtime to refuel and refocus, and communicate clearly what you are hoping for, especially if you want counseling sessions after speaking. Not all speakers are comfortable with personal follow-up."

Jane Rubietta, author and veteran retreat speaker

CHAPTER 4

A Little Cabin in the Woods . . . or Not!

Location, location, location! One of the biggest planning hurdles for your team to clear is the location of your retreat. The following are some things you will want to ask yourselves:

- How much time do we want to spend traveling?
- What lodging style will be comfortable for our participants?
- What are our meeting space requirements?
- What are our audio-visual/tech needs?
- Do we want to eat in a dining hall or do our own cooking?
- What kind of recreational amenities do we need?
- What kind of natural setting do we want?

Once you have answered these questions, you can look for a camp, conference center, or other retreat location that meets your needs. The sooner you start this process, the better, as some camps allow reservations a year ahead of time and will automatically rebook a group that returns annually. The listing in Appendix B is designed to be a starting point for your Retreat Leadership Team in finding a facility that matches your needs. Although the retreat facilities are listed by state, please note that the list is not comprehensive.

I strongly recommend that you do a personal site visit to the location you choose to make sure that it will meet your group's requirements. Arriving at camp on the day of the retreat to discover that the bathrooms are actually one common bathhouse a five-minute walk from your cabins may add a lot of unwelcome stress to your weekend.

In Appendix B, I provide very basic information for at least four camp/conference/retreat centers per state. Each entry includes the camp name and location, a phone number and website, the type of setting, and lodging style, along with a few special features. Generally speaking, I have broken down the lodging into three categories: dorm (multiple beds to a room and shared bathroom facilities), motel (one to two beds per room and private bath), and RV (a campground area with a bathhouse; you supply your own tent or camper). There are wide variations within these categories, so please be sure you check out your desired facility in person and know the type of place you are reserving—rustic, upscale, or something in between.

Where possible, I have noted locations that specifically are open to personal/individual retreats. In addition, while most facilities handle retreats year round, some close for the winter or cannot accommodate you during their residential summer camps. Also, a few facilities are geared just for adults, so make sure to check all your requirements with your chosen site.

Helpful Websites

If the list in Appendix B doesn't provide what you need, you may find the following websites helpful, as I did when preparing this material:

Denominational Listings

American Baptist Churches USA
www.nationalministries.org/education/camps_and_conferences.cfm

Episcopal Church
www.episcopalccc.org/default.htm

Evangelical Lutheran Church in America
http://archive.elca.org/camps/

Presbyterian Church USA
www.pccca.net/

Roman Catholic Church
www.catholiccity.com/links/29/
www.catholiclinks.org/retirosunitedstates.htm

Southern Baptist Church
www.sbccamping.org

United Methodist Church
www.gbod.org/camping/

General Listings

American Camp Association
www.acacamps.org

Christian Camp and Conference Association
www.ccca.org

Directory of Spiritual Retreats, Religious Retreats and Conference Centers
www.findthedivine.com

Oikosent North America (ONA)
www.retreatcenternetwork.org

Adult Spiritual Renewal and Empowerment
www.asrenewal.org

These sites are all searchable by state and often by demographic group or facility requirements. For more possibilities, google your state name and "Girl Scouts," "4-H," or "YMCA." Throughout my research, I found numerous camps run by these organizations that are open to hosting church retreats Happy hunting!

CHAPTER 5

Ready, Set, Go
The Final Details

You are about a month away from retreat, and the excitement is no doubt building. "Is it time yet? Is it time yet?" the veteran retreaters will begin to demand as the date draws near. For the Retreat Leadership Team, however, there are still several things to do.

Retreat Communication

The first task of the RLT is to call any participants who gave initial deposits but have not turned in a registration form. After all the registrations and monies are in hand, write your Final Details Letter (see Appendix A, p.109). At a minimum, this should include the retreat date and location (including an address and phone number) and a packing list (clothes, toiletries, bedding items, outerwear, special retreat supplies, flashlight, bug spray, swimsuit, etc.). You may also want to include your tentative schedule and suggestions for free-time outings or recreation. If you are arranging carpools, be sure to include the lists of drivers and riders, along with instructions for how they are to connect with each other (e.g., rendezvous point or phone number), as well as a map and directions to the retreat center.

Transportation

When setting up your carpools, keep in mind the following:

- The time of day people are available to leave
- The number of seats available in each vehicle. A word of warning: don't fill the car to capacity. Try to leave at least one seat open, especially if you are going to a facility where you have to bring your own bedding.
- The way you will connect riders and drivers (e.g., family members, geographic neighbors, roommates, etc.)
- Any additional information riders and drivers will need about stopping for meals on the way to and from the retreat

Room Assignments

If you have a small group, room assignments are probably not going to be a big deal. If you have a larger group, you may need to assign people not only to rooms but to separate buildings.

One option is to ask for roommate requests on your registration form. Make housing assignments using this information, along with your knowledge of the group's various personalities. The RLT also has the option of not creating any specific groupings and simply letting people find a bed when they get to the retreat. Either way, be alert for those shy or unique participants who may have a hard time finding a spot. The RLT's job is to actively model hospitality so that no one starts the retreat feeling left out, isolated, or unwelcome. And, as silly as it sounds, the RLT may want to wait until participants are at the retreat to give out housing information. Sometimes people get a little worked up over living arrangements when given those details too far in advance.

Need to Know Tip

"What's on a guy's mind when deciding whether or not to go on retreat is, Where will I stay and who will I stay with? We guarantee there's one mattress per man!"

Dale Garwood, servant, Granger Community Church, Granger, Indiana

---

Small Group Formation

How well your group knows each other and how large it is will determine how you break into small groups for discussion or activities. Ideally, you should have a minimum of three participants and a maximum of eight in each small group. The RLT has three basic choices when forming these groups:

1. *Random selection.* Using a variety of methods, the RLT divides participants into small groups without any particular concern for balance (counting off by fours, standing according to height or birth month, etc.). If using permanent name badges all weekend, you can also mark the backs with various symbols that represent the different small groups.
2. *Intentional selection.* In advance the RLT considers the content of the different sessions and thinks about the personalities of the participants. Then groups are assigned with the goal of balance. The RLT should try to form groups that have participants with a mix of ages and stages in life, very social people and rather shy people, public no-holds-barred sharers with patient listeners. These groups can stay together all weekend, or, if your group knows one another fairly well, these groups can be remixed for different sessions.
3. *Free choice.* In this option, an RLT member will start each session by asking participants to get into groups of a certain number. This option, though, has the greatest chance for making a few individuals feel left out or unwanted, especially if they are new to your group and don't have a friend to partner with. However, adults do like to have control over their own lives, and sometimes free choice is the best way to help the majority feel more comfortable and at ease. RLT members should watch for people who might need an invitation to join a small group and facilitate that.

In all of the above methods, however, each RLT member should assign himself or herself to a group and serve as its leader/facilitator. If your retreat has a large number of participants and you don't have enough members on the RLT to facilitate every small group, think about which participants would make strong discussion leaders and ask them ahead of time if they would be willing to serve in that specific capacity. Be sure to give them the discussion questions/material in advance, too.

Special Touches

As a child, I remember going to Milwaukee on a family vacation and spending one night at the Pfister Hotel, an upscale hotel in the city. I was very impressed when the housekeeper came in that night to turn down the bed and leave a chocolate mint on the pillow. What a treat!

So, in keeping with the need to renew and refresh, the RLT can go the extra mile and add a few special touches to the retreat experience. While this may be too touchy-feely for guys, women participants I've known have certainly enjoyed the extra pampering. Again, the rule of thumb is do what works best for your group. Pillow treats are easy and relatively inexpensive. Assign one RLT member the task of buying the mints or candies, and while everyone is in the opening overview on the first night, place a mint on each pillow. The same can be done the second night after dinner or while people are in an evening session. An alternative for guys and/or youth is to leave a snack-size candy bar or pack of gum on each pillow. Treats can be combined with a Bible verse that relates to the theme.

Hospitality kits are a nice surprise, too, and can be done inexpensively with unused sample-size bathroom products RLT members have collected from vacations or business trips, along with a few small purchases. On MomsLINK retreats, our standard hospitality kits included shampoo, conditioner, bar soap, deodorant, feminine hygiene products, ibuprofen, antacids, a toothbrush, and toothpaste. We also set out a roll or two of paper towels and a bottle of liquid hand soap in the bathroom.

Now, guys I have talked to have said, "Don't bother with that." I say, "Cleanliness is next to godliness." So a few bottles of hand soap and extra rolls of paper towels are great to have on hand. Depending on what your facility provides, your RLT members may also want to bring bathmats or large hand towels to use as bath mats, because swampy bathroom floors are just gross, whatever your gender!

Creating Master To-Do and Supply Lists

If you forget to copy a handout or don't bring the snacks, it's not the end of the world. However, in order to avoid feeling harried on your retreat designed to bring you R & R, creating master to-do and supply lists will help you be fully prepared. Using the timeline in this book, go through your own retreat schedule and sessions and make a list of any remaining tasks that need to be done, no matter how small. During your final RLT meeting the week before retreat, assign an RLT member to each item and write his or her name next to it on the list. Make copies for each team member. Also, as a team, go through your retreat schedule from start to finish and make a list of all supplies needed for every time slot, from setting out the bathmats you brought along to distributing the retreat evaluation forms with pens! Every supply should have an RLT member name next to it, too, noting which person is responsible for getting it to the retreat.

Handling Cancellations and Last-Minute Crises

Rule #1: Never say never.
Rule #2: Everything will work itself out.
Rule #3: You are bound financially and legally by the terms of your contract.

If you get a call at the last minute from a participant unable to go on retreat, be understanding and sympathetic but do not offer to refund the money unless (1) you are 100 percent certain the retreat center will let you alter your numbers at the last minute or (2) your group is prepared to cover the lost fee. Your contract should state by which date you can receive what percentage of your money back from the facility. Generally no money will be refunded after your final count is given ten business days before the event. Now, you certainly can call and explain the situation to the retreat center and see what the management says; however, you should be prepared to pay the full amount for the number of attendees you guaranteed, which should also be written in your contract with the center.

Last-minute crises might include a carpool driver's car going into the shop on the day you're leaving for retreat or an RLT member not being able to go because of a sick child. This is why you need master to-do and supply lists that spell out exactly who is doing what and bringing what. Don't panic. Refer to your lists. If the choice is recruiting a reluctant driver at the last minute or several people not being able to go on retreat, you'll get your driver.

Creating Evaluation Forms

The sign of a quality event is when participants are offered the chance to give feedback. A retreat is no different, even with a small group of participants. The RLT needs to know what people thought, and an anonymous evaluation form will give them the information they need to plan an even better retreat the next year. The form (see Appendix A, p. 110) can be simple, using a rating scale of 1 to 10 with 1 being awful and 10 being fantastic.

You should include questions about the housing, the food, the meeting space, the grounds, the amount of time dedicated to sessions and free time, the quality/relevance of the sessions, and the appropriateness of the cost. It is also helpful to add a few open-ended questions, such as, "The best part of retreat was . . ." or "The thing I'd change for next year is . . ." The RLT may want to ask for volunteers for the team for the following year, too. These forms should be copied ahead of time. Bring them to the retreat with a set of pens and a manila envelope in which participants can place their completed evaluations.

CHAPTER 6

R & R for Everyone: Responding to Special Concerns

Group Dynamics

Ladies, if you have ever worked in an all-female office or lived in an all-girls dorm, you know that things can get a little dicey at times when there are no males around. Women can be the best of friends and the worst of enemies, so the Retreat Leadership Team needs to keep that in mind when facilitating the small groups.

For all participants, however, comfort levels of sharing will differ vastly. Some people will want to tell their whole life's story to anyone who is willing to listen (and even to those who aren't!). Others will want to linger in the background, listening to the discussions but not necessarily revealing personal details. And some will participate in a few conversations but not all, and that's okay.

Keep in mind your main purposes for retreat, which are to provide quality time for spiritual self-renewal and quality time for friendship growth and renewal. Encourage your members to participate at the level with which they are comfortable. You never grow if you don't extend your comfort zone a little, but that can be done gradually. Those who have never gone on a retreat before may find it a little intimidating to be asked to give opinions or share personal insights right off the bat, even if they know the other participants well. The retreat structure in this book provides a framework for moving from more general group activities into more intimate, reflective discussions. This will guide you in helping people feel more at ease in sessions.

The RLT also needs to be able to gently redirect participants who monopolize discussions. Leaders need to be ready to tactfully jump in if the conversation strays too far off topic or one person's story becomes the never-ending life saga. Be brave in stepping in where your sense of redirection is needed, but also be kind. Chances are the person who really needs to vent is taking this opportunity because he or she hasn't been able to talk freely before. Certainly no one likes to feel that his or her life experiences are unimportant or uninteresting, yet your job as a discussion facilitator is to ensure that everyone gets a chance to share or vent if desired. Reminding the group of the discussion parameters ahead of time definitely helps avoid conflict down the road, but you will need to be prepared to keep things moving if necessary.

Need to Know Tip

"When a bomb is dropped into the conversation, the leader has a golden opportunity to say, 'This is a safe place. This is exactly the kind of thing that should happen.' How the leader handles this will demonstrate to the group that this is a safe place to share."

Greg Bowman, Group Life Movement, Willow Creek Association

Need to Know Tip

"When a youth says something inappropriate, don't give a big reaction. Keep it cool. If it's an inappropriate comment, call him or her on it and refocus. If you suspect (the youth is talking about) an abuse situation, say, 'You know what, that sounds like a topic you and I need to talk about later' and redirect. Then follow up with that youth after the session."

Calvin VerMulm, Director of Ministries, Inspiration Hills, Inwood, Iowa

---

The other thing you need to work into your weekend is the availability of RLT members or a special volunteer (recruited ahead of time) to talk with people who are ready to take their next step with Jesus. This may be a first-ever baby step, or a lifelong Christian may be moved to rededicate his or her life to Christ. Either way, early in the weekend the RLT needs to let people know who is available for continued conversations, questions, and prayer throughout the weekend.

Need to Know Tip

"Just lay it all out on Friday night. The leaders should say, 'This is a weekend for us all to get right with God. There will be small groups, but if you need to talk to a leader about getting right with God, we're available to you all weekend.'"

Laura Vroom, Executive Director of Manitoqua Ministries, Frankfort, Illinois

---

Confidentiality Policies

Regardless of how well your group members know and are comfortable with one another, one of your first announcements at retreat should be about the confidentiality policy. The bottom line is this: What's said at retreat stays at retreat.

Remind the participants that none of them would like to return home worried that someone else is going to share his or her personal thoughts and opinions with the local hairstylist, restaurant owner, or group member who couldn't come along. All individuals should feel safe in being able to vent if they need to vent, cry if they need to cry, complain if they need to complain, or share previously untold life stories.

Coping Strategies for Newbies

A retreat is supposed to be a relaxing time, a time for rest and rejuvenation. The pressure is not on to "spill your guts." The pressure is supposed to be off, because you are taking time for yourself to renew and refresh your spirit and be a more productive human being, a more efficient professional, a kinder and gentler parent, a more understanding spouse, a more compassionate friend, a more faithful believer.

With that in mind, your Retreat Leadership Team needs to know that while many people are thrilled at the chance to escape real life for a weekend and take time for themselves, there are a few who simply won't go on retreat because they feel they can't leave. There are also those who will go and constantly worry about what they left behind.

In particular, if parents are worried about the ability of their spouses, parents, or other caregivers to take care of their kids while they are gone, remind them that it is only for a weekend. It may be character building for the spouse, and it is really unlikely the children will suffer permanent emotional damage from being left to someone else's devices for the weekend. In fact, it will probably be great fun for everyone. Kids often revel in the relaxed schedules that emerge and the not-so-nutritious meals that may be offered when the primary caregiver is away. Or it may turn out that your stand in is truly a whiz in the kitchen and an amazing housekeeper. What a wonderful surprise that would be! And, even if that's not the case, again, it is only for a weekend. Life will go on, and you will be even better prepared to deal with the craziness because you have gotten much-needed R & R.

There are two caveats here: (1) If enough of your potential participants are having difficulty leaving their children or other responsibilities for several days, you can try a one-night retreat the first time around. I did that with my moms group the first year we went, and by the end of the first hour away at camp, the women who had been so hesitant to leave were complaining because they didn't want to go home so soon! (2) If at all possible, encourage your worried parents (or single parents) to call upon extended family—aunts and uncles, adult cousins, grandparents—to come and stay or take the kids for the weekend. It's okay to ask for a little extra family support to get away and rest.

Do the following to help all your participants feel more at ease:

1. Make sure you give out all retreat center contact information several times in your registration process and especially in your Final Details Letter. Even though people want to get away, most of them probably want to know they can be found in case of emergency.
2. If applicable, make sure all parent participants receive a copy of the Kids' Daily Schedule to leave with those staying at home (see Appendix A, p. 107–108).
3. During retreat, encourage everyone to turn off and put away their cell phones and only check for messages on breaks or during free time. If some insist on being connected at all times, ask that ringers be turned to vibrate only during discussions or large group sessions.
4. Patiently reassure nervous moms (and dads) and make sure the RLT knows if there is anyone who is going to need an extra hug or pat on the back while he or she works through leaving family for the first time.

Need to Know Tip

"For youth, overplan, don't underplan. Have backup plans. You can always just use what you need. Make sure you have enough supervision. Nothing ruins a retreat faster than a kid not getting cared for on retreat. Have a schedule for the event, and give it to the camp so they know where you are and what you're doing."

Laura Vroom, Executive Director of Manitoqua Ministries, Frankfort, Illinois

---

Pinch-Hitting When Things Don't Go as Planned

"Expect the unexpected" is a useful motto; it pays to be prepared. In my many years of planning retreats, like clockwork it seemed that my own kids could sense when I was going to be away, and at least one of them would get seriously ill the day before retreat. But that is why you have a Retreat Leadership Team and a timeline and a master to-do list. Even if one of your key team members can't go at the last minute, your group should still be able to carry on with little disruption and with full confidence.

Other problems may arise on-site, and you should be ready for these too. It may be that in the time between making your reservation and arriving, a larger group booked space at the camp, so your group gets bumped to less spacious accommodations. As long as you still have the same housing requirements listed in your contract, you will probably just need to go with the flow. However, if you now are short beds or do not have a common large group meeting area, your first task is to politely talk to the camp director or host on duty. The retreat center has a right to make the best use of its available space, but as a paying customer, you have a right to get what you contracted for. Be flexible but firm in stating your needs accurately so that the camp has a chance to make things right.

Also, depending on how often the retreat center is used and whether it's oriented more toward summer camps or adult conferences, you may find that additional visitors come to your weekend, such as the occasional mouse or insect.

Agh! you may think to yourself. *Not acceptable!* Yet "wildlife" is by definition wild, and from time to time natural visitors may wander in. The first thing to do, should you encounter such a situation, is not make a big deal out of it that sends your critter-phobic participants over the edge. The second thing to do is to contact the management and have them set traps or bug bait in your building. Unwanted retreat visitors are another reason why it is very important for the RLT to visit your prospective site in advance of making your reservation. You should know what you are reserving and be comfortable with that.

Another possible dilemma is forgotten supplies. Perhaps the DVD you need for Session 3 is sitting on top of your DVD player at home. Decide whether you can just describe the scene and go from there or if you need to find a copy. Unless you are truly out in the boonies, chances are there is a video store within a 20-minute drive. Just ask your camp staff for directions. If your missing items are more along the lines of glue and scissors, contact the camp staff to see if they have any craft supplies they could loan you. Or if your need is greater, ask them for directions to the nearest store that would carry the necessary supplies.

Last of all, don't be afraid to improvise. If a discussion seems to be getting far off track or it just never gets off the ground, stop for a word of prayer or a few songs. You might also ask the group if they would prefer a change of scene and move to an outdoor location or to a different building if possible. Or, you could offer the group a chance to grab some personal quiet time and simply end your session early. As an RLT member, part of your job is gauging the emotional temperature and interest level of your group and helping move things along by redirecting them if you are getting bogged down.

Need to Know Tip

"Have a prayer team that meets regularly to pray for the retreat planning and the event. The rest will come together then."

Jane Rubietta, author and veteran retreat speaker

Leadership Team R & R

The RLT should not return home feeling stressed and exhausted from planning and facilitating the weekend. The goal of retreat is for *all* participants to come home renewed and refreshed, the RLT included. So, as a team, you need to make sure you have done your homework before you leave and that you are prepared for the unexpected.

If everyone on the team holds up his or her end of things, your retreat should go smoothly, even with a minor bump or two along the way. Technically, you are not in charge anyway. God is. Put the Lord at the center of the retreat and trust the Spirit to lead the way and you will be fine.

Need to Know Tip

"Leaders tend to overprogram. They don't leave enough space for these [relaxed] conversations to happen organically. Part of what makes the retreat experience so valuable is the sense of community you've experienced. Know how to whet their appetite for more."

Greg Bowman, Group Life Movement, Willow Creek Association

CHAPTER 7

Revisiting R & R

Making the Most of Your Evaluations

Evaluation sheets—such small tools, such big results! Before you read through your evaluations, know that not everyone will give every item a top rating. Most likely, unless there was a major catastrophe, participants will have enjoyed just getting away, having a little alone time, strengthening their connection with God, and spending time with friends. Most of your reviews will probably be stellar. But be prepared. A handful of 8s on a ten-point scale can throw the most positive RLT member into a funk. However, the key is not to take comments personally. You asked for input, and you got it. Now use it to make next year's retreat even better!

Things marked with 9s and 10s definitely bear repeating next year. Celebrate those high points! Eights are certainly worth trying to duplicate as well, as you see how they fit into your plans. Items ranked 7 or below need your serious review. Were the participants only lukewarm about your facility? Should you consider moving retreat to a different location? Was there something about the food that you could comment on to the retreat center and have changed for next year? Was the drive too long? The cost too much? The sessions too long or not tailored enough to meet your group's needs? Again, remember not to take these things personally. Look at the feedback objectively and figure out what the consensus was on issues that rated low.

Planning Ahead for Next Year

The weekend went by so fast, you can hardly believe it's over. But it's not too late to start your planning for the next retreat. If you liked your facility, talk to the manager before you leave about reserving the same weekend next year (or about how to move your retreat to a different date). If you know you will need to change locations, start your research now so that you can book early for the best dates. Then once you have your reservation secured, just follow the timeline to another rave review retreat!

PART 2

Experiencing Spiritual R & R: Sample Retreats

CHAPTER 8

Women's Retreat #1

Running the Race with Perseverance

Schedule and Plan

Sample Schedule

Friday

6:00 p.m.	RLT arrives at camp to set up
7:30 p.m.	Women arrive at camp, find rooms, settle in
8:30 p.m.	Opening overview: How to Survive Retreat
9:30 p.m.	Munchies and more

Saturday

8:00 a.m.	Breakfast
8:45 a.m.	Opening worship
9:00 a.m.	Team challenge: The Amazing Race Scripture Scavenger Hunt
10:00 a.m.	Session 1: The Faith Fear Factor
12:00 p.m.	Lunch
1:00 p.m.	Session 2: What's the Deal?
2:15 p.m.	Free time (optional craft project)
5:30 p.m.	Dinner
6:30 p.m.	Session 3: God's Apprentice
9:00 p.m.	Munchies, movies, and more

Sunday

8:00 a.m.	Breakfast
8:45 a.m.	Group hike or beginning of extended personal devotions
9:45 a.m.	Personal devotions
10:30 a.m.	Closing worship
11:30 a.m.	Closing activity and evaluations
12:00 p.m.	Depart for home, lunch on the road

Retreat description: This is a laid-back yet interactive women's retreat based on reality TV shows. It is designed for two overnights and one and a half days. Participants will address the parts of life that challenge them and reflect on how their faith and their God-given gifts can strengthen and empower them to live more abundant Christian lives.

Two weeks before leaving, the RLT should send out the Final Details Letter (see Appendix A, p. 109). Make sure your letter tells participants to bring a "luxury" item they couldn't do without on retreat (e.g., lipstick, hairdryer, favorite pillow, perfume, etc.) for the mixer, along with their Bibles. Also at this time, confirm that your facility is supplying a TV/DVD player.

RLT Master Supply List

Hospitality kits (see chapter 5), 1 per bathroom
Housing/roommate assignments
A check for conference center if required, per your contract
Cash for carpool drivers from registration money
Pens, markers, tape, blank sheets of paper, pack of index cards
Poster board, 1 sheet per small group
1 envelope per participant with her name written on it
Strips of paper with participant's name on them for gift-writing activity. If you have 12 participants, you will need 11 strips for each name.
Master set of collection envelopes, 1 for each participant
Copies of retreat schedule for each participant and for cabins and meeting spaces
Copies of retreat sessions for each RLT member or volunteer facilitator
Copies of Amazing Race Scripture Scavenger Hunt, Faith Fear Factor Questions, and God's Apprentice Activity Instructions
Paper cut in the shape of headstones for RIP activity, 1 per participant
CD player (if retreat center does not supply) and meditative/praise/worship CDs
Light colored bandannas (with Run the Race with Perseverance 20__ written on them, optional)
Fabric markers
Craft supplies for group craft: felt rectangles cut on the diagonal to make pennants (1 per person), craft glue, hot glue, fabric paint, ribbon, scissors
Copy of Mel Gibson's *The Passion of the Christ* DVD
Concordance, study Bibles, personal devotions resources
Chocolate coin medals for each participant for Closing Activity (made from gold foil-wrapped coin with neck-sized red, white, and blue ribbon loop carefully hot-glued onto coin)
Movies or board games for free time
Pillow mints and/or bedtime Scriptures
Name tags
Coffee, tea, pop, bottled water, and snacks for breaks if your retreat center does not provide them
Cups, plates, napkins
Small prizes for the scavenger hunt, if desired
Copies of Sunday morning order of worship and any supplies for worship

FRIDAY

Arrival

Upon arriving at camp, the RLT will need to check in at the main building and receive housing assignments. Once in your space, the RLT should unpack, gather supplies for the opening overview, and place hospitality kits in the bathrooms. Then at least half the RLT should return to the main building/parking area to welcome and direct the rest of the participants.

Opening Overview: How to Survive Retreat

Time frame: 1 hour
Supplies: schedules, envelopes with name strips, pens, participants' luxury items

After participants get settled in, gather them for the opening overview: How to Survive Retreat. They need to bring their "luxury items" with them. RLT members should welcome the women and reassure them that this will be a wonderful getaway where they can refresh their minds, bodies, and spirits. Start your time together with worship, a few songs and Scriptures, and a time of prayer, asking God to be present and to transform hearts and lives this weekend. The RLT then needs to introduce the retreat confidentiality policy that "what's said at retreat stays at retreat" and distribute and review the weekend schedule and any camp rules or procedures to be followed. This is also a good time to identify the RLT members or other volunteers who are available to pray with or talk to women wanting to take the next step with Jesus.

Talents and Gifts Activity This next activity is ongoing from Friday night to Saturday dinner. Tell participants that they will need to be watching their fellow retreat-goers for signs of their gifts, talents, and strengths.

Hand out an envelope to each person with her name on it. Inside will be a strip with a name on it for every other person on retreat. (Prepare these ahead of time. If you have a very large group, assign small groups ahead of time and do this activity by small group. Bring extra supplies just in case.) The task before dinner on Saturday is to think of at least one gift, strength, or talent they see in each person, write it on her name strip, and place it in her collection envelope. (By breakfast on Saturday, an RLT member needs to tape a master set of collection envelopes labeled with each participant's name in a common area). Remind participants that it is God who gives us all of our gifts and strengths. Read to the group from Romans 12:3-8, which speaks of our spiritual gifts, and from Galatians 5:22-25, which lists the fruits of the Spirit. Encourage women to draw upon their own knowledge of the Scriptures when trying to identify gifts and strengths in their sisters in the faith. Post the two Bible passages for further reference by the group.

Tell participants that they shouldn't worry if they don't know everyone well. They have twenty hours to get to know people a little better, and there will be plenty of opportunity for discussion and conversation. Take some time now to quickly go around the room and ask people to share their names, hometowns, number of children, professions, etc.

Fear Factor Ice Breaker: Would You Eat This? Taking one question at a time, go around the whole group (or small group if you have already split up) and share answers to the following:

1. What is the scariest or worst meal you were ever served as a kid?
2. What is the scariest or worst meal you think you have served your own family (or you have ever eaten as an adult)?
3. What is the one food you absolutely wouldn't touch with a 10-foot pole?

Luxury Item Next, have participants go around the circle and explain the luxury item that they brought to retreat that they couldn't live without. Then break into small groups and have participants brainstorm one Bible-time luxury item that a woman wouldn't have wanted to travel into the desert without. Share in large group. Remind participants that our modern definition of luxury was probably far different from that of our Bible ancestors. Encourage them to think creatively. This activity is really just for fun and to get people laughing and socializing.

Munchies and More

Break out the snacks and drinks and let people relax. You might choose to build a campfire or set up board games or put in a movie. Some women may opt for going to bed, which is okay too.

Instead of or in addition to pillow mints each night, the RLT may choose to put a devotional Scripture on each woman's pillow or print Scriptures on self-stick address labels and attach them to a mint. Possible verses include Exodus 15:2; Psalm 46:1; and Philippians 4:13.

SATURDAY

Breakfast

Opening Worship

Gather the women before the first activity for a time of worship. Sing a few songs, share some Scripture, pray for the women and this time together. Be intentional about inviting God to be part of this retreat process.

Team Challenge: The Amazing Race Scripture Scavenger Hunt

Time frame: 30–45 minutes, including team sharing
Supplies: copies of the Scavenger Hunt (see Appendix A, p. 111), small prizes if desired, bandannas

Divide the women into teams of eight to ten and give them the list. They will be looking up Bible verses and searching for objects that represent the verses. Award a prize to the first team finished. Allow 30 minutes for the activity, with another 10–15 minutes to share. An RLT member can introduce the activity, saying: *The following verses represent things that we need for survival. While you hunt for objects to symbolize these verses, talk with your team about how God has helped you survive in life.*

Before this activity begins, you may also choose to pass out the bandannas for teams to tie on their heads, arms, necks, or legs to identify their team. Or hand them out as prizes when teams return. During the hunt, half the RLT should stay accessible in a central place in case groups have questions. The other half should go back to do any necessary set up for the morning discussion. Once teams are all back, have them share what they found to represent each item on the list.

Session 1: The Faith Fear Factor
Time frame: 90–105 minutes
Supplies: copies of the Faith Fear Factor handout (see Appendix A, p. 112), Bibles, construction paper headstones, pens

A member of the RLT should preface this discussion with the following guidelines, saying: *You don't have to answer any question if you don't want to. Simply pass to the next person. Anything that's said at retreat in small group needs to stay at retreat. Everyone has a right to feel that what she says is shared in the spirit of trust and confidentiality. Try to stay on topic and let everyone in your group have a chance to share her thoughts. Your leader will help the group work through the questions, so don't be offended if she keeps the discussion moving.*

Divide into (previously assigned) groups and move into your small group areas (bedrooms, other available space, or outdoor location). Ideally, these groups will have five to eight people maximum in them. If you have a lot of participants and you don't have enough RLT members to facilitate, recruit a few more volunteer leaders for these small groups. The facilitator assigned to each group will begin by asking the first question on the Faith Fear Factor handout and sharing first if no one else would like to start. You will stay in these small groups for the entire morning session, so you should bring all necessary supplies with you to the small group meeting area.

Word Wise When you finish the discussion questions, open your Bibles and read silently Hebrews 12:1-13, which speaks of running the earthly race with perseverance, keeping our focus on Jesus and the faithful example he set for us. Then go around the group and read it out loud one verse at a time. Ask the women to think about this passage and how it applies to their lives today. Let women who are comfortable share what this passage means to them. RLT group leaders should be listening for possible testimonies that can be shared in Sunday's worship service.

RIP Activity Give each woman a paper headstone and pen and ask them to reflect on their discussion this morning and think about what they hope people will say about them when they are no longer on this earth. Ask them to come up with a few adjectives, a quote, or a Bible verse describing this Christian they are journeying to become and then to write their names and these words on their headstones. Give the group about 20 minutes to think and write and another 10 minutes to share their headstone sayings. An RLT member can hang these above each person's Talents and Gifts Activity collection envelopes after the session. An RLT member can close your session in prayer, saying: *Thank you, Lord, for being with us here this morning. May your Spirit touch each one of our hearts and minds as we desire to grow closer to you. We pray that no matter what earthly challenges stand before us, we will be able to run our race with perseverance and courage and the support of our brothers and sisters in faith. Let us run in Jesus' name and boldly proclaim our faith in the Good News. Amen.*

Lunch

Session 2: What's the Deal?
Time frame: 1 hour
Supplies: index cards, pens, CD player, CDs, DVD player, TV, *The Passion of the Christ* DVD

One RLT member should take responsibility for facilitating this opening segment.

1. Give each woman an index card and pen. Ask the women to think of one ministry area that really appeals to them. Maybe it is an area in which they are currently serving. Maybe it is an area in which they would love to serve but never had the time or thought they didn't have the talent. Or maybe it is an area that involves risk and they were fearful. This ministry area could be in the local church or out in the world (examples: starting a food pantry at church or serving in an AIDS orphanage in Africa). Ask the

women to write this ministry on one side of the card. Give 5 to 10 minutes of thinking time. Have music playing in the background.

2. Ask the women to turn the card over and write down the biggest obstacle they see in being able to serve in this ministry (or make the ministry grow or run more efficiently if they are already serving in it). RLT members should complete this activity too.
3. The RLT facilitator says: *God knows our passion for serving in the kingdom. The Holy Spirit hears our cries and feels our pain. The Creator shares our love for creation. God has shaped us and formed us in a particular way, at a particular time, for a particular reason. God has equipped us to serve out our passions in Jesus' name. With God, all things are possible, somehow, some way. How will you respond to God's call? What do you say? Deal or no deal?*
4. Direct women to break into the small groups they formed earlier. Ask them to share their cards, front and back, with their small group and answer whether they said "Deal" or "No deal," and why. As a group, read Colossians 1:9-12 and pray for each woman (saying her name and her ministry (e.g., "Lord, we pray for Brenda and her desire to teach young children about your love. We ask that she will be able to fulfill her passion for service no matter what obstacles are in her way"). Exchange cards so that each woman has someone else's card. Encourage the women to continue praying for their partners even after they have left the retreat.
5. Gather your whole group around the TV, dim the lights, and play the clip from *The Passion of the Christ* where Jesus is in the Garden of Gethsemane and is wrestling with accepting the terms of God's deal for our salvation. End the clip as he stomps on the snake (scene 3 in Scene Selection). Before the clip, an RLT member says: *Sin and temptation have been present since God created people. Our Lord had to face down evil so that we might be saved from sin. Thank God that Jesus said, "Deal!"*
6. Move immediately from the end of the clip into group prayer. One RLT member should start the prayer, and one should close it. Leave time in the middle for participants to offer their thoughts too.

Prayer opening: *Lord, we come before you now, humbled that you said, "Deal," when your Father asked you to take on the sins of the world. We can't imagine what our lives would be like if you had passed, hoping for a better offer. We are grateful, from the bottom of our hearts, that you chose death so that we might live. We know this is not a debt to be repaid but an opportunity to live a life worthy of the one to which we have been called by you. Hear us now as we lift up our prayers of thanksgiving and love. . . .*

Prayer closing: *May our words of praise and petition draw us closer to you, O Lord, our Rock and our Redeemer. Amen.*

For additional discussion or quiet reflection time, consider these passages: Luke 22 and Philippians 2:1-11.

Free Time

This retreat has a large afternoon block of free time. The RLT should do a little background research and have a list of free-time options available in the area, such as hiking, shopping, antiquing, or seeing a movie. They can also provide or ask for board games and videos to show. And of course, there's always napping, journaling, curling up with a good book, or catching up with friends!

Optional Free-Time Craft: Faith Flag Supplies: felt rectangles cut on the diagonal to form two pennants (one per person), concordance, Bible, craft glue or hot glue, fabric paint, fabric markers, ribbon or trim, scissors

Directions: On this faith flag you will write or draw a key verse or key symbols that represent your faith in God and team loyalty to God. Be creative! You can also go out onto the grounds and collect items from nature that you would like to add to your flag.

Dinner

Remind participants to make sure they have put the name strips into the envelopes because they will be used in the next session immediately after dinner.

Session 3: God's Apprentice

Time frame: 2 hours

Supplies: God's Apprentice Activity Team Instructions copies (see Appendix A, p. 113), pens, poster board, markers, names/gifts envelope for each woman

RLT directions:

1. Have collection envelopes of names/gifts ready for each participant.
2. Gather the group. Give each participant a pen and an index card. Ask her to write down five things she feels she is good at (these can be personal qualities, professional tasks, or parenting skills or can be hobby-related, church-related, etc.).
3. Depending on your group dynamics, either ask women to get into their morning small group or form new teams for this activity.
4. Hand out envelopes containing strips of paper with affirmations written on them. Ask the women not to look yet.
5. One RLT member needs to serve as facilitator for each team for this activity. She will read the scenario on the handout and walk the team through steps 1–6 but should also fully participate in her team project. Plan to gather as a large group at 8:00 p.m. to allow each team to present its idea.
6. Move into your small groups and begin the God's Apprentice activity.

When your groups have finished presenting their action plans, an RLT member can close in prayer, saying: *Lord, we thank you for giving us different gifts, that together they might work together to glorify you and show your love to this broken world. We pray that even as we dream, even as we hope, even as we plan, even as we prepare our hearts to serve, that you would continue to walk with us. Make us bold. Make us fearless. Make us passionate about serving you. To God be all the glory in everything we do. Amen.*

Munchies and More

Saturday night might be a great time for a campfire, a chick flick, or a night hike with a naturalist. The RLT can use this time to leave another mint and/or Scripture on participants' pillows.

SUNDAY

Breakfast

Group Hike or Extended Personal Devotions

If the weather and your location cooperate, plan a group hike through the woods, along the beach, or on the retreat center grounds. You can also set aside this hour as the beginning of extended personal devotions.

Personal Devotions

Those who went for the hike can now begin personal devotions. Your team may want to put out some additional resources for women to use—devotional books or magazines, study Bibles, poems, or quotes on the themes of faith and perseverance.

Closing Worship

Time frame: 45–60 minutes

Supplies: to be determined by RLT

The RLT can plan a worship service in advance (or you can build planning time into the Saturday free time and encourage attendees to participate). Check your church library for liturgical resources if you want to include a call to worship, prayer of confession, or other group prayers, or write your own. Scriptures may include any of the ones listed previously in this retreat, or the RLT can use a concordance to look up verses under the headings of *strength, strengthen, perseverance, service, devotion,* or *faith*. Retreat participants could also be asked to share any favorite passages they have on these subjects.

If you type up and copy an order of worship, include your praise song and hymn lyrics or bring along songbooks or hymnals. Ahead of time, find an RLT member or a retreat participant who would be comfortable leading the singing and/or accompanying the group for worship. If needed, bring a portable CD player and worship music CDs.

Don't forget to ask the RLT members to listen for stories of faithfulness in the face of challenges that come up in the small group discussions. Ask a few of these women if they would share their testimonies in worship for the morning's message. Your group may also want to bring things for the altar, such as candles and flowers or an offering basket if you plan to take up an offering.

Closing Activity and Evaluations

Time frame: 20 minutes
Supplies: fabric markers, participants' bandannas

Ask the group to bring their bandannas to the common area. Have fabric pens out and let people sign one another's bandannas. When the bandanna signing is finished, ask people to put them on, and take group photos.

Next, pass out the retreat evaluations (see Appendix A, p. 110) and ask participants to complete them so that you have input for next year's planning. Have pens and a large manila envelope available. As people turn in their evaluations, award a chocolate coin medal for surviving the real-life retreat challenge.

Depart for Home, Lunch on the Road

Finish packing and head for home at this point. Make sure your group has followed the retreat center's checkout procedures. Don't forget to leave your check if that is what the management requires. Grab lunch on the road.

CHAPTER 9

Women's Retreat #2
Peace

Schedule and Plan

Sample Schedule

Friday

6:00 p.m.	RLT arrives at camp to get set up
7:30 p.m.	Women arrive at camp, find rooms, settle in
8:30 p.m.	Vesper service
9:30 p.m.	Munchies and more

Saturday

8:00 a.m.	Breakfast
8:45 a.m.	Opening worship
9:00 a.m.	Session 1: The Peaceable Kingdom
11:00 a.m.	Free time
12:00 p.m.	Lunch
1:00 p.m.	Session 2: The Bonds of Peace
3:00 p.m.	Free time
5:30 p.m.	Dinner
6:30 p.m.	Session 3: My Peace I Leave with You
8:00 p.m.	Free time/campfire on the beach

Sunday

8:00 a.m.	Breakfast
8:45 a.m.	Group hike or extended personal devotions
9:45 a.m.	Personal devotions
10:45 a.m.	Closing worship and evaluations
12:00 p.m.	Lunch at camp and depart for home

Retreat description: This is an introspective retreat where the goal is to help women find peace in a variety of relationships: with God, with self, and with others in the world. It is designed for two overnights and one and a half days. Participants will identify the conflicts in their lives that prevent God's peace from prevailing and learn how to find that peace that passes all understanding.

Two weeks before leaving, the RLT should send out the Final Details Letter (see Appendix A, p. 109), which reminds women to pack their Bibles. Also at this time confirm that your facility is supplying a TV/DVD player if you will be watching moves during free time.

RLT Master Supply List

Hospitality kits (see chapter 5), 1 per bathroom
Housing/roommate assignments
A check for conference center, as needed per your contract
Cash for carpool drivers from registration money
Pens, markers, masking tape
Giant Post-it flip chart pad or 4 to 6 sheets of poster board for graffiti pages
Copies of retreat schedule for each participant and for cabins and meeting spaces
Copies of retreat sessions for each RLT member or volunteer facilitator
Copies of vespers order of worship, songbooks or hymnals, audio copy of "Let It Be," Bible
Candles (individual for each woman in a holder, plus candles for lighting during vesper service), matches or lighter, and cards with lighting instructions, see vesper service notes
Copy of *How Sweet the Sound* by T. Wyatt Watkins, Judson Press, 2001 or meditation passage of your choosing
Journal copies for Session 1 (p. 114–115)
Art supplies (optional): colored pencils, watercolor paints, sketch pad, etc.
Copy of *The Gift of Peace* by Joseph Cardinal Bernadin, Loyola Press, 1997
8- to 10-foot lengths of rope or wide ribbon, 1 per every 2 women
Dyad questions (p. 116)
Craft supplies for group craft if adding your own project during free time
Craft supplies for wall hanging project: background material, assorted fancy paper, scissors, craft glue, and simple directions
Concordances, commentaries, and study Bibles
Collection of resources for personal devotion time on Sunday (books, poems, magazines)
Movies or board games for free time
Pillow mints and/or Bible verses
Name tags
Coffee, tea, pop, and bottled water and snacks for breaks if your retreat center does not provide them
Cups, plates, napkins
CD player and praise and worship CDs
Copies of Sunday morning order of worship and any worship supplies

FRIDAY

Arrival

Upon arriving at camp, the RLT will need to check in at the main building and receive housing assignments. Once in your space, the RLT should unpack, gather supplies for the opening overview, and place hospitality kits in the bathrooms. Then at least half of the RLT should return to the main building/parking area to welcome and direct the rest of the participants.

Vesper Service

Time frame: 35–40 minutes
Supplies: CD player and meditative music, order of worship, Bible, song sheets or songbooks, music for song leader if applicable, candles for lighting, individual candles for each woman, matches, copy of *How Sweet the Sound,* if using for meditation

After participants get settled in, gather them for the vesper service. This candlelight evening worship service will set the tone for your weekend, and you will change up the normal retreat order by starting with worship instead of a welcome and the weekend schedule review. Another way to do this, if it works better for your group, is to begin with your welcome, icebreaker, and camp rules and then move to a different location for your worship service so that there is a clear break between activities.

Outside the worship area, have a table stocked with individual candles and holders and small cards that read: "Prepare your heart and mind for worship. Light this candle and enter the room silently. When you feel ready to connect with God, blow out your candle. When all the candles are out, we will begin the service."

Inside the worship area, have meditative music playing on the CD player (or use a live musician if you have one) and have a number of candles set up around the room so that you won't be in total darkness when the women extinguish their individual candles. When all worshippers have entered and the last candle is blown out, begin the service.

Order of Worship

Scripture (An RLT member reads aloud)

Hear the good news from the Gospel of John [read John 1:1-5]. *Let the people of God say, "Amen." (Amen.)*

Call to Worship (An RLT member leads and asks the people to respond after each line with "Amen, let it be.")

From Psalm 85:8-13

L: **Let me hear what God the LORD will speak, for he will speak peace to his people,**

P: Amen, let it be.

L: **To his faithful, to those who turn to him in their hearts.**

P: Amen, let it be.

L: **Surely his salvation is at hand for those who fear him, that his glory may dwell in our land.**

P: Amen, let it be.

L: **Steadfast love and faithfulness will meet; righteousness and peace will kiss each other.**

P: Amen, let it be.

L: **Faithfulness will spring up from the ground, and righteousness will look down from the sky.**

P: Amen, let it be.

L: **The LORD will give what is good, and our land will yield its increase.**

P: Amen, let it be.

L: **Righteousness will go before him, and will make a path for his steps.**

P: Amen, let it be.

Prayer (led by an RLT member)

Lord God, we come to you this evening, people very much in need of peace. We struggle day in and day out with burdens that seem too much to bear, Lord. Weary, weary, we are from fighting the battles of this world. Broken relationships that will not mend. Broken bodies that will not heal. Broken hearts that withdraw from your love. Broken spirits that know not peace. Lord, we cast all our cares upon you. We lay all of our burdens down at your feet. We are trusting, with childlike faith, that because you loved us enough to lay down your life for us, that you will pick us up and show us the path for peace. Hear us, Lord, as we share with you our inmost trials and troubles. [Allow a pause for silent prayer.] *And now, Lord, hear us as we turn our voices to you and our prayers become songs of worship.*

Songs

Recruit a musician/song leader ahead of time. Ideally you will have a guitar or piano player along who can help keep the group singing, but you can also do this a cappella. Suggestions include: "I Cast All My Cares upon You," "Sanctuary," "There Is a Redeemer," and "Jesus Remember Me."

Meditation

An RLT member reads from How Sweet the Sound, "Second Rest," p. 173–185 (or feel free to use another reading or personal story on finding peace that would better meet your group's needs). Preface the passage by saying: *Peace is not a given in our lives. Nor is it the absence of conflict or struggle. Peace is about getting right with God, about reconciling our differences with others and with the Lord and actively taking part in the kingdom work that God asks us to do in his name. In this passage, you'll meet Earl Norris, the eldest member of the Ashgrove Church in Indiana, and hear about his journey from passive church-goer to re-committed believer who discovered that true peace comes first from personal reconciliation with God. In the words of Earl's favorite hymn: "Breathe, O breathe Thy loving Spirit / Into ev'ry troubled breast! / Let us all in Thee inherit, Let us find that promised rest". . . Let the peace of God, that passes all understanding, let it reign as you hear these words.*

Read the story and ask women to reflect on what it says about the power of God to bring peace into our lives and what it means for each person individually in her search for peace. (Allow 5 minutes of quiet reflection. Have very soft meditative music playing in the background. If using this story, you could play the hymn "Love Divine" which is featured in the text.)

Prayer (led by an RLT member)

Lord, we have come together this weekend seeking peace. Hear our prayers. Know our needs. We ask that the power of your love would transform our hearts and minds during this time away, Lord. In the quiet beauty of this place, may we open our ears to hear the message of peace that your Son brings. Forever change us to become instruments of your peace in a discordant world. Amen.

Closing songs

"All Praise to Thee My God This Night" or "Let the Peace of God Reign." An RLT member gives these instructions before singing: *During this closing song, you will be relighting your individual candle. When the song ends, we ask for continued silence for people to pray or be bathed in the Spirit of the living God. When you are ready to leave worship, please take your light and carry it out into the darkness so that the darkness shall not overcome. If you need someone to pray with you, please come forward, and the Retreat Leadership Team will minister to you. We will regather in this worship space for fellowship about 10 minutes after everyone has left the room.*

Transitioning song

"Let It Be." (Have this playing as people relight their candles and move out of the worship space.)

Munchies and More

Time frame: 1 hour

Supplies: snacks, drinks, cups, napkins, small plates

Set up refreshments and welcome your group back to your meeting space. When everyone is settled with a snack, go around the circle and share names and one or two bits of personal information to help break the ice. The RLT should then review the retreat confidentiality policy that "what's said at retreat stays at retreat," as well as the weekend schedule and any camp rules or procedures to be followed. This is a great time, too, to introduce RLT members who are available for continued conversations and prayer about deepening your relationship with Jesus.

Allow women time to unwind and socialize. Bring out a few board games or movies or just let people talk and get to know one another. Some women may also opt to head to bed, which is okay. Part of finding peace is being able to rest.

Instead of or in addition to pillow mints each night, the RLT may choose to put a devotional Scripture on each woman's pillow or print the Scriptures on self-stick address labels and attach them to a mint or other treat. Possible verses include Matthew 5:9, Colossians 3:15, Philippians 4:7, and Romans 12:18.

SATURDAY

Breakfast

Opening Worship

Gather the women before the first activity for a time of worship. Sing a few songs, share some Scripture, pray for the women and this time together. Be intentional about inviting God to be part of this retreat process.

Session 1: The Peaceable Kingdom

Time frame: 2 hours

Supplies: flip chart pages hung around the meeting space, masking tape, markers, Bibles, peace journals (see Appendix A, p. 114–115)

Peace, Baby Ahead of time, label the flip chart pages with these headings: Other Names for Peace, Places of Peace, People Working for Peace, Images or Symbols of Peace, Places in Need of Peace. As women enter, ask them to look at the sheets and write what comes to mind. Once everyone has had a chance to contribute, gather the group and read through the sheets. An RLT member should next ask the group if anyone has a specific memory or experience related to peacemaking (local or global) that she would like to share (allow for three or four stories to be told). Thank the women for sharing.

An RLT member should read Isaiah 11:1-9 after giving the following background information (encourage women to read along in their own Bibles): *This passage from Isaiah 11 explains how God's covenant is going to be fulfilled. From the line of King David, the Messiah will come, and the Messiah is our peace. He will break down the walls that exist between peoples and nations and create the peaceable kingdom. Hear God's word:* (read from Bible)

An RLT member asks the group:

1. What image(s) in this passage do you connect with? Why?
2. If the Messiah is going to bring about the peaceable kingdom, are we off the hook?
3. How do we fit into this big picture plan for world peace?

Give each participant a peace journal that the RLT has prepared from the sample in Appendix A. Participants will be engaging in some personal reflection time now using a version of the study practice Lectio Divina. Ask participants to go out from your meeting space and find a quiet place where they can be completely alone. They will need the journals, Bibles, and pens. They should take the next 30–45 minutes to sit quietly and focus on God's Word, using the journal pages to help them connect. Free time will follow, so if they need additional time to meditate, they can do so. Note: If you want to encourage creative reflection, you can bring a variety of art supplies (watercolors, markers, colored pencils, art quality drawing paper, etc.) and let women know these resources are available to take with them for the reflection time.

Free Time

Those who need it can extend their personal meditation time or return to the cabin to take a nap or read or enjoy the camp surroundings.

Lunch

Immediately preceding or following lunch would be a good time to take a group photo.

Session 2: The Bonds of Peace

Time frame: approximately 1.5–2 hours
Supplies: *The Gift of Peace*, lengths of rope or wide ribbon (8–10 feet long, one piece for every two women), copies of the Dyad questions (see Appendix A, p. 116).

Gather your group and open with a word of prayer. A member of the RLT should then say: *I'd like to share another passage with you from Cardinal Bernadin. Here he is reflecting on his pastoral ministry; however, I'd like you to think about this on a more personal level. Jesus is the pioneer and perfecter of our faith. He is the ultimate role model whose example we are struggling to follow. Listen to the cardinal's words and think about what ministering to one another really means for you. Is it something you enjoy or something that drains you?* (Read from the bottom of page 77 beginning with "As a shepherd . . ." to the end of the first paragraph on page 80, or use your own personal experience or reading material that better meets your group's needs.) *Any thoughts you'd like to share? What in this passage struck you?*

While one RLT member is reading, others should be laying out the rope segments in a crisscross pattern so that it looks like an asterisk or starburst. Your women will make a circle around these ends. If you have a large group, make multiple circles.

Now hear these words from Paul, who was trying to teach the believers in Ephesus what it meant to live in community with one another. [Read from Ephesians 4:1-6.] *Please make a circle around the ropes and pick up the end that lies in front of you. If you don't have an end, please join with your neighbor to the left or right. Jesus calls you to maintain the unity of the Spirit in the bond of peace, bearing with one another in love, showing patience, and speaking with humility and gentleness. You are going to live out that call now as we break into dyads [or triads] for discussion. Please stay bonded to your partner(s) at the other end of the rope, but move out of the circle to stand next to one another.* (Allow groups to form.)

Dyads (or triads if you have a group of three) are a series of questions or open-ended statements that allow you to get to know another person deeply in a rather short amount of time. Your job is twofold: you need to focus on your partner when it is her turn and listen to what she has to say, restating her answer, if needed, to ensure that you understand her message. Your second job is to open up and share honestly with your partner even if you don't know her well. This is an opportunity for us to minister to one another by living a life worthy of the one to which we've been called. Please pick up a dyad question sheet and find a quiet space on the grounds where you can talk. You have an hour to complete the questions. Please come back to our meeting space at __:00. And here's one final but very important guideline. Remember that anything that's said at retreat in small group needs to stay at retreat. Everyone has a right to feel that what they say is shared in the spirit of trust and confidentiality. Thank you for your understanding.

An RLT member distributes the handout and encourages the pairs to find a quiet place to talk. Members of the RLT should participate in this exercise, too, although one pair may want to stay in the meeting space and keep track of the time. When the women return, gather them in a circle for closing prayer and then sing a simple hymn or worship song. (Suggestions: "Go Now in Peace" or "Dona Nobis Pacem," both of which can be done as rounds.)

Closing prayer: *Thank you, Lord, for being with us here this afternoon. We live in such a broken world that is so far removed from the peaceable kingdom you promise. In our daily lives, we come in contact with people—strangers, friends, family members—who are hurting or who have hurt us—and so often we pass right by, unwilling to take the time to offer comfort or reconciliation. In Romans 8 Paul tells us,*

> *"the Spirit helps us in our weakness; for we do not know how to pray as we ought, but that very Spirit intercedes with sighs too deep for words. And God, who searches the heart, knows what is the mind of the Spirit, because the Spirit intercedes for the saints according to the will of God. We know that all things work together for good for those who love God, who are called according to his purpose" (Romans 8:26-28).*

Lord, we pray that we would live a life worthy of the one to which you have called us. Teach us to build up unity of the Spirit in the bonds of peace, even when that's hard, even when that's painful, even when that's frightening. Help us to be the people you want us to be. Amen. Let it be.

Free Time

This retreat has a large afternoon block of free time. The RLT should do a little background research and have a list of free-time options available in the area, such as hiking, shopping, antiquing, or seeing a movie. You can also provide or ask for board games and videos to show. And of course, there's always napping, journaling, curling up with a good book or catching up with friends! If your participants are crafty, your RLT might want to plan a craft that could be done as an option during free time.

Dinner

Session 3: My Peace I Leave with You

Time frame: 1 hour

Supplies: large section of burlap or other material (approximately 3 feet wide by 5 feet long), sheets of scrapbooking paper in various colors, prints, and themes, quick bond fabric/craft glue, scissors (multiple pairs), several copies of the wall hanging directions, Bibles, copy of guided meditation for leader

Encourage the women to bring their pillows and/or blankets or wear their pajamas for this session, as you will be leading a guided meditation and being comfortable is key. To begin, though, ask the women to find their dyad partner(s) and join with another pair to form a group of four.

An RLT member should direct the groups to read John 14:25-27. Each person should read it silently first and then take turns reading a verse out loud until the passage has been read through twice aloud. An RLT member then says: *Jesus says he is leaving us his peace. How would you describe Jesus' peace?* [Give groups 7–10 minutes to discuss this idea and then ask the next question.] *On a scale of 1 to 10, how much do you feel Jesus' peace right now?* [Give groups 5 minutes to discuss this idea, and then ask the next question.] *On the same scale, how much do you feel Jesus' peace back in the "real world"?* [Give groups 5 minutes to discuss this idea, then ask the final question.] *Reflect on this tonight and tomorrow. What can you do to ensure that the peace of Christ that you have experienced on retreat continues to transform your life back in the "real world"? If you want to talk about how to take that next step with Jesus, members of the RLT will be available after this session.*

An RLT member should ask women to get comfortable for the guided meditation. They can stretch out on the floor or curl up on a couch. The meditation will be about 15–20 minutes long. When participants are ready to move out of meditation mode and into the final "art" segment of the session, they should do so quietly. There will be no talking from this point on. The directions for the group wall hanging should be posted by the worktable. Women will be selecting a piece of paper and cutting it into a shape that represents a "place of peace" for them. Participants should follow the directions and complete the task in silence. Women can leave the session when they have finished their "place of peace" for the wall hanging. Free time follows. Share these schedule details with your group before beginning the meditation.

An RLT member should read this meditation slowly, giving ample time for reflection during the specified pauses. The goal is for women to fully relax and visualize this encounter with Jesus and take away some spiritual truth to apply to their lives. Note: Whoever is leading the meditation should practice beforehand by reading through the text multiple times so that it will flow.

An RLT member says: *I'd like everyone to get very comfortable right now. Stretch out, curl up, kick off your shoes, roll your shoulders. From this point on, through the end of the session, we will be silent, except while I lead you through this meditation.*

Please close your eyes now. Take three deep breaths from the bottom of your belly and let them out slowly. [pause] *Do that again, counting to three while you inhale and to three while you exhale.* [pause] *Focus on your breathing. Breathe in, 1-2-3. Breathe out, 1-2-3. In.* [pause] *Out.* [pause]

Imagine your body floating, weightless. [pause] *See yourself on a cloud, in a pool suspended, relaxed.* [pause] *Slowly wiggle your toes, circle your feet, and let them go limp.* [pause] *Now slowly wiggle your fingers, circle your hands at the wrist, and let them go limp.* [pause] *Part by part; see the stress and busyness stored in your brain run down your neck, past your shoulders, along your arms and slide out those limp fingers.* [pause] *Visualize the pain and hurt that is wrapped around your heart letting go like a combination lock unlocking, 3-2-1.* [pause] *Your heart is open. Let that conflict flow out down past your stomach, which is unknotting,* [pause] *down through your legs, [pause] past your ankles* [pause] *and out those limp toes.* [pause]

Take a deep breath, 1-2-3. Let it out, 1-2-3. Again, breathe in, 1-2-3, and out, 1-2-3. [pause]

Your body is strong and healthy, and you are out walking. [pause] *It's a beautiful day.* [pause] *The sun casts a sweet, mellow glow on the world, warming your heart and giving you energy you haven't felt in days, maybe in weeks or even years.* [pause] *The grass under your feet is soft and springy and smells newly cut, that familiar scent reminding you of the change of seasons and new life bursting forth.* [pause] *Birds call to one another in this meadow, trilling and singing to their heart's content.* [pause] *A babbling brook gently burbles over smooth stones, just feet from where you stand.* [pause] *You wiggle your bare toes in anticipation of the refreshingly cool water that will flow over them when you dip them into the stream.* [pause] *You feel at one with God's creation, and you think to yourself: "The Lord is my shepherd. I shall not want. He makes me lie down in green pastures. He leads me beside still waters. He restores my soul. He leads me in paths of righteousness for his name's sake."* [pause] *You walk over to the brook and dip your toes in its healing waters.* [pause] *You smile with delight. The water was every bit as wonderful as you expected.* [pause] *You cup your hand and slowly let the water run through your fingers.* [pause] *When you pull it out, you drink joyfully from the crystal clear liquid. You are refreshed.*

Turning, you step out of the brook and lie down on the bank, gazing at the blue expanse of the heavens that seem to stretch on to eternity. [pause] *Your mind wanders, dancing through years of memories, some good, some not so good.* [pause] *You linger on a situation in your life that has been hurtful, filled with pain and conflict, making you doubt yourself, making you doubt your relationship with God.* [pause] *But here in this place of peace by this babbling brook,* [pause] *on this lush green grass,* [pause] *with the birds singing sweetly,* [pause] *you hear a voice whisper in your ear, "No worries. Look at the birds of the air; they neither sow nor reap nor gather into barns, and yet your heavenly Father feeds them. Are you not of more value than they?"* [pause]

And yet [pause] *you feel the anxiety stir deep within as you return to this piece of your life that you want to go away.* [pause] *You sit up, pondering your situation, how you got to this place in your life, where it's going to lead you.* [pause] *And then you feel a hand on your shoulder and sense someone kneeling behind you.* [pause] *"Friend, even though you walk through the darkest valley, you need not fear evil," the voice reassures.* [pause] *"For I am with you. My rod and my staff, they will comfort you. I will prepare a table before you in the presence of your enemies. I will anoint your head with oil. Your cup will overflow."* [pause]

Your head bows in submission and relief. You know who it is that speaks to you. [pause] *Wonderful Counselor,* [pause] *mighty God,* [pause] *everlasting Father,* [pause] *Prince of Peace.* [pause] *Prince of Peace.* [pause] *Arms embrace you now, wrapping around you tightly, holding on and not letting go.* [pause] *But you are not a captive. Instead, you feel wildly free.* [pause] *You know that your Redeemer lives. He pulls you out of the miry clay and sets your feet on solid ground.* [pause] *Prince of Peace, my Prince of Peace, you say, basking in the warmth of the love that surrounds you.* [pause] *I can do all things through Christ who strengthens me. Jesus, tell me what to do.* [pause] *And so the Savior speaks to you in this moment of heaven on earth and you listen to all he has to say* (long pause, maybe 20–30 seconds)

Surely goodness and mercy shall follow you all the days of your life, and you will dwell in the house of the Lord your whole life long. [pause] *Slowly, slowly, the arms holding you release you, but the sensation of being held lingers on, a permanent imprint on your being.* [pause] *You feel, rather than hear, the soft thud of departing footsteps, yet you are not alone.* [pause] *That voice, that comforting, ever loving, everlasting voice drifts back to you on the fragrant breeze, "Peace I leave with you; my peace I give to you, do not let your hearts be troubled, and do not let them be afraid. My peace I give to you."* [pause]

You lift your head but don't turn to look at the departing figure, for you are not alone, you are never alone. Your Prince of Peace is always with you. [pause] *His peace he has given to you. That's all you need to know.* [pause] *You stay in the meadow as long as you need to, breathing slowly, deeply, mindfully, fully aware of the presence of God and the peace he brings to your life. Amen. Let it be.*

At this point, an RLT member or two should get up and move to the wall-hanging project so that women know it is okay to change gears. However, this should still be a time of silent reflection. As women come to the table, the RLT members can point to the directions and gesture to the available supplies. Using the scrapbooking paper, women will be creating a group wall hanging that illustrates a place of peace for them (the mountains, the lakeshore, the church, a family cabin, a vacation spot, the cross, etc.). Once they have formed their "place" they can glue it onto the wall hanging and then depart the meeting area. Evening free time follows. Note: Ahead of time, fold over the top three inches of the wall hanging and hot-glue the edge to create a pocket for a dowel rod for future hanging.

Munchies and More

The RLT can use this time to leave another pillow mint and/or Scripture on participants' pillows. Free-time options might include a night hike, a fire in the fireplace, a bonfire on the beach, board games, movies, or refreshments.

SUNDAY

Breakfast

Group Hike or Beginning of Extended Personal Devotions

If the weather and your location cooperate, plan a group hike through the woods, along the beach, or on the retreat center grounds. For those who don't want to hike, you can mark this hour as the beginning of an extended personal devotional time. Provide a variety of resources (books on prayer, meditation, devotionals, picture books relating to peace, etc.) and encourage the women to select one and take it with their Bible to a quiet place. Those hiking can start this devotional time when they return.

Personal Devotions

See above. Those wishing an extended time of meditation can forgo the hike and start at 8:45. Your RLT may wish to provide a list of the Scriptures that have been studied this weekend, as well as study Bibles, concordances, and commentaries for those who wish to dig deeper.

Closing Worship and Evaluations

Time frame: 60–75 minutes
Supplies: To be determined by RLT

The RLT can plan a worship service in advance and/or use free time on Saturday to recruit participant help in planning. Check your church library for liturgical resources if you want to include a call to worship, prayer of confession, or other group prayers, or write your own. Scriptures may include any of the ones listed previously in this retreat, or the RLT can use a concordance to look up verses under the headings of *peace, unity, community, love, tolerance, acceptance, neighbor, peaceable,* or *union.* Retreat participants could also be asked to share any favorite passages they have on these subjects.

If you type up and copy an order of worship, include your praise song and hymn lyrics or bring along songbooks or hymnals. Ahead of time, find an RLT member or a retreat participant who would be comfortable leading the singing and/or accompanying the group for worship. If needed, bring a portable CD player and worship music CDs.

Don't forget to ask the RLT members to listen for stories of peace and peacemakers that come up in the small group discussions. Ask a few of these women if they would share their testimonies in worship for the morning's message. Your group may also want to bring things for the altar, such as candles and flowers or an offering basket if you plan to take up an offering.

After closing worship concludes, ask the participants to complete the retreat evaluations (see Appendix A, p. 110).

Pack Up, Have Lunch at Camp, and Depart for Home

Finish packing, then head for home. Make sure your group has followed the retreat center's checkout procedures. Don't forget to leave your check if that is what the management requires.

CHAPTER 10

Men's Retreat #1

Running the Race with Perseverance

Schedule and Plan

Sample Schedule

Friday

6:00 p.m.	RLT arrives at camp to get set up
7:30 p.m.	Men arrive at camp, find rooms, settle in
8:30 p.m.	Opening overview: How to Survive Retreat
9:30 p.m.	Munchies and more

Saturday

8:00 a.m.	Breakfast
8:45 a.m.	Opening worship
9:00 a.m.	Team challenge: Soul Survival Kits
10:00 a.m.	Session 1: The Faith Fear Factor
12:00 p.m.	Lunch
1:00 p.m.	Session 2: What's the Deal?
2:15 p.m.	Free time (optional service project)
5:30 p.m.	Dinner
6:30 p.m.	Session 3: God's Apprentice
9:00 p.m.	Munchies and more

Sunday

8:00 a.m.	Breakfast
8:30 a.m.	Group hike or beginning of extended personal devotions
9:30 a.m.	Personal devotions
10:15 a.m.	Closing activity
10:45 a.m.	Closing worship
11:45 a.m.	Evaluations
12:00 p.m.	Lunch at camp or pack up and depart for home with lunch on the road
1:00 p.m.	Optional continuation of service project at camp

Retreat description: This is a laid-back yet interactive men's retreat based on reality TV shows. It is designed for two overnights and one and a half days. Participants will address the parts of life that challenge them and reflect on how their faith and their God-given gifts can strengthen and empower them to live more abundant Christian lives.

Two weeks before leaving, the RLT should send out the Final Details Letter (see Appendix A, p. 109), which reminds men to bring their Bibles. Also at this time, confirm that your facility will supply a TV/DVD player.

RLT Master Supply List

Paper towel and liquid soap supplies for bathrooms if camp does not provide
Housing/roommate assignments
A check for conference center if required, per your contract
Cash for carpool drivers from registration money if applicable
Pens, markers, tape, legal pad, pack of index cards
Copies of retreat schedule for each participant and for cabins and meeting spaces
Copies of retreat sessions for each RLT member or volunteer facilitator
Bible-time foods for icebreaker: olives, goat's milk, matzo, sardines, dates, etc.
Small card stock headstones for RIP activity, 1 per participant
Mel Gibson's *The Passion of the Christ* DVD
DVD copy of Tony Dungy interview (see book's blog, www.completeretreatguide.com) or laptop with Internet connection to Dungy interview
Casting Crowns "Who Am I" video or just an audio version (for links see this book's blog www.completeretreatguide.com)
Copies of the Faith Fear Factor and God's Apprentice handouts
Copies of the "Sharing the Victory" Tony Dungy article (see this book's blog for link)
Concordance, study Bible, and personal devotions resources
Dog tag for each man with church name/logo imprinted on it
Large wooden cross for worship (can be assembled on site with large tree branches and rope or brought from home, at least 6 feet high or taller, depending on group size)
Hammers and nails for closing activity and worship
Movies or board games for free time
Name tags
Coffee, tea, soft drinks, bottled water, snacks, and paper goods for breaks
Small prizes for the Fear Factor eating contest and survival kit games if desired
Candy bars, gum, and/or Bible verse labels for bedtime snack option
CD player (if retreat center does not supply) and meditative/praise/worship CDs
Sunday morning order of worship and supplies

FRIDAY

Arrival

Upon arriving at camp, the RLT will need to check in at the main building and receive housing assignments. Once in your space, the RLT should unpack, gather supplies for the opening overview, and place paper towels and soap in the bathrooms. Then at least half of the RLT should return to the main building/parking area to welcome and direct the rest of the participants.

Opening Overview: How to Survive Retreat

Time frame: 1 hour
Supplies: music for song leader, song sheets for participants (or PowerPoint lyrics), CD player and praise and worship CDs, Bibles, Bible-time food samples, prizes (if using) for Fear Factor eating contest

After participants get settled in, gather them for the opening overview: How to Survive Retreat. RLT members should welcome the men and reassure them that this will be a relaxing time to get some R & R. They will have both personal downtime and time to meet other men and connect. Start your time together with worship. If you don't have a guitar player/song leader, be sure to bring along a CD player and some of the praise and worship songs the men will know. Share some music, Scriptures, and a time of prayer that will bring everyone into retreat mode. One RLT member should then review the weekend schedule, introduce the retreat confidentiality policy that "what's said at retreat stays at retreat," and share any camp rules or procedures to be followed.

Fear Factor Icebreaker: Would You Eat This? Depending on the size of your group, you can stay together as a whole group to answer these three questions or break into small groups with the men sitting near each other. If breaking into small groups, make sure one RLT member goes with each group and has a copy of the curriculum. (If these groups are formed on the spot at retreat, make sure each RLT facilitator writes down the names of the men in his group.) Also take some time now to go around the circle(s) and introduce yourselves with your names and one or two pieces of personal information (where you live, how long you have been at this church, etc.).

Taking one question at a time, have people share answers to the following:

1. What is the scariest or worst meal you were ever served as a kid?
2. What is the scariest or worst meal you think you have ever eaten as an adult?
3. What is the one food you absolutely wouldn't touch with a 10-foot pole?

Then, for a real-life fear factor challenge, bring samples of Bible-time foods that modern Americans might find strange or unappetizing. Present the food and offer a taste to each person who is brave enough. If you are working with small groups already, each table could send a taster forward for each food. Possibilities include: canned sardines or other salty, dried fish, goat's milk, figs, matzo, dates, olives, roasted quail (or other game bird), lamb, etc. Another option is to have an eating contest using sardines, pitted dates or olives, or goat cheese, etc. You can award a small prize (candy, gum, or mints) to the winner.

Munchies and More

The contest should flow into a time of low-key fellowship. Order in pizzas and/or have men bring their favorite junk food and pop to share. Put in a movie or play some tunes. Break out the cards. Do whatever works to put your men at ease and let them get to know one another.

If your team wants to do the bedtime snacks option, bring a supply of fun-size candy (Skittles, M&Ms, Hershey Bars, etc.) and leave one on each man's bunk before bed. To kick it up a notch, your team can print out relevant Bible verses ahead of time and place on each package. Possible Scriptures include Psalm 18:1-2, Psalm 46:1, and Philippians 4:13.

SATURDAY

Breakfast

Opening Worship

Get your men's energy level up this morning with some upbeat praise songs or hymns. Select a few key Scriptures to share, and close with a prayer that God will be with you during your time together this weekend. This may also be a good time to identify leaders and volunteers who are available to meet one-on-one with men who want to ask more questions or talk about deepening their relationship with Jesus.

Team Challenge: Soul Survival Kits

Time frame: 30–45 minutes, including team sharing
Supplies: Bible for each group, small prizes for winning team (if desired)

Gather your men together and either have them find their small groups from Friday night or divide them into new teams (five to eight men per team). Tell them you are going to build a soul survival kit. Make sure each group has at least one Bible. An RLT member will then announce to the crowd the verses below, one at a time. After the verse is called out to the entire group, each team is to look it up and figure out what it represents. The first team to send a man up to the leader with an object representing that verse scores a point. Proceed through all the verses. You can give small prizes to the team with the most points.

Survival Kit verses include (announce only verses, not the category!):

Food: *Numbers 11:4-9*
Water: *John 4:13*
Shelter: *Psalm 61:3-4*
Clothes: *Matthew 6:28-30*
Family: *Ephesians 2:19*
Friends: *John 15:12-14*
Bible: *Hebrews 4:12*
The Lord: *Micah 6:8*

After you have awarded prizes to the winning team, ask the men to take a few minutes and discuss in their teams this question: *Is anything missing from your own soul survival kit?*

Give men a quick bathroom and coffee break and regroup for the first session.

Session 1: The Faith Fear Factor

Time frame: 90–105 minutes

Supplies: laptop with Internet connection to Tony Dungy interview and projector with screen or DVD of interview with Tony Dungy and TV/DVD player, copies of the Faith Fear Factor handout (see Appendix A, p. 117), Bibles, card stock headstones, pens

This session opens with a 20-minute video clip from a Fellowship of Christian Athletes interview done with Tony Dungy, coach of the 2007 Super Bowl–winning Indianapolis Colts. Gather your men around the screen and preface the clip with this: *Tony Dungy, coach of the Superbowl–winning Indianapolis Colts, is also a Christian who is winning victories for God. He has survived extreme highs and lows, both in his personal and professional life, over the years. Hear what he has to say about how his faith works in real life.*

After the clip, get ready to move into discussion groups. A member of the RLT should remind men of the following guidelines, saying: *Anything that's said at retreat in small group needs to stay at retreat. Everyone has a right to feel that what he says is shared in the spirit of trust and confidentiality. Try to stay on topic and let everyone in your group have a chance to share his thoughts. Your leader will help the group work through the questions, so don't be offended if he keeps the discussion moving. And if there's a question you don't want to answer, you can simply pass to the next person.*

Make sure each person has a copy of the Faith Fear Factor handout. Move into your small group areas (bedrooms, other available space, or outdoor location). The RLT member assigned to each group will begin by asking the first question and sharing first if no one else would like to start. When you finish the Fear Factor questions, move into the Word Wise activity, followed by the RIP activity. If your small group is leaving the main meeting space, bring all supplies with you.

Word Wise When you finish the discussion questions, open your Bibles and read silently Hebrews 12:1-13, which speaks of running the earthly race with perseverance, keeping our focus on Jesus and the faithful example he set for us. Then go around the group and read it out loud one verse at a time or ask for a reader to read the whole passage. Ask the men to think about how these words apply to their lives today. Let men who are comfortable share their understandings with the group. Note: The RLT group leaders should be listening for possible testimonies that can be shared in Sunday's worship service.

RIP Activity Supplies: small card stock headstones, pens

After the Word Wise discussion, tell the men that you are going to close in prayer and then ask them to leave the session quietly, picking up a headstone on the way out. Direct them to continue reflecting on this morning's session by finding a quiet place to think about and (preferably) write down what they would want on their headstone. It might be character traits they aspire to have or a Bible verse that has shaped their lives. It is up to them to decide. Ask them to bring the headstones back to the session after dinner tonight. Then end in prayer, saying: *Thank you, Lord, for being our rock and our salvation, for giving us strength even when we cannot admit our own weaknesses. We pray that no matter what earthly challenges stand before us, we will be able to run our race with perseverance, through the help of our brothers and sisters in faith. May we run in Jesus' name and boldly proclaim our faith in the Good News. Amen.*

Lunch

Session 2: What's the Deal?

Time frame: 75–90 minutes

Supplies: index cards, pens, CD player, praise and worship CDs, TV/DVD player, *The Passion of the Christ* DVD

As your men are coming in to the meeting space, ask them to find and sit with their small groups. Open with prayers; then ask each RLT group facilitator to do the following with their small group:

1. Give each man an index card and pen. The RLT member asks the men to think of one ministry area that really appeals to them. Maybe it is an

area in which they are currently serving. Maybe it is an area in which they would like to serve but never had the time or thought they didn't have the talent. Or maybe it is an area that involves risk and they didn't or couldn't take the chance. This ministry area could be in the local church or out in the world (examples: starting a handyman service for people in need at church or building schools in Mexico). Ask the men to write this ministry on one side of the card. (Give about 10 minutes of thinking time. Have music playing in the background.)

2. Ask the men to turn the card over and write down the biggest obstacle they see in being able to serve in this ministry (or make the ministry grow or run more efficiently if they are already serving in it). RLT members should complete this activity too.
3. Leader says:
   God knows our passion for serving in the kingdom. The Holy Spirit hears our calls for help and feels our pain. The Creator shares our love for creation. God has shaped us and formed us in a particular way, at a particular time, for a particular reason. God has equipped us to serve out our passions in Jesus' name. With God, all things are possible, somehow, some way. How will you respond to God's call? What do you say? Deal or no deal?
4. Ask the men to share their cards, front and back, with their small group and answer whether they said "Deal" or "No deal," and why. As a group read Colossians 1:9-12 and pray for each man (saying his name and his ministry, e.g., "Lord, we pray for John and his desire to work with the youth group"), asking that he would be able to fulfill his passion for service no matter what obstacles are in his way. (*Note:* If you feel your group is open to this, exchange cards so that each man has someone else's card. Encourage the men to continue praying for the man whose card they received even after they have left retreat.)
5. Ask the men to try to stay with their groups. Centrally locate the TV/DVD player. Dim the lights and play the clip from *The Passion of the Christ* where Jesus is in the Garden of Gethsemane and is wrestling with accepting the terms of God's deal for our salvation. End the clip as he stomps on the snake (scene 3 in Scene Selection). Before the clip, an RLT member says: *Sin and temptation have been present since God created people. Our Lord had to face down evil so that we might be saved from sin. Thank God that Jesus said, "Deal!"*
6. Move immediately from the end of the clip back into small group time. RLT leaders ask this question: *What does it mean to you that Jesus said, "Deal"?*

After the men have had a chance to process this question, the RLT member should start the group in prayer. Let the men know there will be time during the prayer for them to offer their thoughts too. Ask for a volunteer to close your time in prayer if you feel your group is up to that.

Sample opening: *Lord, we come before you now, humbled that you said, "Deal," when your Father asked you to take on the sins of the world. We can't imagine what our lives would be like if you had passed, hoping for a better offer. We are grateful, from the bottom of our hearts, that you chose death so that we might live. We know this is not a debt to be repaid but an opportunity to live a life worthy of the one to which we have been called by you. Hear us now as we lift up our prayers of thanksgiving and love. . . .* (Let men respond.)

Sample closing: *May our words of praise and petition draw us closer to you, O Lord, our Rock and our Redeemer. Amen.*

Free Time

This retreat has a large afternoon block of free time. The RLT should do a little research and have a list of free-time options available in the area, such as hiking, golfing, touch football, basketball, softball, etc. They can also provide or ask for board games and movies to show. And of course, there's always napping, snacking, or just hanging out!

Optional Service Project Your RLT may want to discuss ahead of time with your camp or retreat center manager if there are any opportunities for service projects that your group could work on during this free time. Make sure men know in advance that this opportunity will be available, and ask them to indicate their interest on your registration form so you know approximately how many men you will have for the project(s), although you should have the flexibility to let people join in that afternoon. Tell them ahead of time to bring whatever clothes and supplies are needed. It is possible that you could start the project at this time and continue it Sunday after closing worship, extending your weekend by several hours.

Dinner

Before dinner ends, make an announcement reminding the men to bring their headstones back to the last session.

Session 3: God's Apprentice

Time frame: 1 hour

Supplies: copies of Tony Dungy interview from the Fellowship of Christian Athletes *Sharing the Vision* magazine (for a link to a printable copy see www.completeretreatguide.com), pens, Bibles, copies of God's Apprentice handout (see Appendix A, p. 118).

As the men are entering the meeting space, ask them to sit with the small groups they formed earlier. An RLT member will preface this session, saying: *This morning we watched the interview with Tony Dungy. In his everyday life, Tony strives to be God's apprentice. We are going to revisit his example of servant leadership by looking at the four core values of the Fellowship of Christian Athletes on which Tony bases his life.* [Pass out copies of interview.] *In your small group, you are now getting a copy of the Tony Dungy interview that recaps what we watched this morning. Take a few minutes to read through it, and then your small group can move into discussion. Feel free to find a quieter space to talk.*

After the group has worked through the questions, the RLT facilitator will ask the men to take out their headstones. He will say: *Take a few minutes to reflect on what you wanted your headstone to say and how you want to be remembered when you leave this world. Looking back on our discussions throughout the day, is there anything you want to add or change on your headstone? If you haven't yet, jot down your thoughts.* (Have extra headstones available in case someone forgets his.)

Allow the men 5–10 minutes to complete this activity; then move into prayer to wrap up your time together, saying: *Lord, we know that we are far from perfect, that we have much to learn about you and your love for us. We pray that you would be patient with us, your humble apprentices, that you would open our hearts and our minds to your will and engage our hands in your service. We ask that you would continue to walk with us, even when we veer off course. Make us bold. Make us fearless. In the challenge to know you and love you, Lord, we ask that you hear our hearts' desires to join your team. To God be all the glory in everything we do. Amen.*

Ask the men to keep their headstones and bring them to closing worship on Sunday.

Munchies and More

This would be a great time to schedule a bonfire to keep the men bonding. The RLT can also use this time to leave another bedtime snack on men's bunks.

SUNDAY

Breakfast

Group Hike or Beginning of Extended Personal Devotions

If the weather and your location cooperate, plan a group hike through the woods, along the beach, or on the retreat center grounds. You can also set aside this hour for extended personal devotions.

Personal Devotions

Ask the men to take this half hour to reflect on the weekend's message. Provide a list of Scriptures discussed in the sessions. You may also want to set out study Bibles and concordances for men who want to dig deeper.

Closing Activity

Time frame: 20–30 minutes

Supplies: pens, YouTube video of Casting Crowns song "Who Am I?" (for YouTube link see www.completeretreatguide.com), laptop with Internet and/or TV/DVD player (or just play the song, no video), CD with worship music or musician who can play music to transition between video and the beginning of worship, wooden cross (set up at the front of your worship area), nails, hammers

Remind the men that they need to bring their headstones to this final session. Make sure that each man has a pen. An RLT member will preface the song with this statement: *This song you are about to hear asks the question: Who am I? Think about your answer. Reflect on what you wrote on your headstone and how you want to be remembered. Who are you in God's world? When the song ends, take a minute to write down the next step in your faith journey that will help you become the man you want to be in God's eyes. When you are finished writing, go nail your headstone to the wooden cross in the worship circle and have a seat there. You can nail it writing side down if you don't want anyone to see what you have written. We'll begin worship when all headstones have been nailed to the cross. We ask that there be no talking during this preworship activity.*

Play the "Who Am I" video (or just the audio) and let men work through the process of finishing their headstones and nailing them to the cross. As soon as the video ends, you should switch to worship music on the CD player or have your musician begin playing in the background to transition into the worship service opening music.

Closing Worship

Time frame: approximately 30–45 minutes
Supplies: To Be Determined by the RLT

The RLT can plan a worship service in advance. Check your church library for liturgical resources if you want to include a call to worship, prayer of confession, or other group prayers, or write your own. Scriptures may include any of the ones listed previously in this retreat, or the RLT can use a concordance to look up verses under the headings of *strength, strengthen, perseverance, service, devotion,* or *faith.* Retreat participants could also be asked to share any favorite passages they have on these subjects.

If you type up and copy an order of worship, include your praise song and hymn lyrics or bring along songbooks or hymnals. Ahead of time, find an RLT member or a retreat participant who would be comfortable leading the singing and/or accompanying the group for worship. If need be, bring a portable CD player and worship music CDs.

Don't forget to ask the RLT members to listen for stories of faithfulness in the face of challenges that come up in the small group discussions. Ask a few of these men if they would share their testimonies in worship for the morning's message. Your group may also want to bring an offering basket if you plan to take up an offering.

Evaluations

Before everyone leaves the worship area, try to get a group picture, and then pass out the retreat evaluations (see Appendix A, p. 110). Ask participants to complete them so you have input for next year's planning. Have pens and a large manila envelope available. As people turn in their evaluations, award a dog tag for surviving the retreat challenge.

Lunch at Camp or Pack Up and Depart for Home with Lunch on the Road

Finish packing and head for home at this point. Make sure your group has followed the retreat center's checkout procedures. Don't forget to leave your check if that is what the management requires.

Optional Continuation of Service Project at Camp

If you are continuing to work on your service project this afternoon, adjust your schedule accordingly.

CHAPTER 11

Men's Retreat #2
Heroes

Schedule and Plan

Sample Schedule

Friday

6:00 p.m.	RLT arrives at camp to get set up
7:30 p.m.	Men arrive at camp, find rooms, settle in
8:30 p.m.	Opening overview: Hero Worship
9:30 p.m.	Munchies and more

Saturday

8:00 a.m.	Breakfast
8:45 a.m.	Opening worship
9:00 a.m.	Session 1: Real-Life Heroes (includes short break)
12:00 p.m.	Lunch
1:00 p.m.	Session 2: The Bible's Men of Steel
2:30 p.m.	Free time (optional Challenge Course activity)
5:30 p.m.	Dinner
6:30 p.m.	Session 3: Becoming a Hero in God's Eyes
8:30 p.m.	Munchies and more

Sunday

8:00 a.m.	Breakfast
8:45 a.m.	Group hike or beginning of extended personal devotions
9:45 a.m.	Personal devotions
10:45 a.m.	Closing worship
11:45 a.m.	Evaluations
12:00 p.m.	Lunch at camp or pack up and depart for home with lunch on the road

Retreat description: This is an introspective men's retreat that examines the concept of real-life heroes—both biblical and contemporary—and what it means to be a hero in God's eyes. It is designed for two overnights and one and a half days. Participants will identify heroic qualities in biblical role models, in contemporary examples, and in their own personalities and understand how to apply them to further God's kingdom.

Two weeks before leaving, the RLT should send out the Final Details Letter (see Appendix, p. 109), which reminds men to bring their Bibles. Also at this time, confirm that your facility will supply a TV/DVD player.

RLT Master Supply List

Paper towel and liquid soap supplies for bathrooms if camp does not provide
Housing/roommate assignments
A check for conference center, as needed per contract
Cash for carpool drivers from registration money if applicable
Pens, markers, tape, sheets of paper for group work
Giant flip chart or 5 sheets of poster board
Copies of retreat sessions for each RLT member or volunteer facilitator
Copies of retreat schedule for each participant and for cabins and meeting spaces
Copies of handouts: Real-Life Heroes, Hero Qualities, The Bible's Men of Steel, and A Hero in God's Eyes
Copies of the following movies: *Batman Begins, Braveheart, Pride* and *World Trade Center*
Superhero candy or fun-size candy for prizes and/or bedtime snacks option
Movies or board games for free time (suggested films—*Remember the Titans, Glory Road, Hancock*)
Name tags
Coffee, tea, soft drinks, bottled water, snacks, and paper goods for breaks
Sunday morning order of worship and supplies

FRIDAY

Arrival

Upon arriving at camp, the RLT will need to check in at the main building and receive housing assignments. Once in your space, the RLT should unpack, gather supplies for the opening overview, and place paper towel and soap in the bathrooms. Then at least half the RLT should return to the main building/parking area to welcome and direct the rest of the participants.

Opening Overview: Hero Worship

Time frame: 1 hour
Supplies: TV/DVD player, copy of the movie *Batman Begins,* sheets of paper and pens, flip chart Post-it pad or large sheets of poster board (approximately 5), markers, superhero candy prizes

After participants get settled in, gather them for the opening overview: Hero Worship. RLT members should welcome men and reassure them that this will be a relaxing time to get some R & R. They will have both personal downtime and time to get to know some other men and connect. Start your time together this weekend with worship. If you don't have a guitar player/song leader, be sure to bring along a CD player and some of the praise and worship songs your men will know. Share some music, Scriptures, and a time of prayer that will bring everyone into retreat mode.

One RLT member should then review the weekend schedule, introduce the retreat confidentiality policy that "what's said at retreat stays at retreat," and share any camp rules or procedures to be followed. This is also a good time to identify the RLT and any volunteers who are available if men need prayer or want to talk about deepening their relationship with Jesus.

Hero Worship Note: Either before breaking into small groups (if your total size is twenty-five or fewer) or after (if you have twenty-five or more), be sure to go around the circle and introduce yourselves, with your names and maybe one or two pieces of personal information (where you live, how long you have been at this church, etc.).

An RLT member will ask the men to break into groups either by tables or using guidelines from chapter 5. (Make sure an RLT member is placed in each group to act as the group facilitator. If these groups form on the spot at retreat, be sure each RLT facilitator writes down the names of the men in his group.) Then the RLT member will hand each group a piece of paper and a pen and give these directions: *Your group has 10 minutes to make a list of as many comic book heroes as possible. Along with the hero's name, note any special qualities and abilities that each hero possesses.* Give men 10 minutes to make the list. Call time and ask groups for the total number of heroes listed. If desired, award superhero candy prizes to the group with the most heroes (search the web for superhero candy or for links see completeretreatguide.com).

Up front, an RLT member should begin a master list of the top three or four superheroes with input from the groups. Put one hero name at the top of each sheet and then ask for the qualities and abilities that the hero possesses that make him an ideal hero. After 10 minutes or so of brainstorming, the RLT member says this: *We're going to be talking about what it takes to be a hero in God's eyes this weekend. We'll leave these lists up so that you can refer to them tomorrow when we look at Bible heroes. Right now, though, we're going to watch a clip from Batman Begins to get us in a heroic frame of mind for this weekend. This clip shows Bruce after he has gotten out of a Chinese prison and is searching for the man who will train him to fight injustice. It then goes into a flashback of his childhood. Think about what drives Bruce to become a hero and what should drive him.* (Show the approximately 20-minute clip, starting with scene 3 in Scene Selection and going through Bruce hurling his handgun into the river.

While the clip is playing, the RLT should set out snacks and drinks (favorite munchies brought from home, pizza ordered in, warm chocolate chip cookies, and milk if available through your camp dining service).

When the clip ends, have your men turn back to their small groups. The RLT facilitator will then ask: *What motivates Bruce Wayne to become Batman?* [Let the men respond.] *Does he fit with your definition of a hero? If not, how do you define* hero?

Munchies and More

Move from discussion right into social time. If men want to continue to watch the movie, let them do that. Encourage your group to just hang out and relax. Your RLT should use your best judgment to do whatever works for your men to put them at ease and let them get to know one another.

Bedtime Snacks If your team wants to do the bedtime snacks option, bring a supply of fun-size candy (Skittles, M&Ms, Hershey Bars, or superhero theme candy) and leave one on each man's bunk before bed. To kick it up a notch, your team can print out relevant Bible verses ahead of time and place on each package. Possible Scriptures include Philippians 4:8, Hebrews 12:1b-2a, and 1 Peter 3:8-9a.

SATURDAY

Breakfast

Opening Worship

Get your men's energy level up this morning with some upbeat praise songs or hymns. Select a few key Scriptures to share (maybe ones that will follow in the sessions later today) and close with a prayer that God will be with you during your time together this weekend. This may also be a good time to identify leaders and volunteers who are available to meet one-on-one with men who find they want to ask more questions or talk about deepening their relationship with Jesus.

Session 1: Real-Life Heroes

Time frame: 2.5 hours, including a break

Supplies: TV/DVD player, Bibles, copy of the movie *Pride*, copies of the Real-Life Heroes handout (see Appendix, page 119), copies of the Hero Qualities handout (see Appendix, page 120)

Real Life Heroes This session opens with a 22-minute video clip from the movie *Pride*. Gather your guys around the screen. A RLT member can preface the clip with this: *Pride tells the true story of how in 1974 Philadelphia Department of Recreation employee Jim Ellis saved the Marcus Foster pool from closing by teaching 6 inner city kids how to swim, as well as how to believe in themselves and each other. In this clip, Ellis and the team are celebrating a state championship win (which will allow them to compete at Nationals) when they return to their home pool to find a local gang leader taking revenge against Ellis for pulling "his kids" away from gang membership. How Ellis ultimately handles the situation gives his team a lesson in real-life heroism.* (Show clip which starts with Scene 20 in Scene Selection and plays through Scene 24, stopping before the epilogue.)

After the clip, move into your discussion groups from Friday night. A member of the RLT should remind men of the following guidelines: *Anything that's said at retreat in small group needs to stay at retreat. Everyone has a right to feel that what he says is shared in the spirit of trust and confidentiality. Try to stay on topic and let everyone in your group have a chance to share his thoughts. Your leader will help the group work through the questions, so don't be offended if he keeps the discussion moving. And, if there's a question you don't want to answer, you can simply pass to the next person.*

Take the handout copies and go to your small group areas (bedrooms, other available space, or outdoor location). The RLT member assigned to each group will begin by asking the first question on the Real-Life Heroes handout and sharing first if no one else would like to start. Your group has about 40–45 minutes to cover these questions. Then you should return to the large group area for a short break and continuation of the session.

Break (approximately 15 minutes) Ahead of time, the RLT (or your camp staff) should lay out refreshments (coffee, water, pop, snacks) in your large group meeting space. Give the men 15 minutes to take a bathroom break and get snacks. Gather your group for prayer before moving back into small group discussion. An RLT member should say: *Lord, we pray now, as we begin to dig into your Word, that you would open our ears that we might hear what you have to say to us. The Bible is our guide for life. Your Word directs us and leads us. We pray that your Spirit would be among us as we seek your truth. Bless this time we have together that we might trust in you and come to know you more. Amen.*

Hero Qualities Pass out copies of the Hero Qualities handout (p. 120) and let your groups return to their meeting spaces for this final portion of the session. (An option would be to let small groups stay in the large group space and follow the Hero Qualities discussion with the epilogue to *Pride*, scene 24, time code 1:42:45 to 1:43:35, and closing in prayer.) When you finish the questions, the RLT group facilitator can take prayer requests and close your time together in prayer, saying: *Thank you, Lord, for providing the words we need to live our lives. Your book is filled with powerful instructions. Help us to take the time to read it, and please fill our hearts with your truth. We struggle every day to be the men you want us to be. We know that your guidelines are right there in front of us. We pray for forgiveness when we turn away and don't stand up for what's right. We pray that you will give us faithful hearts that live to serve you in all that we do. Hear us now as we ask for help with* [fill in from men's requests or make this a silent confession time]. *These things we ask in Jesus' holy name. Amen.*

Lunch

Session 2: The Bible's Men of Steel

Time frame: 75–90 minutes

Supplies: Bibles, copies of The Bible's Men of Steel handout (see Appendix A, p. 121)

Gather the men together, asking them to sit with their small groups, and have an RLT member give these instructions: *Last night we looked at comic book superheroes. This morning we looked at real-life heroes in history. Now we're going to go back even further in time to God's own men of steel—the men whose stories we might remember, or might not. Either way, they are role models for us, even today, showing what God desires of us in word and deed. Now, each hero may not have all the qualities that we looked at in Session 1, but your group's job is to identify the heroic qualities he does have and decide how his life sets an example for us to follow. One amazing thing about God is that from the beginning of time, he has chosen ordinary people to do extraordinary things in his name. Each group is going to look at a different hero. You will be reporting back to the large group on your findings in about 45 minutes.* Note: Your RLT may want to change or add heroes to the handout list depending on the size and needs of your group.

Ahead of time, the RLT should assign a hero to each group facilitator, and each facilitator should take time to read up on his hero using a study Bible or commentary. If your group is large and you know that you will be using additional facilitators who are not on the RLT, be sure to assign each of those men a hero and ask him to do the same prep work for this discussion session. The participants will be reading several pages of Bible background for their group's hero; however, the discussion will flow better if the leader has the "big picture" vision of the hero's story and can share additional information as needed. For the retreat session, each group member should get The Bible's Men of Steel handout.

When you reconvene as a large group, an RLT member should ask each group to make a report, summing up the individual's heroic qualities and how he can serve as a role model for men today. After all groups have reported, an RLT member can close in prayer, saying: *Lord, we pray to you now like David did, asking for help, putting our trust in you, praising you for deliverance.* [Read Psalm 56.] *Lord, hear our prayer. Let us look to the heroes you lifted up. May we see them for the godly men they were, trying to live their lives in service to you. As you held them accountable, we pray that you will hold us accountable for striving to have a hero's heart. These things we ask and pray in Jesus' holy name. Amen.*

Free Time

This retreat has a large afternoon block of free time. The RLT should do a little research and have a list of free-time options available in the area, such as hiking, golfing, touch football, basketball, softball, etc. They can also provide or ask for board games and movies to show. And of course, there's always napping, snacking, or just hanging out!

Optional Challenge Course Activity If you are at a camp with a challenge course, make arrangements ahead of time to offer this as a free-time option. Note that there may be an additional fee.

Dinner

Session 3: A Hero in God's Eyes

Time frame: 90 minutes

Supplies: TV/DVD player, a copy of Oliver Stone's *World Trade Center,* copies of A Hero in God's Eyes handout (see Appendix A, p. 122)

Gather your men around the TV/DVD player. An RLT member should preface the clip with this: *No doubt most adults in America can tell you exactly where they were and what they were doing on 9/11. No doubt most of those adults also watched, probably repeatedly, the video coverage of that horrific event. On that September day, heroes were born out of ordinary people. Those individuals didn't choose to be heroes. They didn't ask to be heroes. But that's what they became. The virtues they exhibited in their actions—the very ordinary characteristics of kindness, compassion, faithfulness, gentleness, honesty, patience, mercy, perseverance—made them heroes. This clip from Oliver Stone's* World Trade Center *shows a few of those ordinary people who did extraordinary things.* [Play from scene 17, "You Are Our Mission," to the two rescue workers preparing to go down into the rubble together to find the Port Authority policemen who are trapped, about 10 minutes. *Note:* This excerpt includes brief profane and vulgar language. Whichever movie you choose, please preview the material to be excerpted before showing to your group.]

After viewing the clip, ask your men to get in their small groups. An RLT member will pass out the handout and give these instructions: *Take 10 to 15 minutes to read through and think about your answers and/or make notes on the A Hero in God's Eyes handout. Then, as a group, we'll go through the questions together and close in prayer.* Each small group facilitator can then lead the group through the reflection and discussion time.

When his group is ready, the RLT member will say: *Becoming a hero in God's eyes is no easy task. Just look at the example we have to follow. Jesus was and is perfect. Sadly, humankind was and is imperfect. We have been rescued from death by the sacrifice of our Savior Jesus. However, that means we have a duty to live a life worthy of the one to which God has called us. Every day we need to be ordinary people doing extraordinary things to bring about God's kingdom. Lord, make us the men you want us to be. Amen.* [pause] *If anyone has questions or would like to talk about how to have a deeper relationship with Jesus, please come see any of the RLT members now or at any time this weekend.*

Munchies and More

This would be a great time to schedule a campfire to keep the men bonding. The RLT can also use this time to leave another bedtime snack on men's bunks.

SUNDAY

Breakfast

Group Hike or Beginning of Extended Personal Devotions

Time frame: 45–60 minutes
Supplies: devotional resources (see below)

If the weather and your location cooperate, plan a group hike through the woods, along the beach, or on the retreat center grounds. You can also set aside this hour as the beginning of extended personal devotions. Your RLT may want to have a variety of resources available for your men: a list of the Scriptures covered this weekend, inspirational books or copies of stories of heroic figures, men's devotional books, study Bibles and commentaries, etc. You may also want to have RLT members available for men who have questions, need prayer, or want to talk about deepening their relationship with Jesus.

Personal Devotions

Time frame: 45–60 minutes

Encourage your men to take this time to go off by themselves and pray or study God's Word before coming to worship. Ask them to focus on the question: What can I do to be a hero in God's eyes?

Closing Worship

Time frame: 45 minutes
Supplies: To be determined by the RLT

The RLT can plan a worship service in advance. Check your church library for liturgical resources if you want to include a call to worship, prayer of confession, or other group prayers, or write your own. Scriptures may include any of the ones listed previously in this retreat, or the RLT can use a concordance to look up verses under the headings of *strength, strengthen, perseverance, service, devotion,* or *faith.* Retreat participants could also be asked to share any favorite passages they have on these subjects.

If you type up and copy an order of worship, include your praise song and hymn lyrics or bring along songbooks or hymnals. Ahead of time, find an RLT member or a retreat participant who would be comfortable leading the singing and/or accompanying the group for worship, or bring a portable CD player and worship music CDs.

Don't forget to ask the RLT members to listen for stories of heroism in the face of challenges that come up in the small group discussions. Ask a few of these men if they would share their testimonies in worship for the morning's message and/or ahead of time ask an RLT member or retreat participant to give a message during your service. Your group may also want to bring an offering basket if you plan to take up an offering.

Evaluations

Before everyone leaves the worship area, try to get a group picture, and then pass out the retreat evaluations (see Appendix A, p. 110). Ask participants to complete them so you have input for next year's planning.

Lunch at Camp, Pack Up and Depart for Home with Lunch on the Road

Finish packing and head for home at this point. Make sure your group has followed the retreat center's checkout procedures. Don't forget to leave your check if that is what the management requires.

CHAPTER 12

Family Retreat #1
Life Is a Three-Ring Circus

Schedule and Plan

Sample Schedule

Friday

6:00 p.m.	RLT arrives at camp to get set up
7:00 p.m.	People arrive at camp, find rooms, settle in
7:45 p.m.	Opening overview: Life Is a Three-Ring Circus
8:30 p.m.	Munchies and more

Saturday

8:00 a.m.	Breakfast
8:45 a.m.	Opening worship
9:00 a.m.	Session 1: Ring 1: Presenting Noble Noah
11:00 a.m.	Free time with worship-planning option
12:00 p.m.	Lunch
1:00 p.m.	Session 2: Ring 2: Presenting the Divine Daniel
2:15 p.m.	Free time (optional craft project)
5:30 p.m.	Dinner
6:30 p.m.	Session 3: Center Ring: Presenting the Amazing Jesus
8:00 p.m.	Munchies and more

Sunday

8:00 a.m.	Breakfast
9:00 a.m.	Group hike
10:00 a.m.	Family devotional time
10:30 a.m.	Closing activity
11:15 a.m.	Closing worship and evaluations
12:00 p.m.	Lunch
12:30 p.m.	Pack up and depart for home

Retreat description: This is an upbeat, active retreat geared for families, although, depending on your congregation, it may include the larger "church family" with single and/or older adults, as well as entire families. It is designed for two overnights and one and a half days. Participants will see how God functions as the ringmaster in this three-ring circus of life and learn ways to best enjoy the show.

Two weeks before leaving, the RLT should send out the Final Details Letter (see Appendix A, p. 109), reminding families to bring a Bible. Also at this time, confirm that your facility will supply a TV and DVD player.

RLT Master Supply List

Hospitality kits (see chapter 5), 1 per bathroom
Housing assignments
A check for conference center, as needed per contract
Copies of retreat curriculum for all RLT members and additional facilitators
Copies of retreat schedule for participants and for cabins and meeting spaces
Pens, markers, tape, pack of index cards, pack of Post-it notes
Ringmaster costume and parade music
Copies of Circus Survey
Big Top cards
Session 1 Children's Activity supplies: mural paper, markers/crayons, yarn, tissue paper gift bag shreds, construction paper noses/stripes/trunks, glue sticks, glitter, 12-inch cardboard people, masking tape
Recording of Bill Cosby's Noah sketches (available on-line at Amazon or eBay)
Skit props for Life Leveler: carpenter's level; 2 PalmPilots, BlackBerries, or date books; 2 coffee cups; 2 books, magazines, or newspapers; 2 cell phones; 2 calendars (maybe 1 wall and 1 desktop); 1 purse filled with receipts, scraps of paper, and junk; 1 briefcase or wallet filled with receipts, scraps of paper, and junk; a computer printout that says "To Do" in big letters at the top
Veggie Tales video or DVD: *Where's God When I'm Scared?*
Haiku Prayer handout
Prayer Plaque supplies: 6- to 8-inch wooden plaques (1 per family unit), craft paint, brushes, glitter, fancy paper, scissors (fancy paper scissors with styled edges work especially well), glue, decoupage coating, plastic tablecloths, Prayer Plaque directions
Family devotional time resources
Closing activity props: stuffed sheep, a 1 million candlepower flashlight, script for the angel (angel's lines from Luke 2:10-12, 14), a baby doll, recording of song "Amazing Love"
Movies or board games for free time
Pillow treats and/or Bible verses
Name tags
Coffee, tea, soft drinks, juice, bottled water, and snacks for breaks
Plates, cups, napkins
Copies of Sunday morning order of worship and worship supplies
CD player (if retreat center does not provide) and praise and worship CDs

FRIDAY

Arrival

Upon arriving at camp, the RLT will need to check in at the main building and receive housing assignments. Once in your space, the RLT should unpack, gather supplies for the opening overview, and place hospitality kits in the bathrooms. Then at least half the RLT should return to the main building/parking area to welcome and direct the rest of the participants.

Opening Overview: Life Is a Three-Ring Circus

Time frame: 30–45 minutes
Supplies: parade participants, CD player, parade music, ringmaster costume, Circus Survey (see Appendix A, p. 123), snacks, drinks, napkins, cups, plates

Note: Ahead of time, the RLT should have recruited participants for the "opening act," a circus parade featuring, for example, a juggler, a clown, a balloon artist, an acrobat/gymnast, a lion tamer (with a child dressed up in a lion costume), etc. You will need a large gathering area for this part of the program.

After all participants are settled in their housing, gather the group for a time of opening worship with some loud, kid-friendly praise and/or camp songs and words of prayer for the weekend time together.

After worship begin the parade. Start up the marching music and let your circus parade wind around the room a few times for effect. The RLT member who is leading tonight's overview can be dressed as a ringmaster with a red blazer, white dress shirt, top hat, and whistle. The RLT can blow the whistle to stop the parade, ask those participants to be seated, and then reassure the entire crowd that even though life is like a three-ring circus, this weekend will be a great getaway where they can get some R & R for their families and themselves. One RLT member should also introduce the retreat confidentiality policy that "what's said at retreat stays at retreat," as well as any camp rules and procedures to be followed. This is a good time, too, to point out that the RLT members are available for continued questions and conversations about deepening one's relationship with Jesus.

Circus Survey For this icebreaker your families can divide themselves into teams or work as a whole unit if your group is very large. If you have singles or older adult couples, the RLT members should help them connect with the family units. Your teams will be approaching other teams, introducing themselves, and asking the survey questions (see Appendix A, p. 123). As soon as the asking team gets a positive response, the responder should sign his or her initials. The asking team may then answer one question for the other team, but then it must move on to interview other groups. If a team has interviewed all of the other teams and still has questions to be answered, it may go back to the team it started with. Award a bag of cotton candy to the team that accurately completes its survey first. Depending on how familiar your group is with one another, you may also want to quickly run through some of the answers and identify people by name to start building connections.

Munchies and More

Now would be a great time for a campfire or a fire in the fireplace in your gathering area. If headed outside, take s'mores supplies with you and a cooler of bottled water and juice. If staying inside, break out the board games, popcorn, and hot chocolate, and let families relax. If there is an indoor gym space where children can burn off some energy after the car ride to camp or the weather is conducive to a night hike, even better.

At this point, your RLT may want to put a treat on each person's pillow (a mint or small piece of candy). In addition to the treat, the RLT may choose to attach a devotional Scripture with a self-stick address label. Possible Scriptures include Psalm 89:8, 1 Corinthians 13:13, and Ephesians 3:15.

SATURDAY

Breakfast

Opening Worship

Gather your families before the first activity for a time of worship. Sing a few songs, share some Scripture, pray for the group and this time together. Be intentional about inviting God to be part of this retreat process.

Session 1: Ring 1: Presenting Noble Noah

Time frame: 90–120 minutes, including break

Supplies: audio or DVD recording of Bill Cosby's Noah sketches (all 3, for 8 minutes total), CD player, Bibles, skit props (see RTL Master Supply List), Big Top cards (see Appendix A, p. 124), pens

Gather your participants and have them get comfortable. Kids may lie on the floor near their parents. An RLT member asks the group if they know who Noah is. After getting responses, tell the group they are going to hear the story of Noah told in a different way. Ask them to close their eyes and listen and see the story unfold in their mind. Play the three Bill Cosby Noah sketches.

Afterward, have families form discussion groups of 8 to 10 people. Assign one RLT member to each group, and ask the following questions:

1. What did Noah do for God?
2. What did Noah have to do to get his instructions from God?
3. What do you think made it hard for Noah to listen to and obey God?
4. Sometimes our lives get crazy like a circus. There is so much going on, so much to see, so many different people to listen to. What are things that you and your family can do to listen to God more closely and to obey God?
5. In your Bibles, read what King David wrote in Psalm 40:6b-8. What things are you learning about God and keeping in your heart?

When groups are finished with this first set of questions, take a short bathroom break. For the next segment, kids three and older will move to a different space for a kid-friendly activity, and adults will stay in the discussion room. For kids younger than three, encourage parents to bring some toys or snacks. The RLT could also bring a video for the young ones and play it at this time, as well as provide supervision. Two to four RLT members should move with the older children to lead their activity. Two to four should stay with the youngest children. The rest of the RLT members should remain with the adults to facilitate adult discussion groups. *Note:* You may need additional facilitators for this section. Try to allow parents to stay with their peers and use RLT members to staff the kids' activities while additional participant facilitators are used for the adult discussion groups.

Adult Discussion Ahead of time, recruit five players for your *Life Leveler* skit. These could be RLT members or people attending the retreat. You will need two men, two women, one announcer, and one "Vanna White" type of assistant. Other supplies are listed at the beginning of the session.

Skit setting: Announcer stands in the middle of the stage area. One woman and one man are seated off to the announcer's left with their PalmPilots, books or newspapers, and cups of coffee (they are not a couple, so they can be facing slightly different directions and in their own space; they are just representing men and women). The other man and woman are on the opposite side of the stage. The woman is pacing while talking on a cell phone. She also has her purse and a date book. The man can be seated at a desk with his calendar and cell phone and with his wallet or briefcase open. He is rifling through the wallet/briefcase frantically and muttering to himself.

Announcer: *Friends, take a good look. Is this your life?* [Points to man and woman on his left who are calmly entering things into their PalmPilots/date books and, when finished, pick up their coffee cups and begin reading.] *Or, is this your life?* [Points to other side of the stage where man and woman are frantically digging through their purse/briefcase and throwing out paper while making calls on their cell phones and flipping calendar pages.]

If this is you [points to the frantic people], *then you need the Life Leveler.* [The "Vanna White" assistant parades the level back and forth for the audience.] *The Life Leveler, by Trinity Inc., will keep you balanced so this can be your life too* [points to calm man and woman reading].

Through powers we don't fully understand, when the Life Leveler is aligned vertically with your head and horizontally with your heart, it will measure the stress and chaos in your life and give a reading. [Vanna demonstrates on one of the calm people and nods, smiling at the audience. She then moves to one of the frantic people and acts as if she can't even get the level to hold straight. She sadly shakes her head at the audience and pulls a printed to-do list out of her back pocket and hands it to the person.] *Trinity Inc.'s specially designed Life Leveler will also print out a list of things you must do to regain balance and get a stable reading. This amazing product is only available through our unique RetreatTV offer, so call now to order your Life Leveler today!* [End skit.]

The RLT should now divide the adults into groups, and one RLT member should go with each group to facilitate discussion with these questions:

1. Who here needs a Life Leveler? Why? What's going on in your life right now?
2. What do you think would be on that Life Leveler printout for you?
3. Why do you think it's so hard to let God be the ringmaster in our lives? Why can't we just listen to and obey God like Noah did?
4. In your Bibles, read Deuteronomy 6:1-9. Verses 4-9 are called the *Shema* (sheh-MAH) in Hebrew, the Jewish confession of faith. These verses were central to God's people's understanding of their relationship with their Creator and were related to the Ten Commandments (see Deuteronomy 5:1-22). Moses' advice to God's people was as relevant then as it is now. What is one thing you can do to act on Moses' advice?

Children's Activity (going on simultaneously with adult discussion) Supplies: 12 feet of mural paper with a big top circus tent outline drawn on it with three large circles marked for the circus rings; markers or crayons; glue sticks; assorted colors (red, yellow, orange, brown, gray, black) of yarn and gift bag tissue shreds; small red, black, and pink circles for noses; gray construction paper strips for elephant trunks; orange and black construction paper strips for tiger stripes;

assorted construction paper; glitter; 12-inch cardboard people cutouts (can be ordered online from school or craft suppliers

The RLT members working with the kids should take them to a large space where you will be able to play some running games and work on a craft. If your group is large or you have a wide age span, break into two groups (preschool–kindergarten and grades 1–5). Ask the middle and high school students to help you with the younger children.

LISTENING GAMES: An RLT member will tell the group that they are going to play two games that will help them practice listening and obeying: Red Light, Green Light and Mother May I. In Red Light, Green Light, one child stands at one end of the room while the other children line up opposite her. With her back to the group, the child leader calls out, "Green light," and the group runs toward her. When she wants to stop them, she calls out, "Red light," and turns around. Children who don't stop have to go back to the starting line (use your best judgment with the younger children and their ability to stop). The leader repeats this cycle until she is tagged. Then the tagger becomes the leader and the game continues.

With Mother May I, the leader stands at the opposite end of the playing space facing the group. One at a time the children ask the leader about different steps they can take, for example, "May I take four baby steps [or three giant steps, five small steps, three bunny hops, eight monkey jumps, etc.]?" The leader then gives permission, restating the type of step and how many the child may take. The first person to tag the leader becomes the new leader, and the game repeats.

If you have two groups and enough space, you can have two game leaders running the games and a group leader helping each group. Just flip-flop your groups and games after 10 minutes or so.

FOLLOW-UP DISCUSSION: Gather your kids into one group and have an RLT member ask:

1. Was it hard or easy to listen to and obey the game leader?
2. Did you ever get tired of listening to the leader?
3. What would happen if you tried to cheat and do what you wanted, not what you were told to do?
4. In your life, whom do you have to listen to and obey? (moms, dads, teachers, God, et al.)
5. Why is it important to obey God, your parents, your teachers, and others in authority?
6. Think back to the Noah story. What do you think would have happened if Noah hadn't listened to and obeyed God?

FOLLOW-UP CRAFT: Lay your big top mural out over two tables or hang it on the wall. Show the kids the three rings in the big top outline. Label the first ring "Listen and Obey." Give each child a cardboard person and tell them that the person represents them and that they are going to decorate their person like a circus performer and put that person inside the "Listen and Obey" ring. They can turn their person into a lion, a tiger, an elephant, a clown, an acrobat, etc. Set out the craft supplies and let the kids create. RLT members and older teens may need to help the youngest ones get started.

When the performers are finished, make sure that names are on the back, and then use masking tape or sticky tack to place them in the "Listen and Obey" ring. When all the performers are in the ring, an RLT member can close your time with a short prayer, saying: *Lord, help us to listen to and obey you in all that we do. We love you, Lord. Amen.*

Rejoin your children's group with your adult group. Give each family a Big Top card and a pen. Ask families to put their name on the tent and then take a minute to think of one thing they can do to listen to and obey God better and write that thing in Ring 1 in their Big Top. Close the morning with a group prayer or the song "What a Mighty God We Serve." The Big Top cards can stay in the meeting area for future use.

Free Time with Worship-Planning Option

There should be about an hour before lunch for families to relax and hang out, take a walk, play a board game, fish, or play football, basketball, or other sports. The RLT should also let families know that anyone wishing to help plan/lead the worship service can meet at a set location after a 15-minute bathroom break. Encourage kids to come and sign up to be in a skit, read a Bible verse, collect the offering, or lead a song or prayer. You can also have supplies available for children to make rhythm instruments to accompany praise songs (toilet paper and paper towel tubes, rice, beans, beads, aquarium gravel, sand, foil, plastic wrap, glue, rubber bands, etc.).

Lunch

Session 2: Ring 2: Presenting the Divine Daniel

Time frame: 60–75 minutes

Supplies: Veggie Tales video or DVD *Where's God When I'm Scared?* TV/DVD/VCR player, pens, Haiku Prayer handout (see Appendix A, p. 125), Bibles, circus mural hung or laid out in meeting area

Gather the group around the TV and show the Daniel in the lions' den segment of the Veggie Tales movie. An RLT member should preface the clip with this: *This morning we learned that we need to listen to and obey God. We also need to be able to talk to God, to pray to God, both when life is crazy like a three-ring circus and when it's going well. In a minute we're going to see the Veggie Tales version of the story of Daniel and his time in the lions' den. That was definitely not a fun "circus" experience for Daniel. It was scary! It was dangerous! And do you know how he got through it all? He talked to God in prayer. Let's see what happened.* [Show movie.]

After the movie, divide up into groups of eight to ten people. An RLT member should go with each group to facilitate discussion of the following questions:

1. Why do you think Daniel kept talking to God when he was in the lions' den?
2. Do you remember how you learned to pray? Tell us about it.
3. Do you know any prayers by heart? Which ones?
4. What do you think are different ways to pray? (by yourself, in a group, in song, etc.)
5. Hear these words that Daniel wrote later after the lions' den experience. It was another time that he was scared and was trying to listen to and obey God. Let's read from Daniel 10:11-12. What's one thing you and your family can do to be more like Daniel? When families have an answer, ask them to go write it down in Ring 2 on the circus mural.

Follow-up Activity Ask families to form their own group now, and give each family a pen and a Haiku Prayer handout (see Appendix A, p. 125.) A haiku is a simple Japanese form of poetry that has three lines. The first and third lines have five syllables; the middle line has seven syllables. Ask families to read the two examples to each other from the handout and then create their own family prayer that they could use at mealtime, bedtime, or on some other occasion. Tell families to save their prayer, because they will have the opportunity to mount it on a plaque during free time, which comes next. When they finish their prayer, they can find their Big Top card and write one thing in Ring 2 that they can do to improve their prayer lives. Families can complete these activities at their own pace and leave when they are done.

Free Time

This retreat has a large afternoon block of free time. The RLT should do a little research and have a list of free-time options available, such as shopping, visiting museums, or seeing a movie, as well as "at camp" activities like relaxing and hanging out, taking a walk, fishing, playing football or basketball, etc. At some point the RLT may want to organize a game of Capture the Flag, sand volleyball, or some other group activity.

Prayer Plaque Craft Supplies: copies of Prayer Plaque handout (see Appendix A, p. 126), 6- to 8-inch wooden plaques (1 per family unit), ripped up tissue paper squares (assorted colors), brushes, glitter, fancy paper, scissors (fancy paper scissors with styled edges work especially well), glue, decoupage coating, paper bowls for glue mix, plastic tablecloths

Cover tables with plastic for easy cleanup. Dedicate an art area and set out bowls of decoupage glue, brushes, tissue paper, and glitter. Each family will need a copy of the directions and a plaque.

Dinner

Session 3: Center Ring: Presenting the Amazing Jesus

Time frame: 1 hour

Supplies: CD player and praise and worship CDs or praise and worship music for song leader and group, Post-it notes, pens, Big Top mural

Gather your group in your meeting area. An RLT member will lead this session. The following is a sample script to use: *This weekend we have been talking about circuses. How do you feel when you're at the circus?* [Let group answer—amazed, scared, excited, thrilled, happy, etc.] *This is exactly how the disciples felt when they saw Jesus in action. They couldn't believe the things he could do; the way he healed people, taught people, loved people, and forgave people was astonishing. Jesus was simply amazing!*

Now here's the great thing! Some people thought that only grown-ups could understand what Jesus was talking about. A few of the disciples even tried to keep little children away from Jesus, figuring that they would be bothering him. But here's what Jesus said: " 'Let the little children come to me. Don't keep them away. God's kingdom belongs to people like them. What I'm about to tell you is true. Anyone who will not receive God's kingdom like a little child will never enter it.' Then he took the children in his arms. He put his hands on them and blessed them" (Mark 10:13-16, NIrV).

Hey, let's give it up for Jesus! [Lead applause.] *No matter how old or young you are, Jesus welcomes you into a friendship with him. Isn't that amazing? Let's take a minute to think about why Jesus is amazing. Get into your family groups and have each person write down on a Post-it note one reason she or he thinks Jesus is amazing. Maybe Jesus helped you or healed you or a friend or family member or you think his love is amazing or his ability to forgive even after we keep making the same mistakes is mind-blowing. You decide and write it down.* [Give families 5–10 minutes of thinking and writing time.]

Now, one at a time, each family is going to come forward and place your Post-it notes in the center ring. Please read each note out loud as you put it in the circle. [Let families come forward.]

Let's close with a time of praise and worship! (Have song sheets available, as well as a CD player/CDs or a musician.) Some suggested songs include: "Hallelujah/Your Love Is Amazing," "Lord, I Lift Your Name on High," "Awesome God," "Let the Praises Ring," "God Is Great," "All I Want to Do," "Here I Am to Worship," "My Best Friend," "Our Love Is Loud," "My Redeemer Lives," "Shine, Jesus, Shine," and "Blessed Be Your Name."

Munchies and More

If the weather permits, have another campfire outside or get your inside fireplace going. Families can contribute snacks to share, or you can provide the s'mores supplies and popcorn. To continue the circus theme, add in peanuts (if no one has allergies) and cotton candy (available in bags, prespun). The RLT can also use this time to leave another pillow treat and verse on participants' bunks. If the weather is bad or you need another choice, offer a family movie option.

SUNDAY

Breakfast

Group Hike

If the weather and your location cooperate, plan a group hike through the woods, along the beach, or on the retreat center grounds. If your youth are doing a skit for worship and need practice time, your RLT could gather them now and run through any final details.

Family Devotional Time

Provide a variety of materials for families—a list of the Scriptures studied this weekend, picture books that relate to circuses or busyness, devotional magazines for kids, study Bibles, art supplies—and encourage families to take this time to reflect on or respond to their favorite Scripture from the weekend.

Closing Activity

Time frame: 30–40 minutes

Supplies: stuffed sheep, a 1 million candlepower flashlight, script for the angel (Luke 2:10–12, 14), a baby doll, volunteers for shepherds, an angel, Mary and Joseph, Big Top cards, pens, CD player, recording of "Amazing Love"

Gather your group in your meeting area. An RLT member will lead this session and serve as the narrator for the skit. The script follows: *We have spent the weekend talking about how life is a three-ring circus and can be filled with sights and sounds that overwhelm us and distract us. It's easy for us to forget that God is our ringmaster. But when we listen to and obey God and when we talk to God in prayer, we will be amazed at the depth of our relationship.*

We're going to look at one last story this morning. I think you'll recognize it. I need some shepherds [give volunteers toy sheep and put them in front] *and an angel who can read* [give angel his/her script and stand him/her next to the shepherds] *and a Mary and a Joseph* [seat them off to the side].

The narrator reads Luke 2:1-18, encouraging the players to act their parts and allowing the angel to speak his/her lines. Shine the flashlight on the shepherds when the text talks about the bright light that shined all around.

And that's really it, isn't it? Jesus is amazing. He's the star of the show, the main act with top billing. From his humble birth to his death on the cross for each one of us, to the way he lives in our hearts today and forgives our sins, Jesus is amazing! I want you to take a few minutes now to complete the center ring on your Big Top card. In that ring you and your family need to write down a few ways you can get to know the amazing Jesus better when you return home. [Play "Amazing Love" while families work.]

Let's close in prayer. Lord Jesus, there is no one else like you. Every day we want to praise the wonder of your mighty love. We come before you knowing that we make mistakes, knowing that we don't love one another like you love us. And still you forgive us. Still you call us your own. We ask that you take over our hearts, Lord. Give us your peace. Forgive us for the hurtful things we say and do, so that we might be more like you in every way, every day. Amen.

Closing Worship and Evaluation

Time frame: 45 minutes
Supplies: To be determined by RLT

The RLT can plan a worship service in advance. Check your church library for liturgical resources if you want to include a call to worship, prayer of confession, or other group prayers, or write your own (maybe you had youth help you during the worship planning time on Saturday). Scriptures may include any of the ones listed previously in this retreat, or the RLT can use a concordance to look up verses under the headings of *peace, love, balance, prayer, pray, listen, hear,* or *obey*. Retreat participants could also be asked to share any favorite passages they have on these subjects.

If you type up and copy an order of worship, include your praise song and hymn lyrics or bring along songbooks or hymnals. You might also opt for a PowerPoint presentation, but make sure you have a power source and a screen. Ahead of time, find an RLT member or a retreat participant who would be comfortable leading the singing and/or accompanying the group for worship. If need be, bring a portable CD player and worship music CDs.

Don't forget to ask the RLT members to listen for stories on listening to and obeying God, on prayer, or on the power of Jesus' love that may have come up in the small group discussions. Ask a few of these individuals or families if they would share their testimonies in worship for the morning's message. Your group may also want to bring things for the altar, such as candles and flowers or an offering basket if you plan to take up an offering.

Before everyone leaves worship, get a group picture, and then pass out the retreat evaluations (see Appendix A, p. 110). Ask participants to complete them so you have input for next year's planning.

Lunch

Pack Up and Depart for Home

Finish packing and head for home at this point. Make sure your group has followed the retreat center's checkout procedures. Don't forget to leave your check if that is what the management requires.

CHAPTER 13

Family Retreat #2
God's Good Eats

Schedule and Plan

Sample Schedule

Friday

6:00 p.m.	RLT arrives at camp to get set up
7:00 p.m.	People arrive at camp, find rooms, settle in
7:45 p.m.	Opening overview: Breads of the World
8:30 p.m.	Munchies and more

Saturday

8:00 a.m.	Breakfast
8:45 a.m.	Opening worship
9:00 a.m.	Session 1: God's Grocery Store
11:00 a.m.	Free time
12:00 p.m.	Lunch
1:00 p.m.	Session 2: Jesus on Bread
2:15 p.m.	Free time (optional craft project)
5:30 p.m.	Dinner
6:30 p.m.	Session 3: Family Dinners
8:00 p.m.	Munchies and more

Sunday

8:00 a.m.	Breakfast
9:00 a.m.	Group hike
10:00 a.m.	Family devotional time
10:30 a.m.	Closing activity: Food Poisoning
11:00 a.m.	Closing worship and evaluations
12:00 p.m.	Lunch
12:45 p.m.	Pack up and depart for home

Retreat description: This is a fun hands-on retreat geared for families, although depending on your congregation, it may include the larger "church family" with single and/or older adults, as well as entire families. It is designed for two overnights and one and a half days. Participants will look at different images of bread and how God feeds our faith so that we can do his work in this world.

Two weeks before leaving, the RLT should send out the Final Details Letter (see Appendix A, p. 109), reminding families to bring a Bible. Also at this time, confirm that your facility will supply a TV/DVD player for free time movies.

RLT Master Supply List

Hospitality kits (see chapter 5), 1 per bathroom
Housing assignments
A check for conference center, as needed per contract
Pens, markers, crayons, tape and/or sticky tack, ream of copy paper
Ethnic breads, either donated by families or purchased ahead of time
Baskets, metal bowl, napkins, cups, plates
Copies of retreat sessions for each RLT member or volunteer facilitator
Copies of retreat schedule for participants and for cabins and meeting spaces
Copies of Bread of Life handout
Prize for bread game if desired ($5 bakery gift card)
Flip chart pad for graffiti sheets
Several 8-foot sections of mural paper
Bible storyteller costumes (robe, tie, sandals)
Bible story food samples: wafer cookies, cooked chicken, baking powder biscuits or something similar, cornmeal cakes, smoked fish, flat bread
Packages of hot roll mix and all added ingredients, plus one extra packet of yeast
Measuring cups and spoons, baking trays, mixing bowls, nonstick baking spray
Drawing of apple tree with construction paper apples
Movies or board games for free time
Pillow treats and/or Bible verses
Name tags
Coffee, tea, pop, juice, bottled water, snacks, and paper goods for breaks if your retreat center does not provide them
CD player (if retreat center does not provide) and praise and worship CDs
Copies of Sunday morning order of worship and worship supplies

FRIDAY

Arrival

Upon arriving at camp, the RLT will need to check in at the main building and receive housing assignments. Once in your space, the RLT should unpack, gather supplies for the opening overview, and place hospitality kits in the bathrooms. Then at least half the RLT should return to the main building/parking area to welcome and direct the rest of the participants and help them settle in their lodgings.

Opening Overview: Breads of the World

Time frame: 45–60 minutes
Supplies: breads from various countries or ethnic traditions either brought by each family and/or purchased in advance, baskets, napkins, juice and water, cups

Once everyone is unpacked, gather your families together in your large meeting space. You should all be seated on chairs in a circle. One RLT member should officially welcome everyone to the retreat, introduce the RLT, and make sure all participants have their name tags. People can go around the circle and introduce themselves and share one or two bits of personal information. Open your time together by singing some familiar praise and worship songs or hymns. After singing, an RLT member will say: *We're going to spend this weekend talking about God's good eats. There are many stories in the Bible about God providing food for people in need, but God doesn't just feed people who have hungry bellies; God also feeds our faith. When we are fed with the Word of God, we become "full" of God energy and are able to go out and do God's work in this world. Hear what Jesus said to his followers in John 6:35 (NIV): "I am the bread of life. He who comes to me will never go hungry."*

That might sound kind of strange, but we're going to spend this weekend figuring out exactly what Jesus meant by those words. Let's pray about our time together. Jesus, we have come to this weekend to learn more about you. We pray that just as our bellies get hungry, that our minds and hearts will be hungry for you and that you will fill them. Bless our time together. Open our ears and our eyes that we might see and hear your truth. We thank you for all the ways that you feed us, Lord. Fill us up and then send us out to do your work in this world. Amen.

Close your time of worship with one or two familiar songs and a word of prayer. Then, to work out the wiggles, play a group game called Upset the Bread Basket. This is a takeoff on Upset the Fruit Basket. Choose 3 or 4 types of bread (Italian, French, flat, Irish soda, pita, rye, banana, etc.) and go around the circle, assigning each person a bread name. Remove one chair from the circle. That person moves into the middle and calls out one of the bread types. All the people assigned to that bread jump up and switch seats with one another. The middle caller tries to steal one of the seats too. Whoever is left without a seat is the next person in the middle. If you want everyone to change seats, call out, "Upset the bread basket!" Play for 10 or 15 minutes or until all the kids have had a chance to be in the middle. With a little energy expended, one RLT member can introduce the weekend's schedule, the retreat confidentiality policy of "what's said at retreat stays at retreat," and any camp rules and procedures to be followed. This is also a good time to point out RLT members who are available to those wishing to talk about deepening their relationship with Jesus.

Breads of the World Guessing Game Supplies: ethnic bread samples, baskets, napkins, blank paper, pens, prize (if desired)

Ahead of time the RLT should have purchased or received family donations of ethnic breads (at least ten types; more is fine), cut them into bite-size pieces, and put them in baskets identified with a number. Family units need a blank sheet of paper and a pen. They will be sampling each bread and trying to guess what it is. When they know, they need to write down the basket number and their guess. For an added twist, you can have a family taster who is blindfolded and must rely only on sense of taste and smell to guess, but it might be more fun for the whole family to participate. *Note:* Please be aware of any food allergies in your group ahead of time and either caution participants or adapt this mixer as needed for personal safety and inclusivity. When families have completed the tasting, regather in your circle and reveal the bread names/numbers. If you wish, the family with the most correct guesses could win a small prize (an extra loaf of one of the breads or a $5 gift card to a local bakery).

Munchies and More

Time frame: 1 hour or more

Supplies: leftover bread samples, juice/water, other snacks, cups, napkins, board games, movies, s'mores supplies, etc.

After the guessing game, everyone can enjoy the remainder of the bread. Serve your juice, water, and other refreshments and begin a time of evening fellowship with board games, movies, singing, or maybe even a campfire and s'mores.

At this point your RLT may want to put a pillow treat on each person's bunk (a mint or small piece of candy). In addition to the treat, the RLT may choose to attach a devotional Scripture with a self-stick address label. Possible Scriptures include Exodus 16:4, Deuteronomy 8:6, Matthew 6:33, and Luke 22:19.

SATURDAY

Breakfast

Opening Worship

Gather your families before the first activity for a time of worship. Sing a few songs, share some Scripture, pray for the group and this time together. Be intentional about inviting God to be part of this retreat process. You can also identify RLT members or other volunteers who are available if people have questions, need prayer, or want to talk about deepening their relationship with Jesus.

Session 1: God's Grocery Store

Time frame: 90–120 minutes, including break

Supplies: Graffiti sheets (large pieces of paper), markers, 1 or more 8-foot sections of mural paper, crayons, storyteller costumes (robe, tie, sandals), food samples (enough that everyone can have a "taste") of wafers (similar to a communion wafer or sugar wafer cookie), cooked chicken, baking powder biscuits, johnnycakes (cornmeal cakes/corn bread), fish (a dried or smoked fish that is easily transported), flat bread

Set up three stations (the more spread out the better). You will need one storyteller for each station, so recruit these from your RLT or your participants ahead of time. Note: Your storytellers can certainly read the scripts that follow below; however, the experience will be much more rewarding if the storytellers have the scripts ahead of time and can prepare by reading the story repeatedly in both the Bible and the script so that they are comfortable telling it in their own words.

The first station will be the story of God feeding the Israelites manna and quail (Exodus 16:4-21). The second will be the Elijah stories (1 Kings 17:1-16; 19:1-9). The third will be the story of Jesus feeding the five thousand (Mark 6:30-44). At each station, set out samples of food for participants to taste: Israelites—wafers and chicken; Elijah—baking powder biscuits, chicken, corn bread cakes, water; Jesus—cooked fish and flat bread. Each storyteller will need a costume (robe, sandals, etc.).

Also, hang several sheets of graffiti paper around the room and lay out the sections of mural paper. On the graffiti sheets write the headings: "God Is Good," "Ways I Can Feed the Hungry," and "One Thing I Learned So Far Is." An RLT member needs to explain to participants that if their group is waiting to move to the next storytelling station, they can come to the graffiti sheets and write down ways that they have seen the goodness of God in this world, ways they they can feed the hungry, and one thing they have learned so far.

On the mural sheets they can recreate the story they just heard as a drawing or series of drawings. The story illustration could be a whole group project, added to by various people, or done by individual families. Note: While this morning session is designed for families to participate as a whole, you may want to look at the ages in your group and provide a supervised nursery option for ages two and under if you feel that would be beneficial.

Divide your group into three parts and assign each one a starting station. Family units can stay together. An RLT member should say: *At each station, participants will hear a story, taste the food that God provided in that story, and talk about how God fed people's spirits as well as their bodies. When you have visited all three stations, we will gather together one last time. If you finish at your station and there's still time before switching, please visit the graffiti sheets or the mural paper stations where you can respond to the story you just heard.*

Manna and Quail Station Storyteller says: *Come, people of God, and gather around. Listen to this amazing story of how God fed his people in the wilderness. This is an Old Testament story that is recorded in the book of Exodus, chapter 16. Moses had just led the people out of their lives of slavery in Egypt. Life had been hard in Egypt. God's people were slaves for Pharaoh, the ruler of Egypt. They worked making mud bricks and helping Pharaoh build his empire.*

They prayed for years for relief from this awful life, and God finally answered their prayers. God sent Moses to lead them out of Egypt. Moses started by talking to Pharaoh, but Pharaoh didn't want to let God's people go. Who else would he find to do all his hard work?

When Pharaoh didn't listen, God poured out plagues on Egypt. Each one was worse than the one before. Frogs, gnats, flies, and finally locusts covered the land. The locusts ate the crops and destroyed the land. Things got worse and worse, and after ten awful plagues, Pharaoh finally agreed to let God's people go.

Then God parted the Red Sea, and Moses and God's people walked right across. But God closed that sea on top of Pharaoh's chariots and armies, so they drowned. God's people were safe. Yea, God! But where we find God's people right now in the story is wandering around in the desert, which they'd been doing for the six weeks since they left Egypt.

They were hot, tired, hungry, thirsty, and crabby, and they were getting mad at God. They were beginning to think that maybe life as slaves would have been better. They complained to Moses and his brother, Aaron, who were leading them farther and farther away from Egypt and into the desert. The people said, "We wish the LORD had put us to death in Egypt. There we sat around pots of meat. We ate all of the food we wanted. But you have brought us out into this desert. You must want this entire community to die of hunger" (Exodus 16:3, NIrV).

Here's what God said to Moses, "I will rain down bread from heaven for you. The people must go out each day. Have them gather enough bread for that day. Here is how I will put them to the test. I will see if they will follow my directions" (Exodus 16:4, NIrV).

And so God sent this bread called "manna" every morning, but the people could only collect as much as they could eat that day. They couldn't save it. Some people didn't listen and tried to keep it for the next day. But it became rotten and stunk and was filled with maggots. So they learned to only take what they could eat during the day. And at night quail covered the camp, and the people were able to kill the quail and roast it like chicken. In the morning the manna came again, and the people were fed. For forty years while God's people lived in the wilderness, they ate manna in the morning and quail in the evening. They were fed and they were full. And then, after forty years, they arrived at Canaan, the wonderful land that God had promised them.

After you finish the story, pass around samples of the "manna" and "quail" and lead the group in discussing the following questions:

1. What do you think about God's people complaining after God led them out of slavery? Would you have been complaining? Was God's response fair? Why or why not?
2. Think of a time when you were angry or complaining, maybe to a friend or to your parents. What happened? How was the situation fixed?
3. When God sends the manna and quail to feed the people, God is taking care of their physical hunger. How does God also feed their spirits?
4. In what way do you hunger to know more about God?
5. How can you feed your spirit?

Elijah Station Storyteller says: *Welcome, travelers, gather 'round. Hear the word of the Lord from the book of 1 Kings, chapters 17 and 19. These are the days of Elijah. Elijah was a faithful prophet for God in a very unfaithful time. There was a wicked king in power named King Ahab. His wife, Queen Jezebel, was even more evil. They both worshipped Baal, a storm god who was said to control the rains and the growing seasons. The king and queen followed the advice of the idol-loving prophets of Baal, and some of God's people began to do the same. This was a problem!*

While Elijah was traveling around trying to teach God's people to follow God's rules, not Baal's, God sent a drought to the land. He told Elijah to tell King Ahab that the drought would last for several years. Then God sent Elijah into the wilderness to hide, because this news made King Ahab very mad. God said, "Go east and hide in the Kerith Valley. It is east of the Jordan River. You will drink water from the brook. I have ordered some ravens to feed you there" (1 Kings 17:2-4, NIrV).

So Elijah did what God ordered. The ravens brought Elijah bread and meat, and he drank water from the brook. A while later the brook dried up because there still hadn't been any rain, so God sent Elijah to Zarephath because God had commanded a widow to provide Elijah with food. When Elijah got there, he found the woman and asked for a drink of water, which she provided. Then he asked for a piece of bread, but the widow said, "I don't have any bread. And that's just as sure as the LORD your God is alive. All I have is a small amount of flour in a jar and a little olive oil in a jug. I'm gathering a few sticks to take home. I'll make one last meal for myself and my son. We'll eat it. After that, we'll die" (1 Kings 17:12, NIrV).

But Elijah reassured the widow. "Don't be afraid," he said. "Go home. Do what you have said. But first make a little bread for me. Make it out of what you have. Bring it to me. Then make some for yourself and your son" (1 Kings 17:13, NIrV). The widow went away and did what Elijah told her to do, and there was enough food every day to feed Elijah as well as the widow and her son.

A year or so later, the drought was still on the country. There had been no rain. The crops weren't growing. The people and animals were hungry and thirsty. No one was happy. Elijah sent his assistant Obadiah to give King Ahab a message: Elijah wants to see you. King Ahab found Elijah, and Elijah told him that they were going to have a little contest between Baal and God. King Ahab agreed, thinking his god was so powerful that this would be an easy victory.

And so Elijah set the rules. Both he and the prophets of Baal would each sacrifice a bull. They would kill the bull, cut it up, and place it on the wood on a huge altar they had made, but neither side could light the fire. Elijah told the people that the god who answered first by sending fire down to consume the sacrifice would clearly be the one and only God.

So the prophets of Baal and their believers prepared their bull and began praying. Nothing happened, so they danced around the altar. Then Elijah began to tease them. "Shout louder!" he said. "I'm sure Baal is a god! Perhaps he has too much to think about. Or maybe he has gone to the bathroom. Or perhaps he's away on a trip. Maybe he's sleeping. You might have to wake him up" (1 Kings 18:27, NIrV).

Then, and this is really sad, the Baal worshippers cut themselves and let the blood flow, which is what they did when things looked hopeless. But still nothing happened.

Then Elijah and God's people repaired the altar of the Lord, which had been destroyed, and they sacrificed their bull and placed it on the wood. Then Elijah directed the people to get four jars with water and pour it on the wood. They did this three times. The water even formed a little ditch around the altar. King Ahab was laughing because he thought God's people were fools for making the wood so wet. How would they ever get a fire started? Then Elijah prayed for God to answer him and send the fire so that the people would know he is the one and only God. And the fire of the Lord came down and consumed everything, even the water. Wow!

After that King Ahab told Queen Jezebel everything Elijah had done. Queen Jezebel had been busy killing off the prophets of God as quick as she could, and this news of Elijah's triumph made Jezebel so angry that she vowed to kill Elijah by the next day. Elijah was so afraid that he ran for his life and traveled into the desert. He collapsed under a small tree and prayed to God to take his life. Then he fell asleep.

But an angel of the Lord touched him and told him to eat, and there next to his head was a little cake and a jar of water. So Elijah ate and drank and then went back to sleep. And again an angel touched him and told him to eat and drink because his journey would be long and hard. So Elijah ate and drank, and the food gave him new strength. Then he walked for forty days and forty nights until he arrived at Horeb, the mountain of God.

After you finish the story, pass out the foods that Elijah ate and discuss the following questions with your group:

1. Over and over again in Elijah's time of serving God, he was hungry and God provided food. How do you think that made Elijah feel about God?
2. When God sent Elijah to the widow and Elijah told her to use the last little bit of her flour and oil to make him a meal, how do you think the widow felt? Why do you think she followed Elijah's instructions?
3. What do you think Elijah and the widow learned about God?
4. Can you think of a time that God took care of your needs? Share that story and tell what it did for your faith.

Loaves and Fish Station Storyteller says: *Hear the story of Jesus feeding the five thousand, as told in Mark 6:30-44. Jesus spent the last three years of his life teaching and sharing his love for God. He traveled around the countryside, meeting people where they lived—in towns, on hillsides, along the road. One day he had been out with his disciples teaching all day long. But people were still coming to hear Jesus. Jesus and his friends hadn't even had time to eat, so Jesus told them, "Come with me by yourselves to a quiet place. You need to get some rest." So the friends all got in a boat and sailed away, but the people saw them and figured out where they were going. By the time Jesus came ashore, a large crowd had gathered. Jesus, always the Good Shepherd, wanted to care for these people and feed their spirits, so he began to teach, even though it was late in the day and neither he nor his disciples had eaten.*

Jesus' disciples were not happy. Jesus had promised them a time of rest. They went to Jesus and said, "It's late. There is nothing here for the people to eat. They can go into the nearby villages and buy something."

But Jesus said, "No, you give them something to eat."

The disciples were amazed. They complained to Jesus, "But that would be too expensive. How are we supposed to buy bread for all these people?"

So Jesus said, "How many loaves do you have? Go and see."

Well, the disciples went off, and when they came back, they said, "Five loaves and two fish." Jesus surprised them again by telling the disciples to gather the people on the grass in groups of hundreds and fifties. Then Jesus took the five loaves and two fish and looked up to heaven and gave thanks. Then he broke the food into pieces and gave the pieces to his disciples to hand out to people. Do you know what happened? All of the people ate and all were satisfied. At the end of the evening when the disciples picked up the leftovers, there were still twelve baskets of broken pieces of bread and fish.

After you finish the story, pass around the bread and the fish and discuss the following questions with your group:

1. Why did the disciples want to send the people away from Jesus?
2. Who do you think was more amazed by Jesus being able to feed the crowd, the crowd or his disciples?

3. Why do you think Jesus wanted to keep the people there with him?
4. What do you think the people in the crowd learned about Jesus that night?

When your groups have visited all three stations, come back together. An RLT member can ask the following questions of the whole gathering:

1. What was your favorite story and why?
2. What do you think it means to be hungry for God (spiritually hungry)?
3. Tell me some ways that God fed hungry bellies and hungry spirits.
4. What is one way you can personally feed either a hungry belly or a hungry spirit?

An RLT member can close in prayer saying: *Lord, we thank you for all that you are and all that you do in your lives. We are so thankful to know that you provide for all of our needs and in doing so strengthen our faith in you. We pray that just as you care for us, we would learn from your example and show this same love and concern for others who are in need. We ask you to fill us up to do this work in your world. Amen.*

Free Time

There should be about an hour before lunch for families to relax and hang out, take a walk, play a board game, fish, or play football, basketball, or other sports.

Lunch

Session 2: Jesus on Bread

Time frame: 60–75 minutes

Supplies: yeast-based hot roll mix, hot water, eggs, butter (per package directions), cooking spray, baking sheets, measuring cups and spoons, mixing bowls, mixing spoons

Gather families together and divide into children and adults. Your RLT will need to divide its leadership, as well. Use your older tweens and teens as helpers with the children. The adult and children's discussions/activities occur simultaneously. Your adults can move to a quieter space if needed. You will regather as a whole group to close the session. Note: You will need to make arrangements ahead of time with the camp to use their ovens for the children's activity.

Children's Activity: Parable of the Yeast Gather the children in a circle. An RLT member can say: *This morning we heard how Jesus fed five thousand people with just five loaves of bread and two fish. Jesus didn't want to send the people away even though it was suppertime, because he knew their spirits needed to be fed with stories about God and God's love. Jesus taught stories with lessons that are called parables. In the middle of telling a bunch of longer stories, Jesus told this very short story in Matthew 13:33-34 [NIrV] "The kingdom of heaven is like yeast," he said. "A woman mixed it into a large amount of flour. The yeast worked its way all through the dough."*

Now, does anyone know what happens when you add yeast to dough when you're making bread? [Let kids answer.] *That's right. The yeast makes the dough rise and the bread tastes wonderful. So what do you think Jesus meant when he said that the kingdom of heaven is like yeast?* [Let kids answer.] *If we think about God being the yeast and us being the flour, what happens when God is mixed into our lives?* [Let kids answer.] *That's right. We grow in our faith!*

Let's do an experiment with yeast and bread dough and see for ourselves how this works.

Make sure all participants wash their hands. Clear a large, clean working space for this activity. Then, following the directions on the hot roll mix box follow the instructions for making rolls. (Note: You may need several packages, depending on group size. Plan for one roll for every person on retreat.) Let the children help add the ingredients and knead the bread. You will need to cover your dough and let it rise in a warm place (hopefully in the camp kitchen). While it is rising, you can do the next activity.

Children's Activity: Jesus Is the Bread of Life Gather the children in a circle. An RLT member says: *This next story happens the day after Jesus fed the people with the loaves and fish and is found in John 6:26-29 [NIrV]. When evening came, Jesus and his disciples got in a boat and sailed to the other side of the lake. When* *morning came, the crowd realized that Jesus was gone, so they got into their boats and sailed to Capernaum to look for Jesus. When they found him, they asked, "How did you get here?"*

Here's what Jesus told them, "What I'm about to tell you is true. You are not looking for me because you saw miraculous signs. You are looking for me because you ate the loaves until you were full. Do not work for food that spoils. Work for food that lasts forever. That is the food the Son of Man will give you. God the Father has put his seal of approval on him."

Then the people asked, "What does God want from us? What works does he want us to do?"

Jesus answered them, "God's work is to believe in the One he has sent." Now here's the interesting thing. Remember our story this morning about manna coming from heaven?

The people talking to Jesus knew that story, too, and here's what they said to him, "What miraculous sign will you give us? What will you do so we can see it and believe you? Long ago our people ate the manna in the desert. It is written in Scripture, 'The Lord gave them bread from heaven to eat.'"

Jesus reminded the people that it was not Moses who gave the people bread but God. God fed them when they had hungry bellies and hungry spirits. Jesus said, "The bread of God is the One who comes down from heaven. He gives life to the world" (John 6:33). The people begged Jesus to give them this bread.

So Jesus said to them, "I am the bread of life. No one who comes to me will ever go hungry. And no one who believes in me will ever be thirsty" (John 6:35).

The people talked among themselves trying to figure this out. Jesus told them not to complain and argue. They didn't understand what Jesus was talking about when he told them that people needed to eat his body and drink his blood. They thought he was nuts. But Jesus understood. He was talking to them in stories, trying to give them word pictures to help them understand. Just as our bodies need food and water for energy so that we can live, our spirits need God food; we need the love and the instruction of Jesus in order to live the way God wants us to live. When we listen to Jesus' stories and all the other words in the Bible, we get the energy we need to live holy and faithful lives.

Think about these things while we work with our bread again. Let's see how big it has gotten.

Have the children wash their hands again, and get your dough from the kitchen. Knead for a second time, roll into logs, and cut into 2-inch chunks. Lay the pieces on a baking sheet sprayed with nonstick cooking spray, cover, and let rise again according to package directions.

Gather your kids back in a circle. An RLT member says: *So what do you think of that last Jesus story? Pretty amazing, isn't it?*

Why do you think Jesus talked in stories instead of just ordering people to do this or that?

What are ways that you can learn more about God and Jesus and be fed?

What are ways you can share this God food with other friends or family members?

Once our rolls have risen and baked, you can share them with your family here. What do you think you're sharing besides an actual piece of food? [Let kids answer.] *Amen! Say thank you to God with me for feeding your bodies and feeding your spirits! Amen!*

While you wait for parents to return from their discussion time, play Upset the Bread Basket again. As soon as the rolls have risen for the second time, put them in the oven. If they are ready when the adults return, serve them after closing prayer. If not, ask people to hang around for a few minutes. Free time follows this session.

Adult Discussion: Jesus Is the Bread of Life Supplies:
packet of yeast, copies of the Bread of Life handout (see Appendix A, p. 127), Bibles

Take your adults into a quiet space that will allow for discussion. An RLT member holds up a packet of yeast and asks: *Does anyone know what this is?* [Let people answer.] *Right, dry baking yeast. And what does it do?* [Let people answer.] *Right. When you add it to bread dough, it causes the dough to rise and the bread to bake correctly. What do you think happens if you forget to add the yeast?* [Let people answer.] *Right. The bread won't rise and won't taste very good.*

Jesus used illustrations like this to paint word pictures for people so they might better understand his stories. In Matthew 13:33-34, Jesus tells people that the kingdom of heaven is like yeast that a woman mixes into bread dough. The yeast works all the way through the dough. Is that going to be good bread? It sure is, because the yeast is a part of the mix. What does that say about our lives when God is in the mix?

Now we're going to take a look at another Jesus story in John 6:22-58. Here Jesus is talking to the crowds that had been fed with the five loaves and two fish the day before. Jesus tells them that he is the Bread of Life. He uses literal examples to get them to think about their lives, both physical and spiritual. Let's read that passage.

Give time for people to read silently. Then ask for a narrator, a "crowd" voice, and a Jesus speaker. Have the narrator read the parts not in quotes (all the background story, the dialogue tags, etc.). Have the Jesus speaker read Jesus' direct quotes. Have the "crowd/they" voice read the other lines in quotes. Then break up into a few discussion groups and give each person a Bread of Life handout. An RLT member should stay with each group to facilitate.

When your adult groups finish, return to the children's activity area. Gather the whole group and join in a closing song or two and a prayer. An RLT member can say: *Lord, it is so good to know that you are the Bread of Life, that whenever our hearts and souls hunger and thirst for God, you are there to fill us up. Help us to trust in you to provide for us. Help us to seek you and no one else. Give us the strength to love you enough to live our lives in your name. Amen.*

While you wait for your rolls to bake, you can play Upset the Bread Basket or add to the murals and graffiti pages.

Free Time

This retreat has a large afternoon block of free time. The RLT should do a little research and have a list of free-time options available, such as shopping, visiting museums, or seeing a movie, as well as "at camp" activities like relaxing and hanging out, taking a walk, fishing, playing football or basketball, etc. At some point the RLT may want to organize a game of Capture the Flag, sand volleyball, or some other group activity.

The RLT should also let families know that anyone wishing to help plan/lead the worship service can meet at a set location after a 15-minute bathroom break. Encourage kids to come and sign up to be in a skit, read a Bible verse, collect the offering, or lead a song or prayer. You can also have supplies available for children to make rhythm instruments to accompany praise songs (toilet paper and paper towel tubes, rice, beans, beads, aquarium gravel, sand, foil, plastic wrap, glue, rubber bands, etc.)

Dinner

Session 3: Family Dinners

Time frame: 1 hour
Supplies: flip chart pages for graffiti sheets, markers
Gather your group in your meeting area. An RLT member should welcome the group and say: *So we just finished dinner, right? That was a pretty big family dinner, wasn't it? Do you ever have big dinners with your family, maybe for a birthday or holiday or even once a week? Let's make a list of the different types of family dinners we've been at.* [Make a list on one flip chart page.]

Now what's your favorite part of the family dinners? [Make a list for these responses.]

Okay, remember when we were talking this morning about Moses leading the Israelites out of slavery in Egypt? The night before that happened, God had given the Hebrew people special instructions for their last family dinner in Egypt. They had to roast meat and eat all of it, no leftovers, and they had to make bread without yeast in it so it wouldn't take so long to bake and it could travel with them. That night God brought death to the oldest sons of the Egyptians, but his angel of death passed over the homes of God's people. This "passover" became a symbol of God's faithfulness, and a special family dinner was celebrated each year to mark this time. It is known as the Jewish holiday Passover.

Now we're going to jump ahead hundreds and hundreds of years to when Jesus was celebrating Passover with his disciples. This was on the night of his arrest, the day before he died. Christians call this meal the Last Supper. It was the last family dinner Jesus had with his disciples on earth. In Luke we find Jesus' instructions for the most important family dinner we can share together as believers, the Lord's Supper, or Communion.

Let's read Luke 22:14-22. [Read passage.]

Does that sound familiar? Remember our story from this afternoon when Jesus told God's people he was the

Bread of Life? This is what he was talking about.

So let's make a timeline. Way over here on the left are the Israelites (God's people) eating their final supper in Egypt. This becomes known as the Passover. [Make a horizontal line from edge to edge on a flip chart page and put an X on the far left. Write "Israelites" and "Passover" by the X. Then, in the middle, make another X and write, "Jesus, celebrates Passover, gives instructions for Lord's Supper/Communion."] *And now here is Jesus celebrating the Passover and giving his disciples instructions for what we know as Communion. After Jesus died and rose again and his followers began traveling and teaching in his name, the believers would gather together for big family dinners. They shared everything they had with one another, and they celebrated the Lord's Supper together.*

Hear what Acts 2:42-44 says. [Read the passage and put an X to the right of the Jesus/Passover X and write, "Jesus' followers eat together." Then put a fourth X on the far right side of paper.] *And here we are.* [Indicate fourth X.] *Now what do you think these first three family dinners have in common?* [Make a new brainstorm list.] *Look at that! They all involve God. And that's what God asks us to do in our family dinners—we invite the Lord to the table. What are some ways we can have God at our dinner table?* [Make one final brainstorm list.] *Awesome! Let's close our time together in prayer.*

Lord, it is so amazing to see how you have been faithful to your people in every generation, that you were present in family dinners thousands of years ago and that you are still present today if we invite you to the table. We pray, Lord, that we will be faithful and welcoming to you, that we will ask you to come, not only to dinner, but into our lives, to guide us, to love us, to help us, to forgive us when we forget to include you. Thank you for always being there for us. Amen.

Munchies and More

If the weather permits, make a campfire outside or get your inside fireplace up and running. Families can contribute snacks to share, or you can provide the s'mores supplies and popcorn. The RLT can also use this time to leave another pillow treat and Scripture verse on participants' bunks. If the weather is bad or you need another choice, offer a family movie option.

SUNDAY

Breakfast

Group Hike

If the weather and your location cooperate, plan a group hike through the woods, along the beach, or on the retreat center grounds. If your kids are doing a skit for worship and need practice time, your RLT could gather them now and run through any final details.

Family Devotional Time

Provide a variety of materials for families, a list of the Scriptures studied this weekend, picture books that relate to food or family dinners or bread baking, devotional magazines for kids, study Bibles, and art supplies, and encourage families to take this time to reflect on or respond to their favorite Scripture from the weekend.

Closing Activity: Food Poisoning

Time frame: 30 minutes

Supplies: a big paper cutout tree (three feet or larger) with apples made from red construction paper (one per person) and loosely taped or sticky-tacked onto the tree, dark markers, basket and/or metal bowl, CD player, praise and worship CDs

Gather your group together for this final session. An RLT member can say: *Well, we've spent our time this weekend talking about how God feeds both our bodies and our spirits. Now I have one last question for you before we finish. Has anyone here ever had food poisoning?* [Let people respond.] *It's awful, isn't it? You eat something that probably looked and tasted good at the time, but it was bad, bad, bad. And it does terrible things inside your belly. Food poisoning is not fun! Usually you're sick for several days. Sometimes you even have to go to the hospital. So what happens to our spirits when we don't eat God food, when we feast on things that pull us away from God and his Word? We get food poisoning!*

Can you think back to the Bible stories you know and guess who got the first case of food poisoning? Who ate something they shouldn't have? [Let group respond.] *That's right. Adam and Eve. God created them and put them in this beautiful Garden of Eden*

where they had everything they needed. The only rule God gave them was not to eat from the tree of the knowledge of good and evil. But what happened? [Let group respond.] *That's right. The serpent tempted Eve and encouraged her to take an apple and eat it, and Eve followed the serpent's word, not God's.*

That, friends, was the beginning of sin. Sin is something we do that separates us from God. Adam and Eve separated themselves from God when they ate the apple. They got spiritual food poisoning! Now how do we recover from spiritual food poisoning? [Allow for answers.] *That's right. We ask God for forgiveness, we promise not to sin again, and we try only to eat the Bread of Life, which is Jesus' truth and teachings.*

What we're going to do now is pick apples off of our tree, and each person in your family can write down a sin he or she has done against God—maybe not obeying your parents, maybe saying hurtful things to a friend, maybe telling a lie, maybe going against God's Word. After everyone has written his or her sin on an apple, place the apples in this basket. We'll bring the basket to worship, and during our time of prayer, we will ask God to forgive us for these sins that cause spiritual food poisoning. We'll ask God to heal us and make our hearts new and clean. So go pick those apples!

Give your families time to pick the apples and write on them. Have music playing in the background. Make sure the apples all get placed in the basket and brought to worship. If you want, you can transfer the apples to a metal bowl and burn them up during worship to symbolize how God erases our sins when we ask for forgiveness.

Closing Worship
Time frame: 45–60 minutes
Supplies: To be determined by RLT

The RLT can plan a worship service in advance. Check your church library for liturgical resources if you want to include a call to worship, prayer of confession, or other group prayers, or write your own (maybe you had kids help you during the worship planning time on Saturday). Scriptures may include any of the ones listed previously in this retreat, or the RLT can use a concordance to look up verses under the headings of *bread, fed, feed, hunger,* or *hungry.* Retreat participants could also be asked to share any favorite passages they have on these subjects.

If you type up and copy an order of worship, include your praise song and hymn lyrics or bring along songbooks or hymnals. You might also opt for a PowerPoint presentation, but make sure you have a power source and a screen. Ahead of time, find an RLT member or a retreat participant who would be comfortable leading the singing and/or accompanying the group for worship. If need be, bring a portable CD player and worship music CDs.

Don't forget to ask the RLT members to listen for stories on God providing for our physical and spiritual needs that may have come up in the small group discussions. Ask a few of these individuals or families if they would share their testimonies in worship for the morning's message or perhaps an RLT member would like to give the message. Your group may also want to bring things for the altar, such as candles and flowers or an offering basket if you plan to take up an offering.

Before everyone leaves worship, get a group picture, and then pass out the retreat evaluations (see Appendix A, p. 110). Ask participants to complete them so that you have input for next year's planning.

Lunch

Pack Up and Depart for Home
Finish packing and head for home at this point. Make sure your group has followed the retreat center's checkout procedures. Don't forget to leave your check if that is what the management requires.

CHAPTER 14

Youth Retreat #1

Be True to Yourself

Schedule and Plan

Sample Schedule

Friday

6:00 p.m.	RLT arrives at camp to get set up
7:30 p.m.	Youth arrive at camp, find rooms, settle in
8:30 p.m.	Opening overview: Be True to Yourself
9:30 p.m.	Munchies and more

Saturday

8:00 a.m.	Breakfast
9:00 a.m.	Self-reflection time
10:00 a.m.	Opening worship
10:15 a.m.	Session 1: Who Am I?
11:30 a.m.	Free time
12:00 p.m.	Lunch
1:00 p.m.	Session 2: Who Are You, Lord?
3:00 p.m.	Free time
5:30 p.m.	Dinner
6:30 p.m.	Worship planning and/or free time
7:45 p.m.	Session 3: "Who Do You Say That I Am?"
9:00 p.m.	Munchies and more

Sunday

8:00 a.m.	Breakfast
8:30 a.m.	Personal devotional time
9:15 a.m.	Closing activity: Here I Am, Lord, Send Me
10:15 a.m.	Closing worship
11:15 a.m.	Evaluations
12:00 p.m.	Lunch at Camp, Pack up, and depart for home

Retreat description: This is a reflective, discussion-oriented youth retreat that will help youth explore who God is, who they are as individuals, and what it means to be a child of God. It is designed for two overnights and one and a half days. Participants will address Christian identity issues and understand how to put faith beliefs into daily words and actions.

Note: Your RLT should include youth as well as adult advisers. During sessions that call for an RLT member to lead a portion, you will need to determine if that leadership is best served by adults, by youth, or by an adult-youth team (which may work very well for small group sessions). Ensuring that youth feel that they are valued members of the RLT while not being burdened with adult leadership roles or being put in situations vulnerable will take a little extra coordination on your part.

Two weeks before leaving, the RLT should send out the Final Details Letter (see Appendix A, p. 109), reminding youth to bring their Bibles. Also at this time, confirm that your facility will supply a TV/DVD player.

RLT Master Supply List

Paper towels and liquid soap supplies for bathrooms if camp does not provide, as well as a stash of extra toiletries that leaders can access for participants if needed (deodorant, toothbrush, toothpaste, feminine hygiene products, etc.)
Housing/roommate assignments
A check for retreat center, as needed per contract
Pens, markers, tape, pack of index cards, ream of copy paper
Flip chart pad
Copies of retreat schedule for each participant and for cabins and meeting spaces
Copies of retreat sessions for each RLT discussion facilitator
Remember the Titans, Napoleon Dynamite and *Mission: Impossible 2* DVDs
Copies of Self-Reflection and Life Timeline handouts
Ways of Seeing activity objects, see p. 80
Copies of Identity Crisis, Images of God, and "Who Do You Say That I Am?" handouts
Sculpey or Fima clay, sculpting tools, paper plates, plastic table cloths
CD player (if camp does not provide) and praise/worship/meditative music CDs
Copies of Sunday Devotions handout
Snacks, drinks, cups, plates if camp does not provide
Movies or board games for free time
Name tags
Pillow treats and/or Bible verses

FRIDAY

Arrival

Your entire group might be arriving together. If that's the case, have an RLT member designated to check in for the group; then direct people to where they need to be. Otherwise, if your RLT arrives early, they can register, settle in, place hospitality supplies in the bathrooms, and greet the other participants when they arrive and show them to their living quarters.

Opening Overview: Be True to Yourself

Time frame: 90–120 minutes
Supplies: copy of *Napoleon Dynamite* or *Remember the Titans* DVD, TV/DVD player, snacks, drinks, cups, napkins

Option A: After participants get settled in, gather them for the opening overview. If you are able to get your group outside, do it! Take a night hike, possibly led by the retreat center staff. Do a blindfolded trust walk in the dark, on which the blindfolded youth walk in a line with hands on the shoulders of the person in front of them, guided by a non-blindfolded adult leader. (Other leaders should be positioned along the line for safety.) Play the amoeba game, in which the group has to move as a huge, undulating circle across the camp, up and down a hill, around a building, etc. If you are stuck inside, try large group games like Upset the Fruit Basket (see p. 67–68) or team charades. Basically you want to burn off some of the pent-up car ride energy and get your youth moving and laughing. Whole group or multiple team activities work well at this stage of the retreat.

After 30 minutes or so of physical activity, RLT members should gather participants, do an official welcome to retreat, and let the group introduce themselves with names and a piece or two of personal information (home town, length of time at church, grade in school, favorite food, etc.). Open with a few praise songs and a prayer for God to transform lives on this retreat. Let them know what your rules are, but also let them know that the goal is to have fun, make friends, and help them deepen their relationships with the Lord. Be sure to identify adults who are available to meet one-on-one with youth who have questions, need prayer, or want to talk about deepening their relationship with Jesus.

One RLT member should talk about camp rules and procedures to be followed, introduce the retreat confidentiality policy that "what's said at retreat stays at retreat," and also talk about appropriate ways of sharing:

- Don't talk over someone else.
- Be respectful of time; make sure that everyone who wants to share has a chance to do so.
- Be a patient listener.
- Don't make fun of other people's answers.

An RLT member introduces the key verse (see below) for the weekend and prefaces the *Napoleon*

Dynamite clip, saying: *Napoleon is an interesting and unique character for lack of other words. Just looking at him, people might make snap judgments about his value as a person. We enter Napoleon's life just after he has dropped off a drawing and an invitation to Trisha to go to the high school dance with him. She's not impressed.* (Play clip that starts about 90 seconds into scene 12 where Trisha is pulling Napoleon's invitation out of the brown envelope and ends about 10 minutes later as he is walking down the street in the suit he just bought for the dance.) After watching the opening clip, ask youth to form groups with three to five other people around them, making sure that there is both an adult and youth RLT member in each group, and answer the following questions:

1. Do you identify with Napoleon Dynamite, or do you know people like Napoleon?
2. What does this key verse mean to you? "The LORD does not look at the things man looks at. Man looks at the outward appearance, but the LORD looks at the heart" (1 Samuel 16:7b, NIV).
3. What does it mean to be true to yourself?

Option B: After the RLT introduces the key verse, preface the *Remember the Titans* clip with this: Remember the Titans *is a film set in the 1980s after a Virginia high school district integrated. The championship white football team is now being merged with an all black team to form one new unit. A new head coach has been brought in, and the scene we're starting with shows his first team meeting, to which the white football team players have not attended...yet. Focus on the character of Louie and the snap judgments that all of the players are making about one another in these initial group gatherings.* Play the first clip (Chapter 4). When that scene ends at time code 14:21, skip to Chapter 7, time code 22:08, and play into Chapter 8 where Louie talks to Rev about being white trash, time code 26:42. After watching the clips, ask youth to form groups with three to five other people around them, making sure that there is both an adult and youth RLT member in each group, and answer the following questions:

1. Do you identify with Louie, or do you know people like Louie?
2. What does this key verse mean to you? "The LORD does not look at the things man looks at. Man looks at the outward appearance, but the LORD looks at the heart" (I Samuel 16:7b, NIV).
3. What does it mean to be true to yourself?

Have each group close in prayer when they are ready. An RLT leader says: *Lord, as we gather this weekend, we have so many questions about you. Open our minds and help us to understand more about who you are, about who we are as your children, and about what you want from us. Help us to grow hearts that reflect your love for us. Amen.*

Munchies and More

This is a time for fellowship and fun. Get a campfire going with s'mores or order in some pizzas and/or have youth bring their favorite junk food and pop to share. Put in a movie or play some tunes. Break out the cards and play Spoons. Do whatever works for your youth to put them at ease and let them get to know one another.

If your team wants to do pillow treats, bring a supply of fun-size candy (Skittles, M&Ms, Hershey Bars, etc.) and leave one on each youth's bunk before bed. To kick it up a notch, your team can print out relevant Bible verses ahead of time to place with the candy. Possible Scriptures include Isaiah 55:8, 2 Corinthians 3:18, and Ephesians 4:1.

SATURDAY

Breakfast

Self-Reflection Time

Time frame: 45 minutes

Supplies: copies of the Self-Reflection handout (see Appendix A, p. 128), pens, Bible for each youth (each should bring his or her own), meditative music, CD player

Gather your youth, asking them to bring their Bibles with them. Give them each a Self-Reflection handout and a pen, and tell them that they need to find a quiet spot to think and reflect. If possible, create a space in another meeting area with comfy pillows, soft instrumental/meditative music, and mood lighting. Offer youth the opportunity to go there or find a spot outside or back on their bunks. There is to be no talking during this portion, no cell phones, and no iPods. After 40 minutes, send RLT members to gather the youth back in your meeting area.

Opening Worship

Transition from personal meditation time to group discussion by singing three or four praise and worship songs, reading the key verse, and opening your discussion time in prayer.

Session 1: Who Am I?

Time frame: 90 minutes
Supplies: Bibles, pens, copies of Life Timeline (see Appendix A, p. 129)

Nothing but the Truth Icebreaker Regather your group in a circle. Have each person share one true and one false statement about himself or herself. Ask the group to guess which is the truth. After everyone has shared, ask: *Did anyone's truth really surprise you? Why?*

Life Timeline Now break into small groups. Make sure each group has at least one adult and one youth RLT member. An RLT member should hand out the Life Timeline sheets and give youth 20–25 minutes to complete them. Regather and have an RLT member ask the following:

1. Looking at this snapshot of your life, do you see any common themes, people, interests, or directions? Tell us about them.
2. As you have grown and developed new friendships and possibly changing family relationships, what roles have God and Jesus played? Has your relationship with the Lord changed at all? For better or for worse?
3. Read Psalm 139:14-17 in your Bibles. When you look at the unfinished end of you timeline, who do you want to become? What hopes, dreams, and goals do you have for the future? What do you think God has in store for you? Take a few minutes to write down some of your ideas about you in the future. (Give youth about 10 minutes to reflect and write.)
4. Ask each person to share at least one future goal or dream.

When your group is finished, have an RLT member close in prayer, saying: *Lord, we thank you for making us the individuals we are. We thank you for our gifts and talents. We thank you for creating us to be unique in a world that pushes us to conform. We pray that even as we wonder about who we are, even as we search to find our purpose in life, that you will be with us every step of the way. We ask for your guidance. We ask for your love. We ask for your forgiveness when we push away your gift of friendship. For all that you do and all that you are, Lord, we praise you. Amen.*

Free Time

Time frame: 30–45 minutes

Your group has just done some major self-reflection and processing. They need time to decompress. Let youth hang out in their rooms, in the meeting area, or outside on the grounds. A few RLT members may want to start up an informal game of football, basketball, or Frisbee. Just help your youth relax!

Lunch

Session 2: Who Are You, Lord?

Time frame: 105–120 minutes
Supplies: Ways of Seeing activity supplies (four objects located in four different rooms or areas: one should be a cross, the others should be unique or unusual objects [an antique toy or tool; a sculpture, statue, or trinket from a foreign country; a weird cooking implement; etc.]), blank paper for Ways of Seeing notes, pens, flip chart, markers, copies of Identity Crisis discussion handout (see Appendix A, p. 130), copies of Images of God in the Bible handout (see Appendix A, p. 131), Bibles, snacks, and drinks for break time

Ways of Seeing Gather your group and pass out a sheet of blank paper and a pen to each person. Divide into four random groups. Tell groups in what order they need to go to observe the four objects you have placed in the four areas (mix it up so that not every group is observing the same object at the same time). Tell them that they are to record their impressions of the object on the paper but that there is to be no talking at this stage of the activity. Give the groups 10–15 minutes to observe all four objects and make their notes. Ask them to return to the meeting area.

An RLT member can lead the following discussion. Hold each object up one at a time and ask these questions of the large group (write all responses on flip chart sheets):

1. What is this thing?
2. What is your first reaction to this thing?
3. What is it used for?
4. Do you have any personal connection or memory related to this thing?

Point out that depending on each person's life experiences and individual perspectives, the objects are all seen slightly differently.

Ask: *What does seeing things from a slightly different perspective say about our understanding of who God is?*

Say: *So you might use these things or relate to these things or understand these things in different ways, but the bottom line is—the thing is what it is—like God is what God is. In fact, God said exactly that to Moses when he was preparing Moses to bring God's people out of Egypt. "God said to Moses, 'I AM WHO I AM'" (Exodus 3:14, NIV). Hang on to that thought, that God is who he is, no matter what.*

Note: You will now be returning to your small groups, each with an RLT member or pair to facilitate. Each group should find its own space for discussion. They will stay together for the remainder of the session, so the RLT members should make sure they have all necessary handouts and supplies.

Identity Crisis Make sure everyone has an Identity Crisis handout (see Appendix A, p. xxx) and a Bible. Go around the circle, with each member taking a turn starting a question by reading and answering it. After each question is read and answered by the first person, the other group members can also share their thoughts.

Break Let the youth take a 10–15 minute stretching break. Keep them close but let them walk around outside or play a quick game of freeze tag or something to get them moving. You might also choose to have fresh fruit, energy bars, juice, and bottled water available for them to snack on.

Images of God in the Bible In your small group, take turns (or work in pairs) looking up the following Scriptures and decide what category to put them in on the Images of God chart/handout (see Appendix, p. 131). Have praise and worship music playing in the background while they work.

After you have the chart completed, an RLT member will ask the following:

1. Which images of God do you like best?
2. Which images of God are harder for you to understand?
3. Which image of God is the one you most connect with? Why?
4. Is there an image you feel is missing? What would you add? Why? Do you have a Scripture verse that you feel illustrates this image?

Direct your group members to take 5–10 minutes of personal quiet time now on their own away from other people. An RLT member may say: *Choose the "Image of God" verse you most relate to from all the verses you looked up, copy it on the back of the handout, and complete the following sentence: Lord, to me you are . . .*

When participants are finished, they may start free time.

Free Time

This retreat has a large block of free time now, depending on your camp's meal schedule. After the two heavy-duty sessions today, it would be good to give your youth time to unwind. Have snacks available and DVDs, music, and board games that they can use. Give them an hour or so of completely unstructured free time. You might want to offer the option of a large group game like Capture the Flag or softball for those who need to burn off a little energy before dinner.

Dinner

Worship Planning and/or Free Time

After dinner and before you begin the third session of the day, set aside time to plan Sunday's worship service.

Youth who don't wish to participate in the planning can have free time for this hour. Otherwise, gather any youth who wish to play an instrument, lead songs, read Scripture, share a testimony, do a skit based on your theme, etc., and let them plan the worship service with adult guidance. You may need to do some prep work ahead of time in terms of bringing resources that you would like to use or props for a skit or a skit script. Your RLT can prepare some basic materials ahead of time during the regular retreat planning and bring them along to this session.

Session 3: "Who Do You Say That I Am?"

Time frame: 60–75 minutes

Supplies: copies of "Who Do You Say That I Am?" handout (see Appendix A, p. 132), Bibles, assorted colors of Sculpey or Fima clay, plastic tablecloths, small paper plates, sculpting tools, markers, praise and worship CDs, CD player

Gather your group and ask people to get in their small groups from Session 2. Distribute the "Who Do You Say That I Am?" handout and make sure everyone has a Bible.

An RLT member will say: *We've looked at who you are as an individual and who you think God is. Now we're going to think about how God sees us. There are a few of God's own words that can help us understand what we mean to God. Let's check them out. Go ahead and work through the handout with your small group.*

When you have gone through all the questions on the handout, an RLT member can ask: *Would anyone like to share how you see God at work in your life, re-forming the broken or damaged parts of your soul?* (Let youth who are willing share. It might help start the discussion to have either the youth or adult RLT member share first. If no one else wants to share, don't push.)

An RLT member can close this portion in prayer before moving to the last activity, saying: *Lord, we know that we are far from perfect, that we have much to learn about you and your love for us. We pray that you would be patient with us, that you would be willing to re-form us again and again, no matter how many times we walk away from you, no matter how many times we follow our will and our way, not yours. We pray that you would forgive us our sins, Lord, and be at work in us to shape us to do your work in this world. To God be all the glory in everything we do. Amen.*

After prayer, return to the large group or craft space, which should be set up with long tables covered in plastic tablecloths and set with clay, paper plates, and sculpting tools (Popsicle sticks, forks, plastic knives, etc.). The first group to reach the work area can turn on praise and worship music to have playing in the background. An RLT member can say: *We're going to take some time now to create. Think about what we've talked about all day: who you are, who God is, who God says that you are to him. Use the clay to create a sculpture that reflects how you think God sees you. It could be a vase or container of some sort like we talked about in this session, or it could be a statue of an object that you think symbolizes your life to God right now. When you're done, write your name on a plate and place your sculpture on it. We'll display them all in our meeting area. When you're finished, you can go help start the campfire or hang out here with us until everyone is through.*

Munchies and More

This would be a great time for a campfire. If the weather is not cooperative, see if you can have a fire in an inside fireplace. Set out snacks, board games, and movies, and get ready to kick back for some much needed R & R. It's been a busy day! The RLT can also use this time to leave another pillow treat on the bunks.

SUNDAY

Breakfast

Personal Devotional Time

The RLT should give everyone a breakfast reminder so no one misses the meal. Before breakfast ends, give participants a copy of the devotional handout (see Appendix A, p. 133) and ask them to find a quiet place inside or out where they can read and reflect on these verses before worship.

If the weather and your location cooperate, plan a group hike through the woods, along the beach, or on the retreat center grounds.

Closing Activity: Here I Am, Lord, Send Me
Time frame: 20–30 minutes
Supplies: *Mission: Impossible* 2 clip, TV/DVD player, Bibles, index cards, pens

Gather your group and watch the opening scene from *Mission: Impossible* 2 where Tom Cruise's character receives his next mission assignment, should he choose to accept it. An RLT leader can preface the clip with this: *Watch this scene and think about the catch phrase in* Mission: Impossible: *"Your mission, should you choose to accept it. . ." Do you hear God issuing that challenge to you?* (Show the first ten minutes of the movie, from the very beginning through Ethan throwing away his video-message sunglasses as they self-destruct in a ball of flames.)

Break into the same small groups from last night. As a group find and read the following passage: 1 Samuel 3:1-19. This is the story of the call of Samuel, a youth who became a prophet for God. While Samuel was scared about being called by God, he did accept God's assignment to serve God. He trusted God's will and followed God's way.

An RLT member can pass out the index cards and pens and say: *Think about everything we've talked about this weekend. What is one thing you think God is calling you to do? It might be a first step, such as accepting Jesus as your Savior and getting to know him better. Or you might feel called into service for God. Write this action step down on your index card.* [Give youth 5–10 minutes to reflect and write, and then close in prayer.] *Lord, we pray that as we take our next step with you, you will be by our side, giving us your wisdom, your love, and your strength so that we might go out and do good work in this world in Jesus' name. Amen. If anyone would like to talk further about your next step with Jesus, I'll stick around until it's time for worship.*

Either have youth keep these cards or write their name and address on the backside so that you can mail the cards to them a month or so after the retreat.

Closing Worship
Time frame: 45 minutes
Your RLT will have planned this worship service in advance. If you need songbooks or song sheets, make sure you have located them ahead of time for your group. You also will need to know ahead of time whether you are going to be using a live musician or CDs and a CD player so that you can make arrangements.

Don't forget to ask the RLT members to be listening during small group time for stories of how youth have struggled to claim their own identity as children of God in the world or how they have answered God's call to serve. Before worship ask a few of these youth if they would share their testimonies for the morning's message. Your group may also want to bring an offering basket if you plan to take up an offering.

Evaluations
Before everyone leaves worship, get a group picture, and then pass out the retreat evaluations (see Appendix A, p. 110). Ask participants to complete them so that you have input for next year's planning.

Lunch at Camp, Pack Up, and Depart for Home
After lunch, finish packing and head for home. Make sure your group has followed the retreat center's checkout procedures. Don't forget to leave your check if that is what the management requires.

CHAPTER 15

Youth Retreat #2

coNectd 24/7

Schedule and Plan

Note: Ideally this retreat should take place at a camp that has a team-building challenge course or low or high ropes course that you can utilize during the Saturday afternoon session. This may incur an additional cost for your group. If the facility you select does not have such amenities, you will need to do a little brainstorming to come up with an alternative. (See Session 2 notes.)

Sample Schedule

Friday

6:00 p.m.	RLT arrives at camp to get set up
7:30 p.m.	Youth arrive at camp, find rooms, settle in
8:15 p.m.	Opening overview: coNectd 24/7
9:45 p.m.	Munchies and more

Saturday

8:00 a.m.	Breakfast
8:45 a.m.	Opening worship
9:00 a.m.	Session 1: Lost or Found?
10:45 a.m.	Personal reflection time
11:30 a.m.	Free time
12:00 p.m.	Lunch
1:00 p.m.	Session 2: Staying coNectd Challenge
3:00 p.m.	Free time
5:30 p.m.	Dinner
6:30 p.m.	Free time and worship planning session
7:45 p.m.	Session 3: d/c (Disconnected)
9:00 p.m.	Munchies and more

Sunday

8:00 a.m.	Breakfast and personal devotional time
9:15 a.m.	Group hike
10:00 a.m.	Closing activity: Reconnecting
11:00 a.m.	Closing worship
11:45 a.m.	Evaluations
12:00 p.m.	Lunch at camp, pack up, and depart for home

Retreat description: This is a thought-provoking, issue-wrestling youth retreat that will help youth explore their basic need to be connected to other people and to God. It is designed for two overnights and one and a half days. Participants will identify ways that they stay connected to one another and see how the desire for connection also applies to our need for God. Moreover, they will consider how being "coNectd 24/7" to the world (and not necessarily to God) can cause problems in their lives.

Note: Your RLT should include youth as well as adult advisers. During sessions that call for an RLT member to lead a portion, you will need to determine if that leadership is best served by adults, by youth, or by an adult-youth team (which may work very well for small group sessions). Ensuring that youth feel that they are valued members of the RLT while not being burdened with adult leadership roles or being put in situations that could expose their own youthful vulnerability or inexperience will take a little extra coordination on your part.

Two weeks before leaving, the RLT should send out the Final Details Letter (see Appendix A, p. 109), reminding youth to bring their Bibles. Also at this time, confirm with your facility that they will supply a TV/DVD player.

RLT Master Supply List

Paper towels and liquid soap supplies for bathrooms if camp does not provide, as well as a stash of extra toiletries that leaders can access for participants if needed (deodorant, toothbrush, toothpaste, feminine hygiene products, etc.)
Housing/roommate assignments
A check for retreat center, as needed per contract
Pens, markers, tape, legal pad, pack of index cards, ream of copy paper, one pack of stationery
Copies of retreat schedule for each participant and for cabins and meeting spaces
Copies of retreat sessions for each RLT discussion facilitator
Flip chart or graffiti sheets
Copy of *Lost* (season 1, disk 1)
Copies of Lost or Found handout, Self-Reflection handout, Whose Truth Is Truest? handout, and Sunday Devotions handout
Art supplies for self-reflection time
Balderdash board game, with copies of game rules
Pillow treats and/or Bible verses
Snacks, drinks, cups, plates, napkins
CD player (if camp does not provide) and praise and worship CDs
Copies of Sunday morning order of worship and worship supplies
Name tags

FRIDAY

Arrival

Your entire group might be arriving together. If that's the case, have an RLT member designated to check in for the group and then direct people to where they need to be. Otherwise, if your RLT arrives early, they can register, settle in, and greet the other participants when they arrive and show them to their living quarters.

Opening Overview: CoNected 24/7

Time frame: 90–120 minutes
Supplies: prelabeled graffiti sheets (see notes below), snacks, drinks, cups, plates, napkins

After participants get settled in, gather them for the opening overview. If you are able to get your group outside, do it! Take a night hike, possibly led by the retreat center staff. Do a blindfolded trust walk in the dark, on which the blindfolded youth walk in a line with hands on the shoulders of the person in front of them, guided by a non-blindfolded adult leader. (Other leaders should be positioned along the line for safety.) Play the amoeba game, in which the group has to move as a huge, undulating circle across the camp, up and down a hill, around a building, etc. If you are stuck inside, try large group games like Upset the Fruit Basket (see p. 67–68) or team charades. Basically you want to burn off some of the pent-up car ride energy and get your youth moving and laughing. Whole group or multiple team activities work well at this stage of the retreat.

After 30 minutes or so of physical activity, RLT members should gather participants, do an official welcome to retreat, and let the group introduce themselves with names and a piece or two of personal information (home town, length of time at church, grade in school, favorite food, etc.). Open with a few praise songs and a prayer for God to transform lives on this retreat. Let them know what your rules are, but also let them know that the goal is to have fun, make friends, and help them deepen their relationships with the Lord. Be sure to identify adults who are available to meet one-on-one with youth who have questions, need prayer, or want to talk about deepening their relationship with Jesus.

One RLT member should talk about camp rules and procedures to be followed, introduce the retreat confidentiality policy that "what's said at retreat stays at retreat," and also talk about appropriate ways of sharing:

- Don't talk over someone else.
- Be respectful of time; make sure that everyone who wants to share has a chance to do so.
- Be a patient listener.
- Don't make fun of other people's answers.

An RLT member will then introduce the theme for the weekend—coNectd 24/7—and ask participants to complete the graffiti sheets, which should have been posted in advance in your meeting space. Sheets have the following headings: "cell phone," "BlackBerry," "iPhone," "e-mail," "IM," "MySpace page," "Facebook page," "Second Life avatar," "landline phone," "snail mail," "handwritten notes," "personal website," "blogging," "hanging out in person," "other (please specify)."

Ask students to walk around and sign all the sheets that apply to them as ways in which they stay connected to other people. If they sign on the "other" sheet, please have them write what that "other" way is. Ask them to go back through and count how many sheets they signed.

Now post a second set of graffiti pages that have the following headings: "go to worship regularly," "participate in youth group regularly," "participate in a small study group regularly," "do service projects," "hang out with other Christians," "sing/play with a worship team," "teach Sunday school," "pray regularly," "use a daily devotional," "read my Bible regularly," "participate in a Second Life church or web-based Christian group," "hang out on Christian blogs or websites," "e-mail/IM with other Christian teens," "write Christian poetry or prayers," "hang out with non-Christians and be open about my faith with them," "other (please specify)." Ask students to sign the pages that apply to them and then count up how many pages they (honestly) signed.

An RLT member should say: *If the first set of sheets represents how we stay connected to the world and the second set of sheets is how we stay connected to God, how balanced are you? Are you equally connected to people in the world and to God or not? Form a group with two or three other people around you and share your answers.* [An RLT member or youth-adult pair should make sure to each take a group and bring enough index cards and pens for each person and distribute.] *Now, when you're done with that question, shift your brain to survival mode and take a minute to write down the top five things you would bring if you were stranded on a desert island. You can assume that for some crazy reason, you can get a wireless signal. You just have no clue where you are.* [Give 3–5 minutes to write, then ask group members to share answers. Give 5–10 minutes for discussion.] *Now assume that you cannot get a wireless signal. Do your top five items change? Discuss those changes with your group.* [Give 5–10 minutes for discussion.] *Now imagine that God has packed a survival kit for you. Write down the five things you think God has packed in your survival kit. Share your list with your group when you're done.* [Give 5 minutes to think and write and 5–10 minutes to discuss answers.]

An RLT member should regather the entire group and say: *Let's share a few of the things in God's survival kit* [make a list on a blank graffiti sheet]. *God desires to be coNectd to us 24/7, but we often tune God out or turn God off. This weekend we're going to look at the ways that we connect ourselves to the world and to God and see how we can improve our communication. Let's ask God's blessing on that process.*

Lord, as we gather this weekend, we have many questions about you—who you are, why you would want to know us, why you would want to be connected to us 24/7 even when we choose to push you away. Help us to reexamine our own lives and find ways to stay connected to you, even though we live in the real world. Help us to follow Paul's challenge from the book of Romans not to be conformed to this world but to be transformed by the renewing of our minds, so that we may discern what is the will of God—what is good and acceptable and perfect. Amen.

Munchies and More

This is a time for fellowship and fun. Get a campfire going with s'mores or order in some pizzas and/or have youth bring their favorite junk food and pop to share. Put in a movie or play some tunes. Break out the cards and play Spoons. Do whatever works for your youth to put them at ease and let them get to know one another.

If your team wants to do pillow treats, bring a supply of fun-size candy (Skittles, M&Ms, Hershey Bars, etc.) and leave one on each youth's bunk before bed. To kick it up a notch, your team can print out relevant Bible verses ahead of time to place with the candy. Possible Scriptures include Psalm 119:105, Proverbs 2:6, and John 15:7.

SATURDAY

Breakfast

Opening Worship

Get your group connected to God this morning by singing three or four praise and worship songs, reading a selected verse, and opening your discussion time in prayer.

Session 1: Lost or Found?

Time frame: 90 minutes

Supplies: TV/DVD player, copy of *Lost: Season 1* (disk 1), Bibles, Lost or Found handout (see Appendix A, p. 134), pens, art supplies for reflection response (paint, markers, paper, collage materials, glue, writing paper, etc.)

Gather your group around the TV/DVD player. An RLT member says: *We're going to watch part of the pilot episode of the TV show* Lost. *The basic premise is that a group of people on board a flight from LA to Sydney crash on a remote island and must figure out how to survive. As you watch, look for ways that they have to work at staying connected. Think about what you might do if placed in the same situation.* (Show the first 15 minutes of the pilot, part 1, through the character Charlie saying to Sayeed, "I'm on it," in regard to building the fire.)

Break your participants into groups. Make sure a youth-adult RLT pair are assigned to each group. Groups will stay together for the remainder of the discussion sessions. Ask groups to spread out to individual meeting places and discuss the questions on the Lost or Found handout. They will need their Bibles.

When your discussion wraps up, an RLT member should say: *Truly, the only thing that disconnects us from God and makes us feel lost is sin. Sin is tricky. Sin is misleading. Sin encourages us to think that any choice we feel like making is God-honoring, instead of using God's Word and the wisdom of other believers to guide us. The key to staying connected to God 24/7 is to reject sin and live a life worthy of the one to which God called us. We're going to close this session with a time of self-reflection so that you can explore this idea a little deeper on your own.*

Personal Reflection Time

Distribute Self-Reflection handouts with verses and instructions printed on them (see Appendix A, p. 135). A few adult RLT members can hang out in the indoor spaces (meeting space, chapel, cabins), and a few can circulate the grounds so that they are available to youth who need prayer or need to talk about what they are reading.

Free Time

There is a small amount of free time between the reflection time and lunch. Students who wish may continue their personal reflection time up until lunch.

Lunch

Session 2: Staying coNectd Challenge

Time frame: 2–3 hours total

Supplies: none unless your facility does not have a ropes course. See below if you need to plan for this time on your own.

Ahead of time, your RLT should communicate with the camp your goal for the challenge course time, which is to help youth realize how vital it is to have good, positive communication in relationships. Ask your camp facilitator to use the following Bible verses as the foundation for the activities for the afternoon: Psalm 34:11-18, Romans 12:2, and Romans 12:3-5. The first Romans verse appeared earlier in the retreat and asks us to not be conformed to the world but transformed by the renewing of our minds. The second Romans passage talks about how we all have different gifts and abilities yet all belong to the same body of Christ. The Psalms passage encourages us to turn away from evil and do good and tells us that when we are righteous, the Lord hears us and rescues us from our troubles.

All of these verses support a philosophy of Christian community where believers model faithful living and encourage one another, where they allow each person to contribute to God's work in this world according to his or her gifts, and where they always treat one another with respect and compassion, just as God treats us. Staying connected to God is at the heart of these three passages, which, in turn, can guide us in our earthly relationships.

If you do not have a facilitator who will run the afternoon's events, you will need to create your own challenge activities to help youth understand the value of good communication and to see how God gives us the wisdom and skills to stay connected to each other and to him. You might want to do a blindfolded trust walk as a group (see page 85), changing the order of the walkers from time to time and/or letting students lead or colead the walk. Or you could have students pair up and lead one another in a shorter blind trust walk, switching roles after 5–10 minutes. You could also create a series of challenges that involve not using hands, feet, vision, etc. and/or require that youth communicate in ways other than speaking to accomplish the tasks. Youth Specialties (www.youthspecialties.com) has a number of activity books, as does Group (www.grouppublishing.com), so you could also look through those resources and come up with a collection of activities. Another option might be to plan a service project at the camp but hinder the students in some way (use only one hand, only boys can talk, girls can speak only two words at a time, etc.) so that they must focus on listening, communicating, and cooperating with one another to get the job done.

Free Time

This retreat has a large block of free time now. After the team-building exercises, it would be good to give your youth time to decompress. Have snacks available and DVDs, music, and board games they can use. Give them an hour or so of unstructured free time. Then you might want to offer the option of a large group game, such as Capture the Flag or softball for those who need to burn off a little energy before dinner.

Dinner

Free Time and Worship Planning Session

After dinner and before you begin the third session of the day, set aside time to plan Sunday's worship service. Youth who don't wish to participate in the planning can have free time for this hour. Otherwise, gather any youth who wish to play an instrument, lead songs, read Scripture, share a testimony, do a skit based on your theme, etc., and let them plan the worship service with adult guidance. You may need to do some prep work ahead of time in terms of bringing resources that you would like to use or props for a skit or a skit script. Your RLT can prepare some basic materials ahead of time during the regular retreat planning and bring them along to this session.

Session 3: d/c (Disconnected)

Time frame: 75–90 minutes

Supplies: Balderdash board game, copies of the Balderdash game rules (one for each small group), Bibles, Whose Truth Is Truest? handout (see Appendix A, p. 136)

Gather your group and break into smaller groups of 5 to 6 youth (these can be your small groups from earlier, even if larger than 6). Make sure at least one adult and/or youth RLT member is in each group. Divide your Balderdash cards evenly among the groups and distribute with a copy of the Balderdash rules. Explain the activity this way: *Tonight we're going to look at how we decide whose truth is truest and how truth can connect us to or disconnect us from other people and/or God. To get started we're going to play a little bit of Balderdash. Your group leader has the game directions. Basically, in each round, the group will be given a word and each person will create a defini-*

tion for it. Then the definitions will be read and players will vote on whose definition they feel is the truest. Points are awarded based on these votes. Give small groups about 30 minutes to play. Note that unless one is a phenomenal wordsmith, the way the game is won is by manufacturing the most creative "truths."

After 30 minutes, reconvene as a large group. One RLT member asks: *So what were some of your most creative definitions?* [Let groups answer] *Was there any concrete way to know whose truth was truest?* [Let groups answer].

Distribute the Whose Truth Is Truest handouts and ask groups to find a quiet place for discussion. Note: for added discussion points on question #3, leaders can do a web search ahead of time on cyber bullying and print out examples of youth who wrestled with the virtual world's version of whose truth is truest and lost. See book's blog (www.completeretreatguide.com) for links. When each group is finished, the RLT member can close in prayer: *Lord, there is so much in this world that we don't understand and probably never will; so much pain, so much anger, so much sin to separate us from you. Yet you remain a constant presence in our lives if we just open our hearts and minds to you. Forgive us when we disconnect from you, when we accept the world's truth as your truth. Help us to be believers who lead by example because we are connected to you, 24/7. Amen.*

Note: If there are youth in your small groups who are struggling to reconnect to God, you can pray for them by name, laying hands on them or otherwise encouraging them to get right with God. In addition, leaders should be watching for and available to youth who would like to ask more questions or talk about their relationship with Jesus after this session in particular.

Munchies and More

This would be a great time for a campfire. If the weather is not cooperative, see if you can have a fire in an inside fireplace. Set out snacks, board games, and movies, and get ready to kick back for some much needed R & R. It's been a busy day! The RLT can also use this time to leave another pillow treat on the bunks.

Sunday

Breakfast and Personal Devotional Time

The RLT should give everyone a breakfast reminder so that no one misses the meal. Before breakfast ends, give participants a copy of the devotional handout (see Appendix A, p. 137) and ask them to find a quiet place inside or out where they can read and reflect on these verses before worship.

Group Hike

If the weather and your location cooperate, plan a group hike through the woods, along the beach, or on the retreat center grounds.

Closing Activity: Reconnecting

Time frame: 30–45 minutes
Supplies: blank paper, pens, pencils, markers, stationery

Gather your group and have an RLT member give these instructions: *All weekend we have been talking about being connected to and disconnected from God. In our final session, your job is to think about how to reconnect with God when sin separates you. And think big picture. What do you want other youth to know about the value of staying connected to God?*

For the next 20–30 minutes, you will be creating a hard copy version of a virtual communication that helps others get coNectd to God 24/7. You can write a blog post, create an e-mail, design a web page, write a text message, lay out a drawing, author an online devotional. Be creative! Before we end, you'll have a chance to share what you did. If you want to work with a partner or two, that's okay, too.

Allow youth 20–30 minutes to work; then regather the group and let them explain what they created. (Provided that the samples are appropriate, encourage youth to take these home and e-mail them to friends and family, put them on their blogs or on their MySpace or Facebook pages, or ask permission to post things on your church website to help connect others to God.)

An RLT member can close in prayer, saying: *Lord, we desire to stay connected to you 24/7. Forgive us when we disconnect from you. Fill us with the power of your love and the knowledge of your goodness that we might be encouraged to share your good news with the world, so that we might be in the world but not of it. Amen.*

Closing Worship

Time frame: 45 minutes
Supplies: To be determined by the RLT

Your RLT will have planned this worship service in advance. If you need songbooks or song sheets, make sure you have located them ahead of time for your group. You also will need to know ahead of time whether you are going to be using a live musician or CDs and a CD player so that you can make arrangements.

Don't forget to ask the RLT members to be listening during small group time for potential testimonies. Perhaps some youth have wrestled with the issue of figuring out whose truth is truest. Others may have felt disconnected and have now reconnected to God. Before worship, ask a few of these youth if they would share their stories in worship for the morning's message (or perhaps one of your RLT members will give the message).

Evaluations

Before everyone leaves the worship area, try to get a group picture, and then pass out the retreat evaluations (see Appendix A, p. 110). Ask participants to complete them so you have input for next year's planning.

Lunch at Camp, Pack Up, and Depart for Home

After lunch, finish packing and head for home. Make sure your group has followed the retreat center's checkout procedures. Don't forget to leave your check if that is what the management requires.

CHAPTER 16

Older Adults' Retreat #1
Still Worthy

Schedule and Plan

Sample Schedule

Friday

6:00 p.m.	RLT arrives at camp to get set up
7:00 p.m.	People arrive at camp, find rooms, settle in
7:30 p.m.	Vesper service
8:30 p.m.	Fellowship

Saturday

8:00 a.m.	Breakfast
8:45 a.m.	Opening worship
9:00 a.m.	Session 1: Age Defiers
11:00 a.m.	Free time
12:00 p.m.	Lunch
1:00 p.m.	Session 2: Hands-on Service
5:30 p.m.	Dinner
6:30 p.m.	Session 3: Worthy in God's Eyes
8:00 p.m.	Free time

Sunday

8:00 a.m.	Breakfast
8:45 a.m.	Morning walk or extended personal devotions
9:45 a.m.	Personal devotions
10:45 a.m.	Closing worship
11:45 a.m.	Evaluations
12:00 p.m.	Pack up, eat lunch, and depart for home

Retreat description: This is a service-oriented retreat where the goal is to help older adults celebrate their age and stage in life and know that they are still worthy in God's eyes as able servants. It is designed for two overnights and one and a half days and can include both singles and couples, men and women. Participants will focus on the stories of Noah, Abraham, Sarah, and Elizabeth and will be involved in hands-on service Saturday afternoon. They will leave the retreat with a renewed sense of value and purpose.

Two weeks before leaving, the RLT should send out the Final Details Letter (see Appendix A, p. 109), reminding participants to bring their Bibles. Also at this time, confirm that your facility will supply a TV/DVD player for free time movies.

RLT Master Supply List

Hospitality kits (see chapter 5), 1 per bathroom
Housing/roommate assignments
A check for conference center, as needed per contract
Cash for carpool drivers from registration money
Pens, markers, masking tape
Giant Post-it flip chart pad or 4–6 sheets of poster board for brainstorming activity
Copies of schedule for each participant and cabins and meeting spaces
Copies of retreat sessions for RLT and all facilitators
CD player and meditative/praise/worship CDs
Copies of vesper service order of worship with all music, song sheets, songbooks
Copy of *The Giving Tree* by Shel Silverstein
Copies of Age Defiers and Worthy in God's Eyes handouts
Concordances, commentaries, and study Bibles
Collection of resources for personal devotion time on Sunday (books, poems, articles, etc.)
Movies, cards, or board games for free time
Pillow treats and/or Bible verses
Name tags
Coffee, tea, soft drinks, bottled water, snacks, and paper goods for breaks
Copies of Sunday morning order of worship and worship supplies

FRIDAY

Arrival

Upon arriving at camp, the RLT will need to check in at the main building and receive housing assignments. Once in your space, the RLT should unpack, gather supplies for the opening overview, and place hospitality kits in the bathrooms. Then at least half the RLT should return to the main building/parking area to welcome and direct the rest of the participants. Be alert for any special needs and address them with grace-filled hospitality.

Vesper Service

Time frame: 35–40 minutes
Supplies: CD player and worship music or songbooks/hymnals and music for song leader, copies of your order of worship

After participants get settled in, invite them to get a cup of coffee or tea and gather them for the vesper service. Ask them to engage in silent reflection once they enter the worship area. For meditative music, have a mix of familiar/favorite hymns and classical music playing on the CD player (or maybe you have a team member or participant who can play for you). If you will be using a preprinted order of worship, distribute copies as people walk in.

ORDER OF WORSHIP

Silent Meditation

Scripture (an RLT member reads aloud)

Hear the good news from Paul's letter to the church in Ephesus. [Read Ephesians 4:1-6, 15-16.] *Let the people of God say Amen. (Amen.)*

Call to Worship

From Psalm 92:1-4, 12-15
L: **It is good to give thanks to the LORD,**
P: To sing praises to your name, O Most High;
L: **To declare your steadfast love in the morning,**
P: And your faithfulness by night,
L: **To the music of the lute and the harp,**
P: To the melody of the lyre,
L: **For you, O LORD, have made me glad by your work;**
P: At the works of your hands I sing for joy.
L: **The righteous flourish like the palm tree, and grow like a cedar in Lebanon.**
P: They are planted in the house of the LORD; they flourish in the courts of our God.
L: **In old age they still produce fruit; they are always green and full of sap,**
P: Showing that the LORD is upright;
ALL: He is my rock, and there is no unrighteousness in him. Amen.

Prayer (an RLT member leads)

Lord, we come before you as servants who have been working long and hard in your name. We wonder, though, Lord, if it is enough—if we can still be of use to you. Our bodies may be weary, but our hearts and hands are willing to serve, Lord. We pray that you will fill us, feed us, heal us, renew us. Help us to live the lives worthy of the ones to which you've called us.

Grant us the wisdom and the faith to discern your will in our lives and act upon it, Lord. We know we can still do good work in this world in your name. Amen.

Songs

An RLT member or ensemble begins singing and leads the group in a number of hymns or worship songs; ideally you will have a guitar or piano player along who can help keep the group singing, but you can also do this a cappella. Suggestions: "They'll Know We Are Christians by Our Love," "Be Thou My Vision," "Come Thou Fount of Every Blessing," "God of Our Life throughout the Circling Years," "To Every Generation."

Meditation

An RLT member reads Shel Silverstein's *The Giving Tree* or a meditation of your choosing. Introduce the book by saying: *In this allegory, the tree never stops giving. Even when old age takes its toll, the tree still draws on herself to continue to serve the boy.* When finished reading, the RLT member should reread the opening verse from Ephesians 4:1 and ask the group to reflect on that as it relates to the story or the meditation that was just shared. Give three to five minutes of time to reflect with soft music playing.

Prayer (an RLT member leads)

Lord, may all that we say and all that we do be pleasing to you. Give us the strength to live each day to the fullest, glorifying you in every word and deed. Amen.

Closing Song Suggestions

"All Praise to Thee My God This Night" or one of your group's favorite hymns

Fellowship

Time frame: approximately 1 hour
Supplies: snacks, drinks, cups, napkins, small plates

Set up refreshments and welcome your group back to your meeting space. When everyone is settled with a snack, go around the circle and share names and one or two bits of personal information to help get people comfortable with one another.

The RLT should then review the weekend schedule and share camp rules and procedures to be followed. This is a good time to identify the leaders and volunteers who are available if people have further questions, need prayer, or want to talk about deepening their relationship with Jesus.

Allow participants time to unwind and socialize. Bring out board games or decks of cards, or just let people talk and get to know one another. Some people may opt to head to bed, which is okay too.

In addition to doing pillow treats (small mint or candy placed on each participant's pillow) at night, the RLT may choose to put a devotional Scripture on each participant's pillow or print Scriptures on self-stick address labels and attach them to the mints. Possible Scriptures include Micah 6:8, Galatians 6:9, and Philippians 1:6.

SATURDAY

Breakfast

Opening Worship

Gather your group for a time of praise and worship. Sing favorite hymns and songs. Read a few passages of Scripture and be in prayer together, asking God to bless this time and transform hearts and minds in Christ Jesus.

Session 1: Age Defiers

Time frame: 2 hours
Supplies: flip chart, markers, tape, Bibles, copies of Age Defiers handout (see Appendix A, p. 138)

An RLT member starts this session with a little brainstorming, saying: *What qualities, strengths, and advantages do older adults bring to service opportunities?* Make a list on the flip chart. Hang that list up and start a new page.

Next ask: *Name some older adults (famous mission workers or simply people you know) who have continued to do good work in God's name, even into their seventies, eighties, nineties, and beyond.* Note: If this list does not contain any Bible personalities, ask the group to consider that category and add those names to the page. Review the lists with the group and say: *This morning we're going to take a look at a few of God's servants who were still worthy and still working, even in their old age. These individuals can serve as role models for us and remind us that God uses each of us according to the gifts and talents we have been given. Just because we're older and perhaps a little tired doesn't mean that we stop using those gifts.*

Divide into groups and make sure an RLT member is in each group to facilitate discussion. Give everyone a Age Defiers handout, and let groups find their own meeting spots. The RLT member should facilitate his or her group's discussion. A time of personal reflection will follow this session and flow into free time. Also remind groups to take stretching, bathroom, and coffee breaks as needed to keep everyone comfortable.

Free Time

Those who need it can extend their personal meditation time or return to the cabin to take a nap, read, or enjoy the camp surroundings.

Lunch

Immediately preceding or following lunch is a good time to take a group photo.

Session 2: Hands-on Service

Time frame: approximately 4 hours
Supplies: to be determined

Ahead of time the RLT should arrange with the camp to do a service project either at camp or in the surrounding community. This project needs to be something that could be done by everyone or have various parts that would accommodate the various gifts and talents of the participants. Be sensitive to mobility, vision, and hearing issues, and have options available for those who can't be as physically active as others. Camp projects might include building a ramp or working on a structure in progress, painting, cleaning, sewing, organizing storeroom areas, clearing brush/landscaping, etc. Community projects might include any of the above and/or running an afternoon vacation Bible school for children, preparing an evening meal for a homeless shelter, stocking a food pantry, rocking babies at a daycare or women's shelter, sorting clothing at a resale shop, etc. If at all possible, get participant input into the projects while you are in the planning stages, and be sure to let all of your participants know final project details so they can pack accordingly (clothing or special supplies).

Dinner

Session 3: Worthy in God's Eyes

Time frame: 1 hour
Supplies: Worthy in God's Eyes handout (see Appendix A, p. 139), pens, Bibles

Gather your group and have an RLT member introduce the session this way: *John Wesley, an English evangelist who started the Methodist Church, believed that you should do all the good to all the people in all the places you are able for as long as you are able. Service was a way of life, as far as he was concerned, and one's age did not automatically put limitations on one's ability to serve. That's what we are going to look at tonight, and we are going to use God's Word to encourage us.*

Divide into your discussion groups from earlier and distribute the Worthy in God's Eyes handout. This handout contains a variety of Scriptures on serving. The RLT member facilitating each group can lead the people through the questions.

To close your session, regather the group as a whole. An RLT member can ask for a few participants to share their key verse or service opportunity and then end with a hymn. Be sure to let people know, after the closing prayer, that if anyone would like to talk further about deepening her or his relationship with Jesus, the RLT members are available for prayer and advice.

Free Time

Free-time options might include a night hike, a fire in the fireplace, a campfire on the beach, board games, movies, or refreshments. The RLT can use this time to leave another pillow treat and/or Scripture on participants' pillows.

SUNDAY

Breakfast

Morning Walk or Extended Personal Devotions

If the weather and your location cooperate, plan a group stroll through the woods, along the beach, or on the retreat center grounds. For those who don't want to walk, you can mark this hour as the beginning of extended personal devotions. Provide a variety of resources (see below) and encourage participants to select resources and take them with their Bibles to a quiet place. Those walking can start this devotional time when they return.

Personal Devotions

See above. Those wishing an extended time of meditation can forgo the walk and start at 8:45. Your RLT may wish to provide a list of the Scriptures that have been studied this weekend, as well as study Bibles, concordances, commentaries, or other devotional materials for those who wish to dig deeper.

Closing Worship

Time frame: 45–60 minutes

The RLT can plan a worship service in advance. Check your church library for liturgical resources if you want to include a call to worship, prayer of confession, or other group prayers, or write your own. Scriptures may include any of the ones listed previously in this retreat, or the RLT can use a concordance to look up verses under the headings of *serve, servant, service, community, love, neighbor, good works,* or *duty.* Retreat participants could also be asked to share any favorite passages they have on these subjects.

If you type up and copy an order of worship, include your praise song and hymn lyrics or bring along songbooks or hymnals. Ahead of time find an RLT member or a retreat participant who would be comfortable leading the singing and/or accompanying the group for worship. If need be, bring a portable CD player and worship music CDs.

Don't forget to ask the RLT members to listen for stories of service, especially in recent years, that come up in the small group discussions. Ask a few of these participants if they would share their testimonies in worship for the morning's message. You may also ask one of your RLT or group members to give a message using Paul's advice to Timothy in 1 Timothy 4:11-16, explaining that "age" could be substituted for "youth" in this passage. God's Word still applies.

Evaluations

Before everyone leaves the worship area, pass out the retreat evaluations (see Appendix A, p.110). Ask the participants to complete them so that you have input for next year's planning.

Pack Up, Eat Lunch, and Depart for Home

Finish packing, load your cars, and have one last meal together at camp. Make sure your group has followed the retreat center's checkout procedures. Don't forget to leave your check if that is what the management requires.

CHAPTER 17

Older Adults' Retreat #2
Wisdom

Schedule and Plan

Sample Schedule

Friday

6:00 p.m.	RLT arrives at camp to get set up
7:00 p.m.	People arrive at camp, find rooms, settle in
7:30 p.m.	Opening overview
8:30 p.m.	Fellowship

Saturday

8:00 a.m.	Breakfast
8:45 a.m.	Opening worship
9:00 a.m.	Session 1: Pillars of Wisdom
11:00 a.m.	Free time
12:00 p.m.	Lunch
1:00 p.m.	Session 2: For Future Generations
3:00 p.m.	Free Time
5:30 p.m.	Dinner
6:30 p.m.	Session 3: Stories around the Fire
8:00 p.m.	Fellowship

Sunday

8:00 a.m.	Breakfast
8:45 a.m.	Morning walk or extended personal devotions
9:45 a.m.	Personal devotions
10:45 a.m.	Closing worship
11:45 a.m.	Evaluations
12:00 p.m.	Lunch at camp and depart for home

Retreat description: This is a discussion-oriented retreat where participants will reflect on God's wisdom and its impact on their lives, as well as look at what wisdom they can pass on to future generations. It is designed for two overnights and one and a half days and can include both singles and couples, men and women. Participants will focus on the stories of Solomon, Philip and the Ethiopian eunuch, and Jesus in his boyhood. They will also reflect on Jesus' parables and create a book of wisdom to bring back to their church family.

Two weeks before leaving, the RLT should send out the Final Details Letter (see Appendix A, p. 109) and remind the people to bring their Bibles. Also at this time, confirm with your facility that they will supply a TV/DVD player for free time movies.

RLT Master Supply List

Hospitality kits (see chapter 5), 1 per bathroom
Housing/roommate assignments
A check for conference center, as needed per contract
Cash for carpool drivers from registration money
Pens, markers, masking tape
Giant Post-it flip chart pad or 6 to 8 sheets of poster board for brainstorming activity
Copies of schedule for each participant and cabins and meeting spaces
Copies of retreat curriculum for all RLT members and discussion leaders
CD player (if retreat center does not supply) and meditative/praise/worship CDs
Copies of Pillars of Wisdom handout
Completed For Future Generations handouts from congregation and extra blank forms
3-ring binder and clear page pocket inserts (2–3 dozen inserts, depending on number of completed For Future Generations forms)
Concordances, commentaries, and study Bibles
Collection of resources for personal devotion time on Sunday (books, poems, devotionals, articles, etc.)
Movies, cards, or board games for free time
Pillow treats
Name tags
Coffee, tea, pop, bottled water, snacks, and paper goods for breaks if retreat center does not provide them
Video camera, tape, tripod, and microphone if using for Session 3
Copies of Sunday morning order of worship and worship supplies

FRIDAY

Arrival

Upon arriving at camp, the RLT will need to check in at the main building and receive housing assignments. Once in your space, the RLT should unpack, gather supplies for the opening overview, and place hospitality kits in the bathrooms. Then at least half the RLT should return to the main building/parking area to welcome and direct the rest of the participants. Be alert for any special needs and address them with grace-filled hospitality.

Opening Overview

Time frame: 75–90 minutes
Supplies: Bibles, flip chart, markers

After participants get settled in, invite them to gather in your meeting space and go around the room introducing yourselves and sharing a piece or two of personal information. Then open your time together with a few favorite hymns or praise songs and a word of prayer.

Next, an RLT member can introduce the weekend's theme, saying: *This weekend we're going to be looking at wisdom. This world is full of people who think they know everything—and tell you so. But as believers we need to remember that true wisdom comes from God. Listen to this passage from the book of Proverbs.* [Read Proverbs 1:2-7.] *And it's okay to ask God for wisdom. James 1:5 says, "If any of you is lacking in wisdom, ask God, who gives to all generously and ungrudgingly, and it will be given you."*

To get us moving in the right direction, we're going to do a little brainstorming. Form a group with three or four other people [make sure an RLT member is in each group to facilitate], *and share one bit of "advice" you received over the years that truly was helpful and came from a parent, teacher, friend, sibling, etc.* [Allow 5–10 minutes for sharing.] *Now think of a bit of wisdom you gained over the years that came from God, something that taught you a lesson, strengthened your faith, or put life in perspective for you.* [Allow 10–15 minutes for sharing.]

An RLT member should regather the entire group and ask for participants to share the best of the best from their groups. Write down the best advice and the best examples of wisdom on two large sheets of poster board or flip chart paper. Hang these in your meeting space. An RLT member can close the group in prayer, saying: *Lord, we come before you this weekend with hearts that still want to know you more, even after all these years. We hunger for the true wisdom that comes only from you. Help us, Lord, to discern your wisdom and then share it with those who follow in our footsteps. You are the way, the truth, and the light, and we want to be your lights that shine in the world for all to see. Amen.*

Fellowship

Time frame: approximately 1 hour
Supplies: snacks, drinks, cups, napkins, small plates

Give people a chance to stretch and take a bathroom break while the RLT sets out refreshments. Then gather again in a circle. The RLT should then review the weekend schedule and share any camp rules and procedures to be followed. This is also a good time to identify leaders and volunteers who are available if people have further questions, need prayer, or want to talk about deepening their relationship with Jesus.

Allow participants time to unwind and socialize. Bring out board games or decks of cards, or just let people talk and get to know one another. Some people may opt to head to bed, which is okay too.

In addition to doing pillow treats (small mint or candy placed on each participant's pillow) at night, the RLT may choose to put a devotional Scripture on each participant's pillow or print Scriptures on self-stick address labels and attach them to the mints. Possible Scriptures include Psalm 90:12, Psalm 100:5, Proverbs 4:10, and James 1:5.

SATURDAY

Breakfast

Opening Worship

Gather your group for a time of praise and worship. Sing favorite hymns and worship songs. Read a few passages of Scripture and be in prayer together, asking God to bless this time and transform hearts and minds in Christ Jesus.

Session 1: Pillars of Wisdom

Time frame: 90–105 minutes
Supplies: flip chart, markers, tape, Bibles, copies of the Pillars of Wisdom handout (see Appendix A, p. 140), pens

An RLT member starts this session with a little brainstorming, asking: *What Bible figures do you see as wise? Give me a name and a brief example of his or her wisdom.* Make a list on the flip chart. Review the list with the group and say: *This morning we are going to take a look at a few of God's servants who were very wise, and their wisdom truly came from God.*

Divide into groups and make sure an RLT member is in each group to facilitate discussion. Give everyone a Pillars of Wisdom handout, and let groups find their own meeting spot. A time of personal reflection will follow this session and flow into free time. Also remind groups to take stretching, bathroom, and coffee breaks as needed to keep everyone comfortable.

Free Time

Those who need it can extend their personal meditation time or return to the cabin to take a nap, read, or enjoy the camp surroundings.

Lunch

Immediately preceding or following lunch is a good time to take a group photo.

Session 2: For Future Generations

Time frame: 90–120 minutes
Supplies: 3-ring binder, clear page pockets to hold each completed form, copies of previously completed For Future Generations forms and blank forms for extras, pens, Bibles, concordances

Ahead of time, the RLT should contact various leaders of the congregation, as well as the members and staff, and ask them to complete the For Future Generations form (see Appendix A, p. 141). This form asks people to identify areas of church life where wisdom is needed. This could range from questions about building and property maintenance to tips for running a church fundraiser dinner, to faith stories that will help others overcome struggles and challenges. Ahead of time, collect these forms, make multiple copies of them, and bring them to this session.

Gather your group and explain that you are going to make a church wisdom book. An RLT member says: *Inquiring minds from our congregation want to know what godly wisdom you have acquired over the years, especially as it relates to our particular church. This afternoon you'll record some of this wisdom for future generations.*

Pass out the forms that were completed by the congregation, and let the participants review them. Then have an RLT member say: *Let's pray as we begin to consider what wisdom we have to share. Lord, we have journeyed with you for many years now, and we have been greatly blessed by your presence in our lives. As we look back on our life experiences, we pray that we would be able to recognize the wisdom you granted us along the way and that we might now be equipped to share that wisdom with those who will follow us. We pray, Lord, that we might be living examples of your faithfulness and that others would grow in godly wisdom because of what you will help us offer to them. May all that we do glorify your holy name. Amen.*

As you continue to look through these questionnaires, think about which ones relate to your life. Where do you have wisdom to share? Maybe it's a few verses of Scripture that helped you deal with a particular earthly struggle. Maybe it's the trick for getting the boiler fixed quickly on a cold winter night. Maybe it's wisdom you gained in helping people who are hurting and need hospitality. Or maybe it's a personal faith story you can share to encourage someone else. Feel free to work with a partner or in a group. You can write your response directly on the form or take a blank form and copy the question and your answer. And if you have a piece of wisdom to share that hasn't been asked about, please complete a blank form as needed. The responses will be placed in this binder, and our church wisdom book will be presented in next Sunday's worship service.

Allow people time to think and consider their answers. Encourage those who might appear uncertain about the value of their godly wisdom, and support teams of people working together on this project. One or more RLT members could serve as recorders for those who are uncomfortable writing down their thoughts and would prefer to dictate. As people finish, they can head out for free time. However, if some would really like to keep adding to the wisdom book, leave it out during free time and let participants continue to work.

Free Time

This retreat has a block of free time in the afternoon. The RLT should do some research ahead of time and make a list of possible free-time activities: golf, hiking, shopping, movies, etc., or provide board games and cards. Napping or just sitting and relaxing are great options too.

Dinner

Session 3: Stories around the Fire

Time frame: 60–90 minutes
Optional supplies: campfire or fireplace fire, video camera, tripod, and tape(s)

Gather your group around the fire and have an RLT member introduce the session this way: *Tonight we're going to sit back and tell stories around the campfire, just the way our Bible relatives did. They passed their faith stories along, generation to generation, telling of the greatness of God and how he was at work in their lives. Hopefully, you've been thinking this weekend about how God has blessed you with wisdom, how you have learned to discern God's will, and how your life has been transformed by your faith. Take a few minutes to think of a God story. This could be a personal story or simply a story you heard and treasured, but it should be a story that reveals God's ability to change lives and impart wisdom to those who believe in him. We'll just take volunteers to get started, and then if you have a story to share, let us know. Thank you for sharing your hearts.*

Note: The RLT should be ready with a few stories to encourage the group. Also, if one of your team members or participants is skilled with a video camera, you can record this storytelling session with the purpose of showing it to the congregation back home and/or adding a copy to your newly made church wisdom book. This taping can be as informal as setting up the camera close enough to pick up the voices but far away enough to see the group, or it can be as formal as having a volunteer operate the camera and zoom in on each storyteller, although a less obvious method will probably work better and calm any "on camera" nerves. Tapes can easily be converted to DVDs with computer software at home or be taken to a camera store for conversion. Having a copy to share reinforces the weekend's theme of passing on wisdom to future generations. What a legacy to leave your church!

Fellowship

Free-time options might include evening refreshments, board games, card tournaments, or movies. The RLT can use this time to leave another pillow treat or Scripture on participants' pillows.

SUNDAY

Breakfast

Morning Walk

If the weather and your location cooperate, plan a group stroll through the woods, along the beach, or on the retreat center grounds. For those who don't want to walk, you can mark this hour as the beginning of extended personal devotions. Provide a variety of resources and encourage participants to select resources and take them with their Bibles to a quiet place. Those walking can start this devotional time when they return.

Personal Devotions

See above. Those wishing an extended time of meditation can forgo the walk and start at 8:45. Your RLT may wish to provide a list of the Scriptures that have been studied this weekend, as well as study Bibles, concordances, commentaries, or other devotional materials for those who wish to dig deeper.

Closing Worship

Time frame: 45–60 minutes

The RLT can plan a worship service in advance. Check your church library for liturgical resources if you want to include a call to worship, prayer of confession, or other group prayers, or write your own. Scriptures may include any of the ones listed previously in this retreat, or the RLT can use a concordance to look up verses under the headings of *age, generation, wisdom, wise, wisely, learn, teach,* and *grow.* Retreat participants could also be asked to share any favorite passages they have on these subjects.

If you type up and copy an order of worship, include your praise song and hymn lyrics or bring along songbooks or hymnals. Ahead of time find an RLT member or a retreat participant who would be comfortable leading the singing and/or accompanying the group for worship. If need be, bring a portable CD player and worship music CDs.

Don't forget to ask the RLT members to listen for stories of godly wisdom that come up in the small group discussions. Ask a few of these participants if they would share their testimonies in worship for the morning's message. You may also ask one of your RLT or group members to give a message using Ecclesiastes 3:1-8 and 9:13-18, which give advice for wise living.

Evaluations

Before everyone leaves the worship area, pass out the retreat evaluations (see Appendix A, p. 110). Ask the participants to complete them so that you have input for next year's planning.

Lunch

Pack Up and Depart for Home

Finish packing and head for home at this point. Make sure your group has followed the retreat center's checkout procedures. Don't forget to leave your check if that is what the management requires.

CHAPTER 18

Personal Retreats

Personal retreats are by nature very individualized, and the suggestions here are truly that—suggestions. Use them as you see fit. However, the basic retreat goal is still the same. You are giving yourself a time-out from the world to reconnect with God. Perhaps even more than a group retreat, a personal retreat is about reconciling yourself with the Lord.

Need to Know Information

1. If you've never done a personal retreat before, you may want to start small. Just go away for a morning or afternoon. Too much quiet time may feel unfamiliar and even stressful if you're not accustomed to it.
2. Just as you would for a group, make plans in advance if you will be using a retreat center, especially if your retreat will include overnight accommodations or meals. Even if your chosen facility mainly serves individuals, you don't want to show up for your retreat and discover that a group will be using the entire space that day.
3. Pray for your personal retreat time in the week(s) before you leave. If you have a prayer partner, spiritual director, or pastor, ask that person to be praying for you too.
4. Be comfortable. Bring a pillow and a favorite blanket. Wear your comfy clothes. Bring special treats and plenty of water or other beverages. Pack or wear your walking shoes if you plan to spend time outdoors. If you like to sing to God, bring your iPod or CD player and praise and worship CDs.

Need to Know Tip

"Listen to your body and listen to your soul, but don't necessarily listen to your brain. When I first went on personal retreats, I'd go away and be such a Puritan about it. I didn't bring enough food. That was stupid. That's part of listening to your body."

Jane Rubietta, author and veteran retreat speaker

5. Don't forget your Bible, your journal or notepad, and any study materials you have collected. Note: A study or reference Bible, a commentary, and a concordance will all be wonderful companions for you in providing background information on your readings.

6. Leave an emergency contact note with a spouse or close friend, just so someone knows where you are and what you're doing.

Need to Know Tip

"Even though it's a personal retreat, the number one thing is not to go alone. It's easy to cancel at the last minute. Having the commitment of another person holds you accountable. You can carpool, share meals, or share a room but go your separate ways during the day."

Brenda Jank, Director of Personal Retreat Ministries, Camp Lutherhaven, Albion, Indiana

---

Brenda's excellent advice aside (see above), your personality will determine if you should plan a personal retreat with a friend. Some people need that accountability; others truly need to go it alone. You be the judge.

Suggested Personal Retreat Themes

For the three themes that follow or any others that you choose (love, wisdom, faithfulness, forgiveness, etc.), use a study Bible and commentary to help with background information and put the story in context. Spend time reading and rereading these passages slowly. Consider the background material. Try reading several chapters before and after these passages to get the big picture view. Reread the stories that really appeal to you, highlighting key phrases that connect you to the story.

If you are having trouble making sense of the passage, make a list identifying the five Ws and one *H*: *Who* is the main character? *What* is happening in this story? *Where* is it taking place? *When* is it taking place? *Why* is there a conflict or struggle? *How* is that conflict being resolved? When you need to rest, rest. In all of your reflection and study, don't forget to take time just to be with God during your time away.

Wilderness

Look at biblical examples of God's people in the wilderness:

Jacob wrestles with God: *Genesis 32:22-32*
The Israelites after leaving Egypt: *Exodus 15:22–16:35*
Elijah: *1 Kings 16:29–19:21*
John the Baptist: *Matthew 3*
Jesus' temptation: *Luke 4:1-13* or *Matthew 4:1-11*

Questions for Reflection

1. Why did God allow Israel to be in a wilderness situation? What did it do for the people's faith in God?
2. Whose story do you most relate to? Go back and read it again. What do you identify with in this story? What truth do you find in this passage?
3. The wilderness is a barren place, removed from all comforts and familiar things in life. Loneliness and struggle are often part of the biblical wilderness experience. When in your life have you been in the spiritual wilderness? Reflect on these wilderness periods, making notes in your journal. Perhaps start a timeline and see if you can find a pattern. Think about other life-changing events that were taking place at the same time. Look for God's presence (or your perceived absence of God) in your timeline and mark those entrances (and exits). Ask yourself what caused you to enter this wilderness and how you moved out of it (or plan to move out of it). Spend time in prayer talking to God about these wilderness experiences. What truth can you take away from this conversation?

Additional Resource

Grace Points: Growth and Guidance in Times of Change by Jane Rubietta, Intervarsity Press, 2004.

Peace

Look at peace from a variety of perspectives:

The Beatitudes: *Matthew 5:1-12*
Transformed by Peace: *Colossians 3:12-17*
The Peaceable Kingdom: *Isaiah 11:1-9*
The Peace of God: *Philippians 4:4-7*
Peace with Others: *Ephesians 4:1-5*
Jesus' Peace: *John 14:25-27*

Questions for Reflection

1. Make a list of people you would call peacemakers. In what ways did they or are they working for peace? What do you admire about their efforts? How are you helping their efforts?
2. God calls you to work for peace in this world. Peace is not the absence of conflict. Peace is a process. It is about working to bring about reconciliation, whether that is within a personal struggle with sin or in a difficult relationship or with individuals who are far from God. Reconciliation is what draws us close to God again and washes away our sin. Reflect on the areas of your life where you are in need of peace. You can make categories: personal peace, peace with friends, with neighbors, with family members, with God, in the world, etc.
3. For each situation you have listed, ask yourself:
   a. Why was/is it difficult to maintain the unity of the spirit in the bonds of peace in this situation?
   b. What responsibility did/do I take for restoring peace in this situation?
   c. If I honestly listened to God in this situation, I think God would ask me to . . .
   d. For me, following God's instructions would be . . .
4. Go back and reread the Ephesians, Philippians, and Colossians passages above. What words and phrases do you hear repeating over and over? Make a list of the qualities God wants you to have so that you can be a peacemaker in his name. Reflect on the qualities you already possess. Now reflect on those you want to develop. Spend time in prayer asking God to help you become a peacemaker for him. Reread Jesus' words in John 14:27. You do not have to be troubled or afraid in working for peace, because Jesus has left his peace with you. It's guarding your heart and mind. Let it be.

Additional Resources:

Resting Place: A Personal Guide to Spiritual Retreats, Intervarsity Press: 2005 and *Quiet Places: A Woman's Guide to Personal Retreat,* Abounding Publishing: 2005 by Jane Rubietta, both with accompanying music CDs, both designed for personal retreat use.

Job

Read Job's story, using the Contemporary English Version or other paraphrased Bible. This book reads like a dual courtroom drama, with Job as the prosecuting attorney and God working for the defense on the one hand, and Job's friends serving as the prosecution with Job defending himself on the other. The best thing about Job's story is that it reflects every one of us. Who among us hasn't suffered and cried out to God in our distress, asking why a certain crisis was happening? Trials are trials, and we all face them because life is filled with human sin and brokenness. But God is fair and just and merciful and wise, and that is what comes through in Job's story.

Take your time reading through the forty-two chapters. Pause after each section and make notes on Job's attitude and emotional state. Compare your life to Job's. When have you shared his feelings? Were you brave enough to cry out to God? What happened? What impact did/do your sufferings have on your faith? Spend time in prayer talking to God about God's presence in your life and your need for God's wisdom and guidance.

Additional Personal Retreat Tools

1. Fast only with the permission of your personal physician. Consider fasting as a way to empty yourself of the ways of the world, to get in touch with the basic needs of brothers and sisters who are suffering in the world, and/or to be more aware of your dependence on God. If you choose to fast, be sure to bring enough water (or juice), so that you don't get dehydrated, and get plenty of rest.
2. Adapt the monastic practice of *lectio divina* to your study needs. This is a traditional form of meditation and prayer that involves reading a Scripture passage in four steps:
   - *Lectio,* or repeated reading of the text until certain phrases and key words begin to resonate with you.
   - *Meditatio,* or continued reflection on those key phrases so that you begin to truly understand God's Word.
   - *Oratio,* or a conversation (prayer) that begins between you and God about God's truth.

  This conversation might actually be you voicing your thoughts to God, or you might respond through writing, art, music, or some other form.
- *Contemplatio,* or a time of silence in which you rest in the awareness of God's presence.

3. Consider making an appointment with your retreat facility's spiritual director if you would like additional guidance or prayer during your retreat. Many Roman Catholic retreat centers offer this support service for all guests, whether Catholic or not. Be sure to check this out in advance if you plan to incorporate it into your retreat time.
4. Don't be afraid to get outside. Many people find great renewal and refreshment by being out in nature. Go for a long hike, paddle a canoe, sit by a pond, walk a prayer labyrinth, climb a hill just to admire the view of God's creation. Don't limit yourself to an inside space while on retreat.

APPENDIX A

Reproducible Forms

List of Reproducible Forms by Chapter

Kids' Daily Schedule

Friday late afternoon activities: ______________________________

Friday dinner Time: ________ Menu: ______________________________

Friday bedtime: Baths for ______________________________

Bedtime routine for ______________________ Time: ________ bottle or snack/story/nightlight/music

Other important information: ______________________________

Bedtime routine for ______________________ Time: ________ bottle or snack/story/nightlight/music

Other important information: ______________________________

Bedtime routine for ______________________ Time: ________ bottle or snack/story/nightlight/music

Other important information: ______________________________

Middle of the night feedings—who/what/when? ______________________________

Saturday morning breakfast/morning bottles: ______________________________

____

Saturday morning/afternoon routine/activities: ______________________________

____

____

Saturday lunch Time: ________ Menu: ______________________________

____

Nap time: ______________________________ bottle/story/nightlight/music

Nap time: ______________________________ bottle/story/nightlight/music

Other important nap information: ______________________________

Afternoon bottles: ______________________________

Typical afternoon activities: ______________________________

Saturday dinner: Time: ________ Menu: ______________________________

____

Saturday bedtime routine: Baths for ______________________________

Bedtime routine for ____________________ Time: ________ bottle or snack/story/nightlight/music

Other important information: ______________________________

Bedtime routine for ____________________ Time: ________ bottle or snack/story/nightlight/music

Other important information: ______________________________

Bedtime routine for ____________________ Time: ________ bottle or snack/story/nightlight/music

Other important information: ______________________________

Middle of the night feedings—who/what/when? ______________________________

Sunday morning breakfast/morning bottles: ______________________________

____

Sunday morning/afternoon routine/activities: ______________________________

____

Sunday lunch Time: ________ Menu: ______________________________

____

Nap time: ______________________________ bottle/story/nightlight/music

Nap time: ______________________________ bottle/story/nightlight/music

Other important info: toys/TV/friends ______________________________

____

____

____

____

____

Camp contact information: ______________________________

My cell phone: ______________________________

Final Details Letter

Date

Greetings!

Your Retreat Leadership Team is in the final countdown. Are you? Retreat is rapidly approaching, and we have been praying and planning and praying some more about our time together.

This letter confirms your participation in the retreat. We have your RSVP. Now we just need you!

We leave on *(date)* and should return by *(time)* on *(date)*. The retreat center contact information is as follows: *(retreat center contact info—name, address, emergency phone number, etc.)*. Directions are also enclosed with this letter *(insert if arranging carpools and your carpool information)*. To make your departure smoother, we have also included the Kids' Daily Schedule for you to leave with whoever is staying with your children while you're away *(insert if your group includes parents leaving children at home)*. Our program begins at *(time)* on *(day)*, so we hope you will be able to get away in time and join us for our opening session.

When packing for retreat, remember that you want to be comfortable. You also definitely want to bring *(insert necessary items here: toiletries, medications, sleeping bag and pillow, towel and washcloth, Bible, casual clothing, flashlight, bug spray, walking shoes, a favorite snack to share, etc. Note: If you are doing a special work project, outdoor activity, or craft and your participants need to wear or bring certain items, list that information here too)*.

We are confident that this is going to be an wonderful time of rest and relaxation that will encourage you in your walk with the Lord! If you have any questions about the retreat, please contact *(list RLT member's name, phone, and email)*.

Grace and peace to you,

Your Retreat Leadership Team

(Insert a key verse from retreat here.)

Retreat Evaluation

Please respond to the following questions using a 10-point scale, with 1 being the lowest rating (awful/never/no way) and 10 being the highest (fantastic/always/absolutely).

1. Overall I would rate the retreat as a ___.
2. I would rate the food as a ___.
3. I would rate the lodging as a ___.
4. The schedule gave me enough downtime. ___
5. The theme/topic was relevant to my life. ___
6. Overall sessions were well prepared and helped me grow in faith. ___
7. I would rate the individual sessions as follows:
   Fri. evening ___ Sat. morning ___ Sat. afternoon ___
   Sat. evening ___ Sun. morning ___
8. I would rate the Sunday morning worship service as a ___.
9. My favorite part(s) about retreat was/were:

10. The thing(s) I would change for next year would be:

11. If you were new to retreat, how welcome did you feel? (circle one)
    very welcome/comfortable   somewhat welcome   not at all welcome
12. The price I paid was (circle one):   too low   just right   too high
13. If you would be interested in serving on the Retreat Leadership Team, please give us your name, phone number, and email address here:

14. Please use reverse side to make any additional comments. Thank you!

Running the Race with Perseverance Women's Retreat

Amazing Race Scripture Scavenger Hunt

Your team will be looking up the following verses and then hunting for an object to represent this verse. While you are hunting, discuss with your team how God has helped you survive in life.

Scripture Scavenger Hunt verses include:

Food: *Numbers 11:4-9*

Water: *John 4:13*

Shelter: *Psalm 61:3-4*

Salvation: *1 Peter 1:3-9*

Clothes: *Matthew 6:28-30*

Family: *Ephesians 2:19*

Friends: *John 15:12-14*

Running the Race with Perseverance Women's Retreat

Faith Fear Factor Questions

1. Who is one person whose faith you admire? Why?
2. Who or what regularly pushes your buttons and challenges your ability to stay faithful to the will and Word of God?
3. What earthly fears do you have that keep you from being the Christian you really want to be?
4. What is one thing you have experienced in life that really affected/tested your faith?
5. What do you do to refocus or renew your faith?
6. What stumbling blocks have challenged you in your faith journey? What strengths have you developed as a result of those stumbling blocks?
7. What's a good piece of advice that a faithful Christian passed on to you?
8. What advice would you give a new Christian about her faith journey?
9. What do you think is God's view of your faithfulness right now? Why is that? Is there anything you would like to do to change that perception? If so, what?
10. Do you have a favorite Scripture verse that helps you refocus your faith? Please share it with us.

For extended discussion or private journaling time, consider these Scriptures as well: Psalm 23; Isaiah 44:6-8; Luke 12:22-34; Philippians 2:12-18; 1 John 4:15-18

Running the Race with Perseverance Women's Retreat

God's Apprentice Activity Instructions

The scenario: While you may not know each team member well, you are all connected through your church. One of you in this small group has been called by God to start a special ministry or mission outreach. The rest of you have been called to help.

1. Take a few minutes to review the things you listed on your paper about your own strengths. Now open your gift envelope and take a look at what other people see as your gifts and strengths.

2. Now take a few minutes, and on the back side of your list of strengths, write down three or four of your ministry or mission interests. Share your interests with your small group and take 15 to 20 minutes to decide what kind of ministry or mission you will develop, based on an area of common interest. You all will need to be in agreement. Assume that you have the necessary financial support of your church to get this project up and running. Be creative! Be bold! What will your ministry or mission do? Whom will you serve? Where will you be based? What will your ministry or mission name be?

3. Now think about what needs to be done in this ministry or mission. What kind of roles are required—for example, teachers, counselors, administrative workers, fund-raisers, mentors, cooks, drivers, organizers, musicians. Take 10 to 15 minutes for everyone to jot down her ideas for what needs to be done to get this project off the ground. Share these in your small group and come to a consensus on the essential ones. Have one person write down all the roles on your poster board.

4. Go around and share a few of your strengths and gifts from your envelope. Take 15 to 20 minutes to look at your role list and think about everyone's gifts and strengths. Who can do what? Who is called to do what? Write down names next to specific tasks on the poster board. Everyone should have at least one job to do.

5. Now take 20 to 30 minutes to brainstorm an action plan to get your project up and running. Write it out in some form on the back of your poster board. Decide who will do what and in what order. If you have time, create a logo or mission statement for your project.

6. Leave 15 to 30 minutes at the end of your session for teams to present their ministry and mission projects. If appropriate, take your ministry and mission ideas back to your church council and see if you can't make at least one of them a real part of your faith community and/or its work in this world.

This is a four-page journal created by photocopying the following two pages back to back and folding in half.

More of my thoughts on being a peacemaker and working for reconciliation in this world:

Peace Women's Retreat

Peace Journal

"Blessed are the peacemakers, for they will be called children of God" (Matthew 5:9, NRSV). I want to be blessed and be called a child of God. Here are ways I can be a peacemaker in this world:

Ephesians 2:13-19

1. Read this passage slowly, focusing on each word and phrase. What portions of the text do you really connect with?

2. Repeat those words or phrases silently or out loud. How or why do these particular portions of text connect you to God? What images are called up as you meditate on these words?

3. How do you feel about what you have read? Show God what you think of God's Word by drawing a picture, writing a poem, creating a prayer, offering a song, making some notes, talking to God.

4. Be mindful of God's presence with you. Close your eyes. Open your ears and your heart.

In light of the Ephesians passage, here are the places in the world where I see a need for peace:

Peace Women's Retreat

Dyad Questions

Directions: Dyads (or triads) are a series of questions or open-ended statements that allow you to get to know another person deeply in a short amount of time. Your job is twofold: First, you need to focus on your partner when it is her turn and listen to what she has to say, restating her answer if necessary to ensure that you understand her message. Your second job is to open up and share honestly with your partner even if you don't know her well. This is an opportunity for us to minister to one another by living a life worthy of the one to which we have been called. Please find a quiet space on the grounds where you can talk. You have an hour to complete the questions, taking turns answering them in order. Please return to this meeting space in one hour. Finally, please remember that anything that is said at retreat in small group needs to stay at retreat. Everyone has a right to feel that what she says is shared in the spirit of trust and confidentiality. Thank you for your understanding.

1. My name is . . .
2. I was born in . . .
3. I grew up in . . .
4. I fill my days by . . .
5. One word that describes me right now is . . .
6. One word that describes my relationship with God right now is . . .
7. A place where I feel at peace is . . .
8. When it comes to relationships with friends, neighbors, and colleagues, I think that unity of the spirit in the bonds of peace is ____________ because . . .
9. I have found it hard to maintain bonds of peace with a particular friend, neighbor, or colleague because . . .
10. What I did (or what I could do) to restore peace with this friend, neighbor, or colleague is . . .
11. If I honestly listened to God in this situation, what I think God would ask me to do is . . .
12. Following God's instructions would be . . .
13. When it comes to relationships with family members, I think that unity of the spirit in the bonds of peace is ______ because . . .
14. I have found it hard to maintain bonds of peace with a particular family member because . . .
15. What I did (or what I could do) to restore peace with this family member is . . .
16. If I honestly listened to God in this situation, what I think God would ask me to do is . . .
17. Following God's instructions would be . . .
18. When it comes to relationships with other church or organization members, I think that unity in the spirit in the bonds of peace is ____________ because . . .
19. I have found it hard to maintain bonds of peace with a particular church or organization member because . . .
20. What I did (or what I could do) to restore peace with this church or organization member is . . .
21. If I honestly listened to God in this situation, what I think God would ask me to do is . . .
22. Following God's instructions would be . . .
23. (Take a moment to read Ephesians 4:1-6.) When I read through this passage, what really hits me is . . .
24. In regard to unity of the Spirit in the bonds of peace, I need prayers for . . .

Running the Race with Perseverance Men's Retreat

Faith Fear Factor Questions

1. Who is one person whose faith you admire and why?

2. Who or what regularly pushes your buttons and challenges your ability to stay faithful to the will and Word of God?

3. What other stumbling blocks have challenged you in your faith journey? What strengths have you developed as a result of those stumbling blocks?

4. What earthly fears or worries do you have that keep you from being the faithful Christian you want to be?

5. What do you think is God's view of your faithfulness right now? Why is that? Is there anything you would like to do to change that perception? If so, what?

Running the Race with Perseverance Men's Retreat

God's Apprentice Questions

Tony Dungy strives to be God's apprentice in his life. In the interview he talks about the ways in which he lives out the core values of the Fellowship of Christian Athletes that help him do that. Let's take a look at them:

Integrity

1. What does it mean to be a man of integrity?
2. Do you know any men of integrity? How have they demonstrated this strength of character?
3. Proverbs 13:6 says, "Righteousness protects the innocent; wickedness is the downfall of sinners." How does that verse fit into your life?

Serving

1. Whose apprentice are you?
2. Genesis 1:27 says, "So God created humankind in his image" (NRSV). In what ways do you see yourself reflecting the image of God through service, or how can you begin reflecting the image of God through service?

Teamwork

1. We are called to live in community with one another. That requires cooperation and teamwork. What things about teamwork do you find frustrating?
2. What is rewarding about teamwork?
3. How does being a player on God's team make you a better individual?

Excellence

First Corinthians 12:31 says, "But strive for the greater gifts. And I will show you a still more excellent way" (NRSV). As God's apprentice, you are still learning, still striving to reflect the image of your Creator in all that you do. What God-skills do you hope to perfect someday?

Heroes Men's Retreat

Real-Life Heroes

Take some time to work through the following questions with your small group.

1. What do you think of the way Jim Ellis initially handles the vandals? Is he being a hero or not?

2. What does his speech on the bus reveal about the kind of man he really is?

3. What heroic qualities do you think he passed along to his team that enabled them to compete at Nationals?

4. What other examples of real-life heroes can you think of (either historical or contemporary)? What makes the person heroic in your mind?

5. Are these heroic qualities similar or different than those in the list of superhero qualities we made last night? How so?

6. In comic book superhero stories, the classic battle is always good versus evil and fighting for justice. How do those fantasy tales mirror real life?

7. Where is God in these real-life battles of good versus evil?

Heroes Men's Retreat

Hero Qualities

Consider these heroic qualities through the lens of Scripture. Read each passage silently; then have a volunteer read it aloud. In your group discuss these two questions for each selection:

1. What is this passage saying about (key word)?

2. What really hits home for me personally in these words?

Endurance: Hebrews 12:1-4, 12; James 1:12-16

Compassion: 1 Peter 3:8-12

Wisdom: Proverbs 3:5-8

Noble/Just: Philippians 4:8-9

Brave: 1 Corinthians 16:13-14

Loyal: 2 Kings 18:1-6

Truth-seeking: Ephesians 6:11-14

Strong: Joshua 1:7-9

Heroes Men's Retreat

The Bible's Men of Steel

Your group will be assigned one of these heroes. Read the accompanying Bible passages to get information on your hero. Then discuss the questions that follow.

David
Chosen to be the future king of Israel, 1 Samuel 16:1-13
Kills Goliath, 1 Samuel 17
David's plans vs. God's plans, 2 Samuel 7

Joshua
Entering the Promised Land and the conquest of Jericho, Joshua 1–6

Daniel
In captivity, Daniel 1 and 2
In the lions' den, Daniel 6

Jonah
His story, Jonah 1–4

Saul
His conversion from Christian-killer to believer, Acts 9
Paul's ministry, Acts 16:11-40
Paul's miracles, Acts 19:11-20

John the Baptist
His ministry, Matthew 3
Jesus speaks about John, Matthew 11:7-15
John's death, Matthew 14:1-12

The good Samaritan and the father of the prodigal son
The good Samaritan, Luke 10:25-37
The father of the prodigal son, Luke 15:11-32

1. In what ways does your ordinary person act in extraordinary ways?
2. What hero qualities from this morning's study do you see in this man?
3. In what ways do you think his actions please or displease God? Why?
4. What is one quality you admire in this Bible hero and would like to practice in your own life?

Heroes Men's Retreat

A Hero in God's Eyes Questions

1. Have you ever seen a real-life hero in action or read or heard about a real-life hero experience that amazed you? How and why did that situation make an impact on you?

2. Which hero qualities do you think you might already possess?

3. Which of your personality traits are not so heroic?

4. Have you ever been faced with a situation in which you needed to show heroic qualities and do the God-honoring thing and you just couldn't rise to the challenge? What happened?

5. Our ultimate hero is Jesus. He exhibits every one of those hero qualities that we have talked about. We can't even begin to compare to his perfection, yet our goal is to try to be more like Jesus in all that we do. By living a life that follows Jesus' example, we become a hero in God's eyes. What are one or two of Jesus' hero qualities that you aspire to have?

6. List two or three specific actions you can take when you get home that will move you along in this journey of becoming a hero in God's eyes.

Life Is a Three-Ring Circus Family Retreat

Circus Survey

Families may split into smaller units or stay together. Your goal is to find a person who fits each of these descriptions and have him or her sign that line. Before you ask your question, you must first introduce each member of your family.

You can ask more than one question of each person, but as soon as you get a positive response, you need to move on to a new person. If you have talked to everyone in the room but still have blanks, you can reinterview people. Your challenge is to fill in all of the blanks.

1. Find someone who has been to a circus. ______________________________

2. Find someone whose favorite circus food is peanuts. ______________________

3. Find someone who has never eaten cotton candy. ________________________

4. Find someone who is afraid of clowns. ______________________________

5. Find someone who can tell you Bozo the Clown's costume color ____________ and hair color ______________. Name: ________________________

6. Find someone who has walked on a tightrope or ridden a unicycle.
   ____

7. Find someone who has been to a circus museum. ________________________

8. Find someone who can tell you what animals Gunther Gebel-Williams was famous for training. ________________ (animals) Name: ____________________

9. Find someone who knows how circuses travel across the United States: by ____________________. Name: ____________________________

10. Find someone who has seen an elephant balance on a ball. __________________

Life Is a Three-Ring Circus Family Retreat

Big Top Card

Copy this big top on card stock and cut out. Provide one per family.

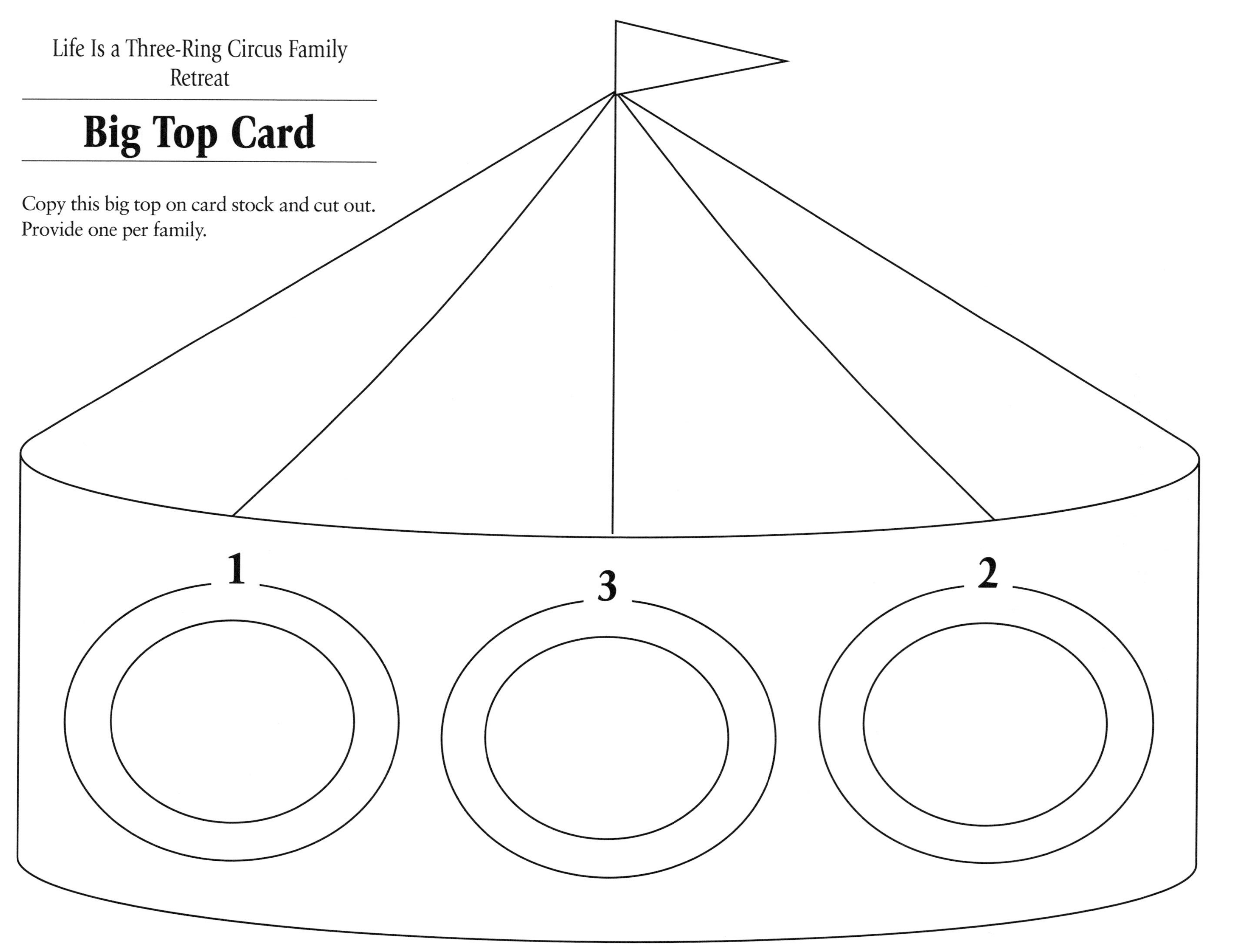

Life Is a Three-Ring Circus Family Retreat

Haiku Prayer Directions

A haiku is a simple Japanese form of poetry that has three lines. The first and third lines have five syllables; the middle line has seven syllables. After reading the samples, create your own family prayer to use at mealtime, bedtime, or some other occasion.

Sample 1
Lord, you are so good.
We love you, Lord, and praise you.
Be with us always.

Sample 2
Thank you, God, for food.
Thank you for our family.
Thank you for your Son!

Your Prayer
Line 1 (5 syllables)

Line 2 (7 syllables)

Line 3 (5 syllables)

Life Is a Three-Ring Circus Family Retreat

Prayer Plaque Directions

1. Find a sheet of fancy paper on which to write your haiku prayer.
2. Cut the paper to fit the wooden plaque, and copy your prayer onto the paper. Set aside.
3. Write your family name on the back of the plaque.
4. Decorate the top and sides of the plaque with a mosaic collage of tissue paper. First brush glue onto the plaque, and then lay the tissue squares on the plaque in an overlapping pattern.
5. Brush glue onto the entire back of your prayer and set on the plaque.
6. Quickly brush the entire plaque (except the back) with a light coating of glue.
7. Set aside to dry.

God's Good Eats Family Retreat

Bread of Life Discussion Questions

Scripture passage: John 6:22–58

1. The people are excited in the first half of the story, begging Jesus for this special heavenly bread. What happens in the second half that upsets them so? What is it that they are not understanding?

2. Why do you think Jesus uses the Exodus reference to explain things to these Jewish people?

3. What was the end result of this story? Do you think the people really got what Jesus was talking about?

4. In verse 57, Jesus says, ". . . so the one who feeds on me will live because of me" (NIV). What is Jesus talking about?

5. Think of a time when you needed to be fed spiritually. What was going on in your life? Who fed you or how were you fed?

6. What connections do you see between this "Jesus is the Bread of Life" story and the stories we looked at this morning: Elijah, the Israelites, and the crowd of five thousand? How do those connections relate to your life today?

7. How spiritually hungry are you feeling these days? What's one way you can make sure you get fed?

Be True to Yourself Youth Retreat

Self-Reflection Questions

1. "The LORD does not look at the things man looks at. Man looks at the outward appearance, but the LORD looks at the heart" (1 Samuel 16:7, NIV). What do people see when they look at you? List a few things:

2. What do you think God sees when he looks at your heart?

3. Is there a difference between how people judge you personally on the outside and how God judges you personally on the inside? Why do you think that is?

4. When you read the Bible, you see that God often chooses people to serve him that the world would have cast aside as unworthy. Take David, for example. He was the youngest of Jesse's sons, a shepherd and a musician, not a mature soldier, yet God chose David to be king of Israel. Read 1 Samuel 16 to see find out more about David. Why do you think God chose him?

5. In preparation for group regathering, think of one true statement about yourself and one false statement. We will be using them for the next activity, in which your goal is to test the group's knowledge of you. So dig deep and see if you can find a way to stump them.

Be True to Yourself Youth Retreat

Life Timeline

Four time periods are identified: birth date, kindergarten, middle school/junior high, present age, and future. For each point on the timeline, participants are asked to complete the following information:

	birth date	kindergarten	middle school / junior high	present age	future
1. The most important people in my life at this point are . . .					
2. My best friend at this point is . . .					
3. My mortal enemy at this point is . . .					
4. In my free time at this point, I love to . . .					
5. My biggest worry at this point in life is . . .					
6. My strengths and talents at this point in life are . . .					
7. My relationship with Jesus at this point in life is . . .					

Be True to Yourself Youth Retreat

Identity Crisis Questions

1. When you imagine God, what do you see?

2. What color(s) do you associate with God?

3. What sound(s) do you associate with God?

4. What kind of music does God like?

5. What do you think is God's favorite place on earth?

6. Has your image of God changed from when you were younger? How?

7. Where or when do you feel close to God?

8. Have you ever literally felt the presence of God? Describe it.

Be True to Yourself Youth Retreat

Images of God

Look up and read the verses on the left and then place them into one of the categories on the right that describe various images of God. You can work with partners within your small group and take 4 or 5 verses to match up and then share your answers.

Genesis 1:1-5
Exodus 20:5
Deuteronomy 4:24
Deuteronomy 7:9
Deuteronomy 7:21
Deuteronomy 32:4
Deuteronomy 32:35
Nehemiah 4:20
Psalm 7:11
Psalm 46:1
Psalm 61:3-4
Psalm 91:2
Jeremiah 1:4-5
Jeremiah 10:10
Daniel 6:26
Jonah 4:2
Micah 5:15
Nahum 1:2
John 3:16
Romans 2:5
1 Corinthians 1:25
2 Corinthians 9:8
Titus 3:4
Hebrews 10:30-31
1 John 1:9
1 John 4:8

Loving God
Creator God
Vengeful God
Forgiving God
Jealous God
Just/Righteous God
Provider God
Faithful God
Everlasting God
Protector/Shelter God
Powerful God

Be True to Yourself Youth Retreat

"Who Do You Say That I Am?"

Genesis 1:26-27

God created us in his image. Based on what we learned about who God is in Session 2, what does that mean for us? Do you feel that you reflect the image of God? Why or why not?

Romans 8:14-17

Children often physically resemble their parents, as well as take on some of their personality traits. This Romans passage tells us that we are children of God and heirs with Christ to the eternal life that God offers to us. An inheritance can be a big blessing. It can also be a big responsibility. What is your response to this amazing inheritance that God has promised you?

Isaiah 64:8

We are the clay in the Potter God's hands. What do you look like? How do you see yourself? Are you beautiful? Useful? Sturdy? Delicate? Able to be used in many ways? Entertaining? Unique? Thought-provoking? Heart-warming? Solid? Many-layered?

Jeremiah 18:1-6

This is really the best news of all. Even though this is an Old Testament passage, it reflects the truth of what Jesus has done for us. Jesus' death on the cross allows us to be remade by God every time we sin. Our mistakes don't mean that God throws us away, unable ever to use us again for his good purposes. God restores us to wholeness because of Jesus' sacrifice. Take a few minutes to think of a time when you made a mistake, when you pushed God away and followed your own will. If you haven't already, ask God to forgive you for this sin. Then think about how God is working in your life to remake you. What signs do you see that the Master Potter is at work?

Be True to Yourself Youth Retreat

Sunday Devotions

Find a quiet place where you can read and reflect on the following verses before worship.

Deuteronomy 7:6-11
Pray for the wisdom to follow God's laws and live in covenant with him.

Daniel 6:16-27
Pray for strength and faith in times of trouble.

Isaiah 51:1-14
Pray for forgiveness from sin and renewal through God's love for you.

coNectd 24/7 Youth Retreat

Lost or Found Questions

1. What were some of the problems the plane crash survivors were facing?

2. Even though technology often helps us communicate, what happens to our lives when technology is suddenly taken away?

3. In what ways does our dependence on technology-enhanced communication help and/or hurt our relationship with God?

4. Can you think of a time when your connectivity to God crashed? What happened? Were you able to restore the connection, or are you still feeling disconnected?

5. Read Proverbs 2:1-11 to yourself. Then have a volunteer(s) read it out loud for your group. What does this passage say you should do? What does it say God will do? If you don't stay connected to God, what are some of the possible consequences?

6. Who is a person whose relationship with God you admire? Why do you think that person has such a strong friendship with God? (What does she or he do to stay connected?)

7. When you feel lost and separated from God, what can you do to reconnect?

coNectd 24/7 Youth Retreat

Self-Reflection Handout

This time is for you and the Lord. You are going to be reflecting on two short passages—Proverbs 8:32-36 and Romans 8:38-39. If you think you might like to draw or paint in response to these readings, take a few art supplies with you before you leave the meeting space.

Find a quiet place where you have space and time to think. Read these verses silently then aloud. What words in these passages stand out to you? Note them here:

Repeat those key words and phrases over and over; then respond to those words. Take a walk and repeat them. Let them echo in your brain. Or paint a picture or write a poem or a prayer that illustrates your understanding of God's truth. Or gather some natural materials (twigs, leaves, stones, etc.) and create a sculpture that reflects your thoughts.

Then rest in the Word. Close your eyes. Shut out the world. Just be in the presence of God.

Free time and lunch will follow your personal meditation time, so you are welcome to continue your alone time right up until lunch if need be. And if you want to talk more about what you're reading and discussing, or if you are wondering about how to deepen your relationship with Jesus, please talk to your group leader or any member of the RLT during the weekend. We would love to help you connect with the Lord.

coNectd 24/7 Youth Retreat

Whose Truth Is Truest?

1. Read the following verses, first to yourself, then out loud in your group: Psalm 119:105, Psalm 119:129-136, and Proverbs 3:5-7. What do these verses say about whose truth is truest? What is one way you can apply these words in your own life? What is one way you can share these words in the world?

2. Think about how much you personally are coNectd 24/7 to people in the world (friends and strangers, Christians and non-Christians). In what ways does 24/7 communication encourage you to disconnect from God and your faith? Are there ways that it encourages you to stay coNectd to him?

3. With so many "voices" in society and on the Internet giving you their versions of the truth, how hard is it to figure out whose truth is truest? How do you determine for yourself whose truth is truest? Can you think of any examples of youth who created/accepted/protested a virtual (e-mail, text message, MySpace post, etc.) truth as truest? What happened? How bad was the disconnect?

4. Sin separates us from God. That's the disconnect that believers struggle with every day. Did you know that the Bible is filled with stories of God's people who faced a disconnect from God because of sin? From Adam and Eve to Cain and Abel to Sarai and Hagar to Jacob and Esau to Jonah to Job to Peter, sin has been causing communication problems with God forever. The good news is that Jesus died for our sins and that amazing sacrifice lets us reconnect to God, over and over again if need be. On a scale of 1 to 10, how connected to God are you feeling right now? Share with your group. What's one action you can take to reestablish or strengthen that connection? Write it down on the back of this sheet and then share with your group. What's one truth you've learned about God this weekend? Write it down on the back of this sheet and then share with your group.

To read more about a few of these disconnected people who lost sight of God's truth for a while, check out:
Genesis 2–3 (Adam and Eve)
Genesis 4 (Cain and Abel)
Genesis 16 (Sarai and Hagar)
Genesis 27 (Jacob and Esau)
The Book of Job
The Book of Jonah
Matthew 26:69-75 (Peter)

coNectd 24/7 Youth Retreat

Sunday Devotions

Find a quiet place where you can read and reflect on these verses before worship.

Proverbs 19:20-21
Pray that you are coNectd 24/7 so that you can know God's plan for your life.

Proverbs 3:5-7
Pray for the wisdom to know that God's truth is truest.

Psalm 32:1-7
Pray that when sin disconnects you from God, you will have the courage to admit your sin and reconnect with him.

Still Worthy Older Adults' Retreat

Age Defiers

In your small group, read the following Bible passages and discuss the questions.

1. Read Noah's story in Genesis 6–9. We know that some of our Bible ancestors lived extremely long lives. Noah lived 350 years after the flood, making him 950 years old when he died. Can you imagine building the ark and filling it with all those animals at the age of 600?
2. What do you think God saw in Noah that made God choose him for this job (see Genesis 6:9), and why was he a better choice than his younger sons?
3. What Noah quality would you like to have in your personality?
4. Read Abraham's story in Genesis 12 and 13, 17 and 22. Through Abraham, God made a covenant with us. God told Abraham that his descendents would be God's chosen people, and that they would be as numerous as the stars in the heavens and the grains of sand in the desert. To know that God was making him the head of his earthly family, when he was old and childless, probably put a lot of pressure on Abraham, but how did he respond (see 13:14-18 in particular)?
5. How have you responded when you felt God was calling you to a difficult task? Have you ever not served God in some capacity because of your age? What happened? Were you able to serve in another way?
6. Take a look at Abraham's wife, Sarah. Read Genesis 18:1-15 and 21:1-15. What is happening in 18:1-8? Abraham and Sarah seem to fully understand the spiritual gift of hospitality. Do you think that gift is easier for older adults to use in service to God than it is for younger people? Why?
7. In Genesis 18:9-15 and 21:1-15 Sarah is told that God will bless her and Abraham with a son and the baby is born. Sarah names him Isaac, which means "he will laugh," because she is filled with such joy. With so many grandparents raising or helping raise grandchildren these days, what example does Sarah set for us?
8. Finally, take a look at the story of Elizabeth and Zechariah, which is similar to Sarah's. Read Luke 1:5-45, 57-80. What does Elizabeth's husband, Zechariah, say in verse 18 that gets him in trouble? Have you ever felt like saying the same thing to God? What happened in that situation?
9. What role does Elizabeth take on for Mary? Why do you think God chose an older woman, and not Mary's own mother or same age relative, to mentor her through this?
10. Even though Elizabeth's son should have received a family name, Elizabeth tells everyone that the baby will be named John, which means "God is gracious." Zechariah confirms the name John. What does this reveal about their response to this opportunity God gave them to serve?
11. In looking at all of these stories of older adults who continued to serve God faithfully throughout their entire lives, whose faith story do you find most inspiring? Why?
12. This final question is for personal reflection. Take your Bible and your handout and find a space, indoors or out, where you can be alone and think. Read back over the stories of Noah, Abraham and Sarah, Zechariah and Elizabeth. Somewhere on your handout, make a list of the personality traits that make these individuals lifelong servants of God. Check any traits you feel you share with these role models. Circle any traits you are inspired to develop. Spend some time in prayer asking God to help you grow in servanthood as you grow in years.

Still Worthy Older Adults' Retreat

Worthy in God's Eyes

Directions: Choose 1 or 2 verses from column A and read them silently several times, looking for the words that really impact you. Then reflect on those words and how they encourage you. After 10 to 15 minutes of reading/study, group members will read their individual verses out loud and share their thoughts. Then repeat this process with the verses in the second column.

Column A
Deuteronomy 6:16-19
Psalm 34:1-14
Isaiah 1:16-17
Amos 5:14-15
Micah 6:8
Matthew 5:43-48
Matthew 25:14-30
Galatians 5:13-14
James 1:22-25

Column B
Galatians 6:7-10
Philippians 1:62
Thessalonians 3:6-13

When you have read, reflected on, and shared the column B verses, make a list of ways in which you have served God over the years, including things you are currently doing, in the church or out in the world (use the back of this handout). Second, list things you would like to do to serve God but never tried for some reason or another. Third, copy your favorite motivational verse from the ones studied this evening and next to it write down one way in which you are going to continue to serve God and live out this verse. Once you complete this half of the handout, share within your group.

Wisdom Older Adults' Retreat

Pillars of Wisdom

In your groups, read through and discuss the following questions and accompanying Bible passages. The last question will take you into a time of personal reflection, so please feel free to find a quiet place to complete this final task.

1. King Solomon was King David's son. He was incredibly wise because he had been given that spiritual gift from God, and for a while, he faithfully used his gift to honor and glorify God. Read Solomon's story in 1 Kings 3:3-15, 16-28 and 1 Kings 4:29-34. In the first section, Solomon is a young man, yet he asks for wisdom from God. What do you think God expects Solomon to do with this gift?
2. In 1 Kings 3:16-28 Solomon gets his first real test. Why was Solomon's decision a wise one? What might a king have done if he relied only on his own wisdom in this situation?
3. Now read 1 Kings 11:9-13. Basically, Solomon got too big for his britches. He liked his gift of wisdom, but he failed to use it to honor God. He took foreign wives and worshipped their idols (see vv. 1-8), and so God punished Solomon for his sin. What does this say to us about how we treat God's gifts to us? If Solomon was so full of God's wisdom, what does that teach us about our vulnerability to sin?
4. Now turn to Acts 8:26-40. This is the story of the disciple Philip who is on the road to Gaza when he comes across an Ethiopian eunuch reading from the book of Isaiah. Philip says to the eunuch, "Do you understand what you are reading?" The man answers, "How can I, unless someone guides me?" (Read the passage silently or out loud.) Who shows wisdom in this passage? What is his response to this gift from God?
5. Has God ever put you in a situation like Philip's? What happened? What was your response to this opportunity to share God's Word?
6. Now turn to Luke 2:41-52 and read these verses out loud in your group. This is the story of the boy Jesus who knows instinctively that he needs to spend time in his Father's house, learning more about him. Sometimes we dismiss children as spiritually immature and not possessing the wisdom of age, but what does the young Jesus teach us in this story? How do his actions and his response to his parents demonstrate true wisdom?
7. Have you ever gained wisdom from an interaction with a child? What happened?
8. The final question is for personal reflection. Take your Bible and this hand out and move to a comfortable, quiet space. You're going to spend some time with one or more of Jesus' parables or teaching stories. Jesus tried to make people wise through his parables, but not everyone caught on. To the crowds he would say, "Let everyone who has ears hear." What are you hearing in Jesus' words today? Underline, copy down or repeat out loud the key phrases that speak to you in the verses you read. Read them several times through, and if you are working with a study Bible, read the corresponding verses in other books of the Bible to deepen your understanding. Pray that God will give you the wisdom to understand what Jesus is saying and the faith to act on those truths. To get you started, look in Matthew 13, 18 or 20, Luke 10:25-37, Luke 12:13-21, Luke 13:15-23, Luke 15 or Luke 16. May you have ears that hear!

Wisdom Older Adults' Retreat

For Future Generations

Dear congregation member, church leader, or church staff person,

The Retreat Leadership Team is asking for your help with our upcoming retreat on wisdom. We will be looking at biblical wisdom to see what we can learn from God and what knowledge God gives us to share with others. We will be tapping into the many years of life experience that our participants have acquired in order to make a church wisdom book that we will share with our congregation and that will be a resource for future generations.

Please use this form to ask any questions you have that our participants might be able to answer in this book. The following are some possible categories:

- What are some "need to know" tips about the church building/grounds/maintenance program?
- What are some "need to know" tips for running big church dinners?
- Hospitality issues—how to be welcoming at church, in your neighborhood, in the larger world
- Stewardship issues—how to be a good steward of God's resources at church, at home, in the world
- Education issues—classroom management, creative teaching, invitation of friends
- Advice for daily living in good times and bad

My questions for our church's wise men and women are:

1.

2.

3.

Name (optional): ______________________________

APPENDIX B

Retreat Sites

**Asterisk indicates a facility's availability for personal retreats.*

ALABAMA

Beckwith Camp and Conference Center
Fairhope, AL
251-928-7844
www.beckwithccc.org
Setting: on Weeks Bay
Lodging: dorm and motel
Special features: pool, nature trails, and challenge course

Camp Lee
Anniston, AL
256-238-8941
www.camplee.org
Setting: Appalachian foothills
Lodging: dorm
Special features: zip line, rock climbing tower, natural rock slide, canoeing, pool, low ropes

St. Bernard Abbey
Cullman, AL
256-734-3946
www.stbernardabbey.com
Setting: Benedictine monastery in a wooded setting with a lake
Lodging: motel
Special features: grotto, walking trails

Springville Camp and Conference Center
Odenville, AL
205-629-6279
www.springvillecamp.com
Setting: in the mountains with woods and a lake
Lodging: motel and dorm
Special features: pool, pond, water trampoline, zip line, hiking, canoeing

Sumatanga
Gallant, AL
256-538-9860
www.sumatanga.org
Setting: Appalachian foothills with a lake
Lodging: dorm, motel, also RV area
Special features: hiking (woods and a paved lakeside trail), pool, lighted cross on the mountain above camp

ALASKA

Birchwood Camp
Chugiak, AK
907-688-2734
www.birchwoodcamp.org
Setting: 160 acres of spruce and birch forest surrounding 35-acre Psalm Lake
Lodging: dorm
Special features: private lake, ropes course, Native American sweat lodge for prayer and meditation

Knox Retreat Center
Fairbanks, AK
907-479-0562
www.binglecamp.org/knox/index.html
Setting: on Harding Lake
Lodging: dorm
Special features: beach, canoeing, fishing, sailing

North Star Bible Camp
Willow, AK
907-495-6378
www.northstarbiblecamp.com
Setting: in Mat-Su Valley with views of Twelve Mile Lake and Denali
Lodging: dorm and motel
Special features: hiking, mountain biking, canoeing, cross-country skiing

Solid Rock Bible Camp
Soldotna, AK
907-262-4741
www.solidrockbiblecamp.com
Setting: lakeside
Lodging: dorm
Special features: horseback riding, snow tube hill

Camp Li-Wa
Fairbanks, AK
907-457-6059
www.campliwa.org
Setting: wooded with lake
Lodging: dorm and motel
Special features: indoor riding arena and equestrian programs

ARIZONA

Camp Ponderosa
Heber, AZ
928-535-5082
www.campponderosa.com
Setting: in the White Mountains in Sitgrave National Forest
Lodging: dorm and motel
Special features: zip line, outdoor amphitheater, climbing tower, hiking trails

The Franciscan Renewal Center
Scottsdale, AZ
800-356-3247
www.thecasa.org
Setting: in resort area close to Paradise Valley
Lodging: motel
Special features: two chapels, healing garden, desert walkways, labyrinth, pool

Friendly Pines Camp
Prescott, AZ
9285-445-2128
www.friendlypines.com
Setting: in Prescott National Forest at elevation of 6,300 feet
Lodging: dorm and motel
Special features: pond, horseback riding, ropes course

Montlure
Greer, AZ
928-735-7534
www.montlure.org
Setting: in the White Mountains
Lodging: dorm and motel
Special features: outdoor chapel, hiking trails, recreational barn

United Christian Youth Camp
Prescott, AZ
928-445-0391
www.ucyc.com
Setting: wooded
Lodging: dorm and motel
Special features: ropes course, two pools

ARKANSAS

Camp Ozark
Mount Ida, AR
870-867-4131
www.campozark.com
Setting: in the Ouachita Mountains overlooking Ouachita River
Lodging: dorm
Special features: hiking trails, indoor gyms, challenge course, climbing tower, waterfront activities

Covenant Camp 8:28*
Fairfield Bay, AR
985-839-2391
www.coveantcamp828.com
Setting: on Greer's Ferry Lake in the Ozark Mountains
Lodging: dorm and motel
Special features: hiking, canoeing, swimming, fishing, near golf

Ozark Conference Center
Solgohachia, AR
501-354-3959
www.ozarkconference.org
Setting: on top of Jenkins Mountain with woods, waterfalls, and ponds
Lodging: dorm and motel
Special features: hiking trails, pool, ropes courses, fishing

Pinecrest Camp
Ozone, AR
479-292-3753
www.pinecrestcamp.net
Setting: wooded area in the Ozarks
Lodging: dorm, motel, also RV area
Special features: stocked pond, close to trails and canoeing

Wyldewood
Searcy, AR
501-305-3000
www.campwyldewood.org
Setting: wooded with lakefront and riverfront
Lodging: dorm
Special features: horseback riding, challenge course, rappelling, pools

CALIFORNIA

Aldersgate Retreat Center
Pacific Palisades, CA
310-454-6699
www.aldersgateretreat.org
Setting: parklike grounds near Pacific Palisades
Lodging: dorm and motel
Special features: close to hiking trails, meditation garden

Hartland Christian Camp
Badger, CA
888-202-4024
www.hartlandcamp.com
Setting: at elevation of 4,500 feet on the northwest border of Sequoia National Forest
Lodging: dorm, motel, also RV area
Special features: archery, canoeing, zip line, paintball, hiking, pool

Idyllwild Pines Camp
Idyllwild, CA
951-659-2605
www.idyllwildpines.com
Setting: in the San Jacinto Mountains
Lodging: dorm
Special features: meadow, creek, mountain views, outdoor amphitheater

Mt. Gilead Bible Camp and Conference Center
Sebastopol, CA
800-576-4508
www.mtgilead.org
Setting: in a forested valley
Lodging: dorm
Special features: zip line, skate park, archery, team initiatives course

Redwood Glen
Loma Mar, CA
650-879-0320
www.redwoodglen.com
Setting: in a redwood forest in the Santa Cruz Mountains
Lodging: dorm and motel
Special features: swimming, Chapel in the Woods, outdoor sports fields

COLORADO

Christ Haven Lodge*
Florissant, CO
719-687-3425
www.christhaven.net
Setting: rolling hills with mountain views
Lodging: motel
Special features: indoor pool

Glacier View Ranch
Ward, CO
303-733-3771
www.glacierviewranch.com
Setting: wooded, on a lake with view of Continental Divide
Lodging: dorm, motel, also RV area
Special features: indoor pool, hiking, canoeing, sled hill

Golden Bell Camp and Conference Center
Divide, CO
719-687-9561
www.goldenbellccc.org
Setting: wooded
Lodging: dorm, motel, also RV area
Special features: high ropes, challenge course, zip line, mini golf, pool

Highlands Presbyterian Camp and Retreat Center
Allenspark, CO
303-747-2888
www.highlandscamp.org
Setting: mountain views
Lodging: dorm and motel
Special features: challenge course, climbing rock, meditation trails

La Foret Conference and Retreat Center
Colorado Springs, CO
719-495-2743
www.laforet.org
Setting: 400 wooded acres with mountain views
Lodging: dorm
Special features: meditation trails, labyrinth, swimming, hiking, ropes course

CONNECTICUT

Camp Hazen YMCA
Chester, CT
860-526-9529
www.camphazenymca.org
Setting: on Cedar Lake adjacent to Cockaponsett State Forest
Lodging: dorm
Special features: hiking trails, climbing wall, challenge course, waterfront activities

Delaware Outdoor Adventure Center
Winsted, CT
860-738-8480
www.delawareoac.com
Setting: wooded with streams and waterfalls
Lodging: dorm
Special features: gardens, climbing wall, arts and crafts building

Holy Family Passionist Retreat Center
West Hartford, CT
860-521-0440
www.holyfamilyretreat.org
Setting: parklike grounds
Lodging: motel
Special features: gardens, trails, chapel

Mountain Lake Bible Camp
New Preston, CT
860-868-2048
www.mtlakebible.org
Setting: in the foothills of the Berkshires
Lodging: dorm
Special features: caves, waterfalls, hiking trails and a 15-acre lake

Willimantic Camp Meeting Association
Willimantic, CT
860-456-2177
www.willimanticcampmeeting.com
Setting: scenic wooded grounds
Lodging: motel; individual homes also available for rent by groups
Special features: pond, walking paths

DELAWARE

Camp Arrowhead
Lewes, DE
302-945-0610, x8
www.camparrowhead.net
Setting: 167 wooded acres on Rehoboth Bay
Lodging: dorm
Special features: ropes course, canoeing, sailing

Felix DuPont Memorial House
Wilmington, DE
302-656-5441
www.dioceseofdelaware.net/memhouse.html
Setting: in the pines two blocks from the ocean, backing to Lake Gerar
Lodging: motel
Special features: chapel, close to Atlantic Ocean

Jesus House Prayer and Renewal Center
Wilmington, DE
302-995-6859
www.jesushousecenter.org
Setting: parklike grounds
Lodging: motel
Special features: walking path, chapels

St. Francis Renewal Center*
Wilmington, DE
302-798-1454
www.stfrancisrenewalcenter.com
Setting: on the historic VanTrump estate
Lodging: motel
Special features: scenic grounds, walking paths

Virden Retreat Center
Lewes, DE
302-831-3714
www.udel.edu/conf
Setting: in the coastal Delaware wetlands
Lodging: motel
Special features: hiking trails, near Cape Henlopen State Park trails and beaches

FLORIDA

Blue Springs Baptist Conference Center
Marianna, FL
800-226-8584, x3900
www.flbaptist.org/bluesprings
Setting: wooded, adjacent to a lake
Lodging: dorm and motel
Special features: pool, ropes course, hiking, canoeing nearby

Lake Swan Camp
Melrose, FL
352-475-2828
www.lakeswan.com
Setting: in the woods with two lakes
Lodging: dorm
Special features: challenge course, hiking trails, waterfront activities

Montgomery Presbyterian Center
Starke, FL
352-473-4516
www.montgomerycenter.org
Setting: on three lakes
Lodging: dorm and motel
Special features: challenge course, ropes course, waterfront activities

Orange Springs Retreat
Orange Springs, FL
800-279-0401
www.orangespringsretreat.com
Setting: 100 acres of rolling hills on the edge of Ocala National Forest
Lodging: dorm
Special features: pool, beach, canoeing, hiking trails, ropes course

Riverside Retreat Center
LaBelle, FL
863-675-0334
www.flumcamps.org
Setting: frontage on the Caloosahatchee River
Lodging: dorm
Special features: nature trails, biking

GEORGIA

Calvin Center
Hampton, GA
770-946-4276
www.calvincenter.org
Setting: lakeside
Lodging: dorm and motel
Special features: challenge course, pool, canoeing, labyrinth

Camp Glisson
Dahlonega, GA
706-864-6181
www.campglisson.org
Setting: lakeside
Lodging: dorm
Special features: gym, challenge course, outdoor amphitheater, waterfront activities

Camp Mikell
Toccoa, GA
706-886-7515
www.campmikell.com
Setting: 460 acres in the northeastern Georgia mountains
Lodging: dorm and motel
Special features: waterfalls and creeks, hiking trails, pool, massage therapy available

Enota Mountain Retreat
Hiawassee, GA
800-990-8869
www.enota.com
Setting: in the Appalachian Mountain Forest
Lodging: dorm, motel, also RV area
Special features: streams and waterfalls on property, hiking trails, ropes course

New Ebenezer Retreat Center
Rincon, GA
912-754-9242
www.newebenezer.org
Setting: on the banks of the Savannah River
Lodging: dorm and motel
Special features: pool, challenge course

HAWAII

Camp Homelani
Waialua, HI
808-637-4131
www.camphomelani.org
Setting: on the beach in a residential area with mountain views
Lodging: dorm and motel
Special features: ocean swimming, outdoor recreation fields

Camp Mokuleia
Waialua, HI
808-637-6241
www.campmokuleia.org
Setting: oceanfront on the North Shore of Oahu
Lodging: dorm, motel and RV
Special features: ropes course, equestrian program, close to Kaiaka Bay Beach Park and numerous hiking trails

Kokee
Kekaha, HI
808-337-1464
www.gbgm-umc.org/kekaha/
Setting: inside Kokee State Park, adjacent to Waimea Canyon
Lodging: dorm and RV
Special features: hiking, fishing

Saint Stephen Diocesan Center
Kaneohe, HI
808-263-8844
www.catholichawaii.org/ssdc/
Setting: lush, wooded property at the foot of the Ko'olau Mountain Range
Lodging: dorm and motel
Special features: hiking, chapel

YMCA Camp Erdman
Waialua, HI
808-637-8874
http://ymcahonolulu.countmein.com
Setting: oceanfront on the North Shore of Oahu
Lodging: dorm
Special features: ocean beach, pool, climbing wall, challenge course

IDAHO

Camp Lutherhaven
Cour d'Alene, ID
208-667-3459
www.lutherhaven.com
Setting: on Lake Cour d'Alene
Lodging: dorm
Special features: hiking trails, challenge course, waterfront activities

Camp Pinewood
McCall, ID
208-634-5598
www.camppinewood.org
Setting: wooded with meadow and lakes
Lodging: dorm, motel, also RV area
Special features: hiking trails, fishing, waterfront activities

Living Waters Ranch Conference and Retreat Center
Challis, ID
208-879-2888
www.livingwatersranch.org

Setting: creek with mountain views
Lodging: dorm and motel
Special features: hiking, snow tubing, near golf, hot springs, and river rafting

Ross Point Baptist Camp
Post Falls, ID
208-773-1665
www.rosspoint.org
Setting: in the pines along the Spokane River
Lodging: dorm and motel
Special features: challenge course, climbing tower, canoeing, hiking trails, beach

Trinity Pines Camp
Cascade, ID
208-382-6200
www.tpines.org
Setting: 198 acres of fields and mountains
Lodging: dorm
Special features: challenge course, zip line, near Cascade Lake

ILLINOIS

Camp Manitoqua
Frankfort, IL
815-469-2319
www.manitoqua.org
Setting: wooded grounds in suburbs
Lodging: dorm and motel
Special features: pond, walking paths, pool, challenge course

Camp Wartburg
Waterloo, IL
618-939-7715
www.campwartburg.com
Setting: wooded
Lodging: dorm
Special features: pond fishing, canoeing, hiking trails

Lake Springfield Baptist Camp
Chatham, IL
217-529-1921
www.lsbconline.com
Setting: on Lake Springfield
Lodging: dorm and motel
Special features: swimming, hiking, recreation fields

Lutheran Outdoor Center
Oregon, IL
815-732-2220
www.lomc.org
Setting: 650 acres of pond, prairie, and forest
Lodging: dorm, motel, also RV area
Special features: pool, hiking trails, labyrinth, team building activities

Pilgrim Park Camp and Conference Center
Princeton, IL
815-447-2390
www.ilucc.org
Setting: woods and prairie
Lodging: dorm and motel
Special features: pool, challenge course, hiking trails, creek

Techny Towers Conference and Retreat Center*
Techny, IL
847-272-1100
www.technytowers.org
Setting: parklike in suburban area
Lodging: motel
Special features: ponds, walking paths, grottos, three chapels

INDIANA

Camp Alexander Mack
Milford, IN
574-658-8431
www.campmack.org
Setting: on Waubee Lake
Lodging: dorm and motel
Special features: ropes course, swimming, hiking, labyrinth, chapel

Camp Tecumseh
Brookston, IN
765-564-2898
www.camptecumseh.org
Setting: 500 acres on the Tippecanoe River
Lodging: dorm
Special features: pools, rifle range, canoeing, hiking, challenge course, climbing tower

Lutherhaven*
Albion, IN
260-636-7101
www.lutherhaven.org
Setting: 72 wooded acres with lake
Lodging: dorm, motel, also RV area
Special features: walking trails, challenge course, canoeing, fishing

Tippecanoe Camp and Retreat Center
North Webster, IN
574-834-4184
www.camptippy.org
Setting: wooded area on Little Lake Tippy
Lodging: dorm
Special features: beach, swimming, canoeing, hiking trails, chapels

Waycross Camp
Morgantown, IN
812-597-4241
www.waycrosscamp.org
Setting: rolling hills
Lodging: dorm and motel
Special features: hiking trails, boating, climbing wall, labyrinth

IOWA

Crooked Creek Christian Camp
Washington, IA
319-653-3611
www.crookedcreekcamp.org
Setting: 300 acres of woods and prairie along Crooked Creek
Lodging: dorm
Special features: nature trails, waterslide, Frisbee golf, rock climbing wall, labyrinth

Forest Lake Camp and Conference Center
Bloomfield, IA
641-684-8908
www.myforestlake.org
Setting: wooded with lake
Lodging: dorm and motel
Special features: paintball, fishing, canoeing, archery

Inspiration Hills
Inwood, IA
712-986-5193
www.inspirationhills.org
Setting: rolling hills, wooded ravines
Lodging: dorm, motel, also RV area
Special features: challenge course, swimming, snow tubing hill, incredible view of the stars

Pine Lake Christian Camp and Ministry Center
Eldora, IA
641-858-3284
www.PineLakeChristianCamp.org
Setting: borders Pine Lake State Park
Lodging: dorm, motel, also RV area
Special features: ropes course, pool, lakefront activities, hiking trails

Village Creek Bible Camp
Lansing, IA
563-535-7320
www.villagecreek.net
Setting: rolling wooded hills
Lodging: dorm
Special features: ropes course, fishing, horseback riding, canoeing, archery

KANSAS

Camp Chippewa
Ottawa, KS
785-242-6797
www.campchippewa.org
Setting: wooded
Lodging: dorm
Special features: trail rides, hiking, fishing, archery, ropes course

Camp Lakeside
Scott City, KS
620-872-2021
www.camplakeside.net
Setting: wooded with lake
Lodging: dorm
Special features: horseback riding, hiking and biking trails, fishing, canoeing, swimming

Forest Park Retreat Center
Topeka, KS
785-234-8024
www.forestparkretreat.com
Setting: wooded valley
Lodging: dorm, also RV area
Special features: hiking, fishing, peaceful grounds

Tallgrass Retreat Center
Matfield Green, KS
620-753-3465
www.tallgrassretreats.com
Setting: prairie
Lodging: dorm
Special features: labyrinth, spiritual direction available

Tall Oaks Conference Center
Linwood, KS
913-301-3004
www.talloaks.org
Setting: 350 wooded acres
Lodging: dorm, motel, also RV area
Special features: horseback riding, challenge course, hiking trails, pool, prayer garden

KENTUCKY

Bethel Mennonite Camp
Clayhole, KY
606-666-4911
www.bethelcamp.org
Setting: wooded
Lodging: motel, also RV area
Special features: hiking trails, waterslide, archery

Cedar Ridge
Louisville, KY
502-267-5848
www.cedarridgecamp.com
Setting: wooded with lake
Lodging: dorm
Special features: hiking trails, canoeing, fishing, ropes course, pool, hayrides

Eagle Ridge Retreat Center
Bowling Green, KY
270-796-5017
www.eagleridgerc.org
Setting: wooded
Lodging: dorm
Special features: walking trails, prayer garden, creek

Loucon Training and Retreat Center
Leitchfield, KY
270-242-7160
www.loucon.org
Setting: wooded with lake
Lodging: dorm and motel
Special features: ropes course, rappelling, canoeing, team building activities, pool

Potter's Ranch
Union, KY
859-586-5475
www.pottersranch.org
Setting: 350-acre wilderness near Ohio River on Gunpowder Creek
Lodging: motel, also RV area
Special features: horseback riding, ropes course, climbing wall, zip line

LOUISIANA

Dry Creek Baptist Camp
Dry Creek, LA
337-328-7531
www.drycreek.net
Setting: pine forest
Lodging: dorm, motel, also RV area
Special features: pool, challenge course, mini golf, canoeing, archery

Harris Baptist Conference and Retreat Center
Minden, LA
318-927-3706
www.harrisbaptist.com
Setting: wooded
Lodging: dorm, motel, also RV area
Special features: pool, pond, ropes course, mini golf

Judson Baptist Retreat Center
St. Francisville, LA
225-634-7225
www.bagbr.org/retreatcenter.htm
Setting: rolling pasture and forest bordered by Thompson Creek
Lodging: dorm, motel, also RV area
Special features: pool, horseback riding, hiking trails

Uskichitto Retreat Center
LeBlanc, LA
337-738-4218
www.campurc.com
Setting: wooded with river
Lodging: dorm, also RV area
Special features: pool, mini golf, ropes course, climbing tower, hiking trails

Tall Timbers Baptist Conference and Retreat Center
Woodworth, LA
318-445-6797
www.lbc.org/talltimbers
Setting: wooded with lake
Lodging: dorm and motel
Special features: adventure course, pool, fishing, game room

MAINE

Blueberry Mountain Bible Camp and Conference Center
Weld, ME
207-585-2410
www.blueberrymountain.org
Setting: wooded mountain terrain with waterfalls
Lodging: dorm
Special features: human-size foosball court, hiking trails, sledding trails

Camp Beech Cliff
Mt. Desert, ME
207-244-0365
www.campbeechcliff.org
Setting: 50 acres of lakefront bordering Acadia National Park
Lodging: dorm
Special features: challenge course, climbing wall, hiking trails

Camp Mechuwana
Winthrop, ME
207-377-2924
www.mechuwana.org
Setting: borders Lake Annabessacook and Lower Narrows Pond
Lodging: dorm
Special features: hiking trails, boating, swimming

China Lake Conference Center
China Village, ME
207-968-2101
www.chinalake.net
Setting: 208 acres on China Lake
Lodging: dorm
Special features: boating, hiking, indoor gym

Farmington Conference Center
Farmington, ME
207-778-9945
www.farmingtonbaptistcenter.com
Setting: wooded
Lodging: dorm, motel, also RV area
Special features: hiking trails, rock climbing, white water rafting, mini golf

New England Camp Cherith
Alfred, ME
207-247-5251
www.newenglandcampcherith.org
Setting: wooded with lake
Lodging: dorm
Special features: canoeing, sledding, snow tubing, archery, hiking trails

MARYLAND

Camp Pecometh
Centreville, MD
410-556-6900
www.pecometh.org
Setting: wooded riverfront
Lodging: dorm
Special features: challenge course, pool, hiking, fishing

Dayspring Retreat Center*
Germantown, MD
301-428-9348
www.dayspringretreat.org
Setting: rolling forest and open fields with streams and ponds
Lodging: motel
Special features: silent retreats only, labyrinth, spiritual direction available

Mar-Lu-Ridge
Jefferson, MD
301-874-5544
www.mar-lu-ridge.org
Setting: in the Catoctin Mountains
Lodging: dorm and motel
Special features: labyrinth, ropes course, rock climbing, canoeing, hiking, pool

Mt. Aetna Camp and Retreat Center
Hagerstown, MD
301-824-6045
www.mtaetnacamp.com
Setting: wooded with pond
Lodging: dorm and motel
Special features: one mile from Appalachian Trail, nature center, ropes course, canoeing

Wellspring
Germantown, MD
301-428-3373
www.wellspringministry.org
Setting: wooded with meadow
Lodging: dorm
Special features: labyrinth, prayer garden, walking trails

MASSACHUSETTS

The Barton Center
North Oxford, MA
508-987-2056
www.bartoncenter.org
Setting: 200 acres of woods with a pond
Lodging: dorm
Special features: hiking trails, ropes course, pool

Cathedral Camp
East Freetown, MA
508-763-8874
www.cathedralcamp.org
Setting: on the shore of Long Pond
Lodging: motel
Special features: boating, fishing, hiking

Friendly Crossways
Harvard, MA
978-456-9386
www.friendlycrossways.com
Setting: peaceful, rural location on the Johnny Appleseed Trail
Lodging: dorm and motel
Special features: four acres of lawn, 40 acres of organic gardens/fields/forest

Grotonwood
Groton, MA
978-448-5763
www.grotonwood.org
Setting: 270 wooded acres on Lost Lake
Lodging: dorm
Special features: Log Cabin Chapel, climbing wall, challenge course, waterfront activities

Lakeside Christian Camp
Pittsfield, MA
413-447-8930
www.lakesideonline.org
Setting: wooded with meadows and lake
Lodging: dorm and motel
Special features: swimming, canoeing, sailing, ropes course, hiking trails

Saint Joseph Retreat Center*
Cohasset, MA
781-383-6024
www.csjretreatcenter.org
Setting: overlooks Atlantic Ocean
Lodging: motel
Special features: labyrinth, spiritual direction and massage therapy available, silent retreats

MICHIGAN

Camp Geneva*
Holland, MI
616-399-3150
www.campgeneva.org
Setting: on the shores of Lake Michigan
Lodging: dorm and motel
Special features: Lake Michigan beach, pool and splash park, challenge course, gym, climbing wall

Lake Huron Retreat Center
Lakeport, MI
810-327-6272
www.lakehuronretreat.org
Setting: on the shores of Lake Huron
Lodging: dorm and motel
Special features: Lake Huron beachfront, outdoor and indoor labyrinths, workout room

Maranatha*
Muskegon, MI
231-798-2161
www.maranatha.gospelcom.net
Setting: in the woods on the shores of Lake Michigan
Lodging: motel
Special features: Lake Michigan beach, hiking trails, climbing tower, gym, mini golf

Presbyterian Camps
Saugatuck, MI
269-857-3751
www.prescamps.org
Setting: in the woods on the shores of Lake Michigan
Lodging: dorm
Special features: Lake Michigan beach, hiking trails, ropes course, canoeing

Wildwood Ranch
Howell, MI
800-969-8090
www.wildwoodranch.org
Setting: 240 wooded acres with two lakes
Lodging: dorms
Special features: wetlands, nature trails, ropes course, equestrian programs

MINNESOTA

Big Sandy Camp and Retreat Center
McGregor, MN
218-426-3389
www.bigsandycamp.com
Setting: in the North Woods on Big Sandy Lake
Lodging: dorm and motel
Special features: waterfront activities, hiking trails, climbing wall, gym, snow tubing

Dunrovin Retreat Center: A Christian Brothers Retreat Center*
Marine on Saint Croix, MN
651-433-2486
www.dunrovin.org
Setting: on the St. Croix River
Lodging: motel
Special features: woodland trails, pond, spiritual direction available

Northern Pines Camp
Park Rapids, MN
218-732-4713
www.northernpinescamp.org
Setting: 40 acres on Fish Hook Lake
Lodging: dorm
Special features: waterfront activities, sledding, cross-country skiing, near golf

Shetek Lutheran Ministries
Slayton, MN
507-763-3567
www.shetek.org
Setting: an island in a Minnesota lake
Lodging: motel
Special features: waterfront activities, fishing, hiking, gym

Timber Bay
Medina, MN
763-478-0500
www.timberbay.org
Setting: wooded with lakefront area
Lodging: dorm, also RV area
Special features: waterfront activities, fishing, hiking and mountain biking trails, snow tubing

MISSISSIPPI

Camp Lake Stephens
Oxford, MS
662-234-3350
www.camplakestephens.com
Setting: wooded with lake
Lodging: dorm and motel
Special features: pool, ropes course, rappelling, fishing, canoeing

Garaywa Camp and Conference Center
Clinton, MS
601-924-7034
www.mbcb.org/business_services/camps/cg/
Setting: parklike grounds in a suburban area
Lodging: dorm and motel
Special features: prayer garden, ropes course, pool

Lake Forest Ranch
Macon, MS
662-726-5052
www.lakeforestranch.com
Setting: wooded with lake
Lodging: dorm and motel
Special features: rock climbing, paintball, ropes course, horseback riding, pool

Pine Lake Fellowship Camp
Meridian, MS
601-483-2267
www.pinelakecamp.com
Setting: wooded with lake
Lodging: dorm, motel, also RV area
Special features: ropes course, boating, swamp trail

Timber Creek Camp
Pulaski, MS
601-536-2130
www.timbercreekcamp.com
Setting: wooded with lake

Lodging: dorm
Special features: waterfront activities, hiking trails, pool, Frisbee golf, challenge course

MISSOURI

The Bear's Den*
St. James, MO
877-543-3943
www.bearsdenretreat.com
Setting: 30-acre woodland with lake
Lodging: motel
Special features: swimming, fishing, canoeing

Hermitage Spiritual Retreat Center*
Pittsburg, MO
816-363-3968
www.hermitageretreats.org
Setting: on the shores of Lake Pomme de Terre in the Ozark foothills
Lodging: motel
Special features: only silent retreats, Stations of the Cross trail, labyrinth

Heartland Presbyterian Center
Parkville, MO
816-891-1078
www.heartlandcenter.org
Setting: wooded, rolling hills
Lodging: dorm and motel
Special features: challenge course, horseback riding, trails, GPS adventures, pool

Lake Doniphan Conference and Retreat Center
Excelsior Springs, MO
816-630-1523
www.lakedon.org
Setting: wooded with lakefront
Lodging: dorm, motel, also RV area
Special features: beach, waterfront activities, pool, hiking trails, golf adjacent

Wilderness Retreat Center
Lawson, MO
816-580-4014
www.wildernessretreatcenter.org
Setting: wooded with lake
Lodging: dorm, also RV area
Special features: hiking trails, fishing, swimming, boating

MONTANA

Camp Bighorn Inc.
Plains, MT
406-826-5595
www.campbighorn.com
Setting: in the mountains
Lodging: dorms
Special features: rifle range, challenge course, mountain climbing, hiking trails

Dickey Lake Bible Camp and Conference Center
Trego, MT
406-882-4572
www.dickeylakebiblecamp.org
Setting: in Kootenai National Forest
Lodging: dorm
Special features: lakefront activities, geocaching, paintball, hiking trails

Glacier Camp and Conference Center
Lakeside, MT
406-844-2114
www.glaciercamp.org
Setting: in the mountains
Lodging: dorm
Special features: canoeing, river rafting, ropes course, challenge course, fishing

Lion's Ridge
Bozeman, MT
406-582-9757
www.lionsridge.org
Setting: wooded with mountain scenery
Lodging: dorm
Special features: hiking trails, snow tubing hills, close to Yellowstone National Park and downhill ski resorts

Trail's End Ranch
Ekalaka, MT
406-775-6401
www.ter.org
Setting: 1,200 acres in the middle of Custer National Forest
Lodging: dorm
Special features: ropes course, zip line, rifle range, craft shop, horseback riding

NEBRASKA

Calvin Crest Camp and Conference Center
Fremont, NE
402-628-6455
www.calvincrest.org
Setting: 250 acres overlooking the Platte River
Lodging: dorm, motel, also RV area
Special features: Meditation Point, outdoor chapel, outdoor movie screen, pool, challenge course

Carol Joy Holling Camp
Ashland, NE
402-944-2544
www.nlom.org
Setting: 317 acres of rolling hills
Lodging: dorm and motel
Special features: challenge course, pool, hiking trails, canoeing, fishing, sledding

Covenant Cedars Bible Camp
Hordville, NE
402-757-3241
www.cedars.org
Setting: wooded with lake
Lodging: dorm, also RV area
Special features: climbing tower, zip line, challenge course, nature trail, pool, canoeing

Maranatha Camp
Maxwell, NE
308-582-4513
www.maranathacamp.org
Setting: wooded with lake
Lodging: dorm, motel, also RV area
Special features: mini golf, team building activities, waterfront activities, pool, archery

Timberlake Ranch Camps
Marquette, NE
308-946-3871
www.timberlake.org
Setting: 700 acres of woods and hills
Lodging: dorm, also RV area
Special features: canoeing, hiking trails, ropes course, climbing wall, fishing

NEVADA

Galilee Episcopal Camp and Conference Center
Glenbrook, NV
775-749-5546
www.galileetahoe.org
Setting: on the shores of Lake Tahoe with mountain views
Lodging: dorm and motel
Special features: beach, watersports, close to extensive hiking trails, golf, skiing

Life-Giving Spring Retreat Center*
Boulder City, NV
702-293-7208
www.lasvegasorthodox.com/retreatcenter/
Setting: overlooks Lake Mead
Lodging: motel
Special features: two chapels, quiet spaces indoors and out

Potosi Pines Camp
Las Vegas, NV
702-875-1980
http://desertsouthwestconference.org/churchmembers/campingyouth/camping_retreat_ministries/potosi_pines_camp/
Setting: high country in the mountains
Lodging: dorms
Special features: hiking trails

Zephyr Point
Zephyr Cove, NV
775-588-6759
www.zephyrpoint.org
Setting: on the shores of Lake Tahoe
Lodging: dorm and motel
Special features: swimming, hiking trails

NEW HAMPSHIRE

Camp Berea
Hebron, NH
603-744-6344
www.berea.org
Setting: wooded on a lake
Lodging: dorm and motel
Special features: rock climbing wall, gym, pool, paintball, challenge course

Camp Calumet
West Ossipee, NH
603-539-4773
www.calumet.org
Setting: on Lake Ossipee
Lodging: dorm, motel, also RV area
Special features: beach, boating activities, swimming

Geneva Point Center
Moultonboro, NH
603-253-4366
www.genevapoint.org
Setting: wooded with lake frontage
Lodging: dorm and motel
Special features: canoeing, fishing, hiking trails, cross-country skiing, arts and crafts

Pilgrim Pines Conference Center
Swanzey, NH
603-352-0443
www.pilgrimpines.org
Setting: wooded with lake
Lodging: dorm, motel, also RV area
Special features: canoeing, hiking trails, sledding, beach

Singing Hills*
Plainfield, NH
888-863-2267
www.singinghills.net
Setting: wooded with pond
Lodging: dorm, motel, also RV area
Special features: hiking trails, pool

NEW JERSEY

Aldersgate Camp, Retreat and Conference Center
Swartswood, NJ
973-383-5978
www.aldersgatenj.com
Setting: wooded on a lake
Lodging: dorm and motel
Special features: ropes course, boating, swimming, hiking trails, discount in December and January

Camp Lebanon
Lebanon, NJ
908-236-2638
www.camplebanon.com
Setting: rolling hills of Hunterdon County
Lodging: dorm and RV
Special features: ropes course, nature trail, recreation fields

Fairview Lake YMCA Camp and Conference Center
Stilwater, NJ
973-383-9282
www.fairviewlake.org
Setting: wooded with lake
Lodging: dorm
Special features: waterfront activities, hiking trails, archery

Johnsonburg Presbyterian Center
Johnsonburg, NJ
908-852-2349
www.campjburg.org
Setting: wooded with lake
Lodging: dorm
Special features: waterfront activities, pool, labyrinth, spiritual direction

Pinelands Center at Mt. Misery
Browns Mills, NJ
609-893-3354
www.mtmisery.com
Setting: wooded with lake
Lodging: dorms
Special features: ropes course, challenge course, lakefront activities, hiking trails

Vacamas
West Milford, NJ
973-838-7534
www.vacamas.org
Setting: in the foothills of the Ramapo Mountains
Lodging: dorm
Special features: challenge course, ropes course, gym, climbing wall, hiking trails, close to Appalachian Trail

NEW MEXICO

Bishop Stoney Camp*
Santa Fe, NM
505-983-5610
www.campstoney.org
Setting: forested countryside
Lodging: dorm and motel
Special features: ropes course, challenge course, pool

Bonita Park Camp and Conference Center
Capitan, NM
575-336-4404
www.bonitapark.com
Setting: 200 acres in Lincoln National Forest
Lodging: dorm, motel, also RV area
Special features: rock wall, mud pit, zip line, indoor pool, skiing nearby

Ghost Ranch
Abiquiu, NM
505-685-4333
www.ghostranch.org
Setting: in remote location at elevation of 6,500-feet
Lodging: dorm, motel, also RV area
Special features: horseback riding, pool, prayer garden, labyrinth, massage therapy available

Manzano Mountain Retreat
Torreon, NM
505-838-1533
www.manzanoretreat.com
Setting: in the mountains
Lodging: dorm and motel
Special features: mountain trails, gym, pool, ropes course, climbing tower

Sacramento Methodist Assembly
Sacramento, NM
575-687-3414
www.sacramentoassembly.org
Setting: in the Sacramento Mountains
Lodging: dorm, motel, also RV area
Special features: trout fishing, mountain biking, outdoor worship areas

NEW YORK

Aldersgate Camp and Retreat Center
Greig, NY
315-364-8156
www.aldersgateny.org
Setting: in the Adirondack Mountains
Lodging: dorm and motel
Special features: boating, hiking trails, human-size foosball court

Camp DeWolfe
Wading River, NY
631-929-4325
www.campdewolfe.org
Setting: wooded bluff overlooking Long Island Sound
Lodging: dorm and motel
Special features: beachfront, wetlands, woodlands, challenge course, climbing wall, canoeing

Koinonia
Highland Lake, NY
800-980-CAMP
www.koinoniany.org
Setting: in the wilderness with two mountain lakes
Lodging: dorm, motel, also RV area
Special features: beach, hiking trails, fishing

Pathfinder Lodge
Cooperstown, NY
607-547-2300
www.abc-nys.org
Setting: wooded hills along Otsego Lake
Lodging: dorm
Special features: swimming, sailing, hiking trails

Presbyterian Center at Holmes
Holmes, NY
845-878-6383
www.presbyteriancenter.org
Setting: wooded with lake
Lodging: dorm and motel
Special features: hiking trails, lakefront activities, fishing, close to Appalachian Trail

Stella Maris Retreat and Renewal Center*
Skaneateles, NY
315-685-6836
www.stellamarisretreat.org
Setting: on Skaneateles Lake
Lodging: motel
Special features: walking paths throughout the parklike grounds

NORTH CAROLINA

Bonclarken Conference Center
Flat Rock, NC
828-692-2223
www.bonclarken.com
Setting: in the mountains
Lodging: dorm, motel, also RV area
Special features: ropes course, zip line, paintball, caving and hiking nearby

Chestnut Ridge Camp and Retreat Center
Efland, NC
919-338-2820
www.campchestnutridge.org
Setting: wooded with lake
Lodging: dorm
Special features: horseback riding, canoeing, ropes course, pool, labyrinth

Holston Presbyterian Camp and Retreat Center
Banner Elk, NC
828-898-6611
www.holstoncamp.org
Setting: high mountain country
Lodging: dorm
Special features: lakefront activities, outdoor chapel

Lutheridge
Arden, NC
828-684-2361
www.lutheridge.com
Setting: wooded with lake
Lodging: dorm and motel
Special features: hiking trails, climbing wall, pottery studio, labyrinth

Mount Shepherd Retreat Center*
Asheboro, NC
336-629-4085
www.mtshepherd.org
Setting: 542 acres of woods with a lake
Lodging: dorm
Special features: ropes course, canoeing, fishing, hiking trails

NORTH DAKOTA

Crystal Springs Baptist Camp
Medina, ND
701-486-3467
www.csbcamp.org
Setting: on Crystal Springs Lake
Lodging: dorm, also RV area
Special features: beach, waterfront activities, gym

FaHoCha Bible Conference
Warwick, ND
701-674-3211
www.fahocha.org
Setting: wooded with lake
Lodging: dorm
Special features: canoeing, pool

Metigoshe Ministries
Bottineau, ND
701-263-4788
www.metigosheministries.com
Setting: in the Turtle Mountains on Pelican and Sandy Lakes
Lodging: motel
Special features: waterfront activities, hiking trails, "live simply" philosophy

Park River Bible Camp
Park River, ND
800-269-2465
www.parkriverbiblecamp.org
Setting: 80 acres with woods and open areas
Lodging: dorm
Special features: waterfront activities, 220-foot waterslide, gym, challenge courses

Sacred Heart Monastery*
Richardton, ND
710-974-2124
www.sacredheartmonastery.com
Setting: rural prairie
Lodging: motel
Special features: chapel, paved walking path

OHIO

Beulah Beach Christian Camp and Retreat Center
Vermilion, OH
440-967-4861
www.beulahbeach.org
Setting: on the shores of Lake Erie
Lodging: dorm, motel, also RV area
Special features: Lake Erie beach, pool, climbing tower, ropes course, paintball

Camp Otterbein
Logan, OH
740-385-5712
www.westohiocamps.com/retreats/otterbein.asp
Setting: wooded with lake
Lodging: dorm
Special features: challenge course, ropes course, hiking trails

Heartland Conference and Retreat Center
Marengo, OH
740-747-0220
www.heartlandretreat.com
Setting: 350 scenic acres of woods, creeks, and open space
Lodging: dorm, motel, also RV area
Special features: challenge course, ropes course, hiking trails

Kirkwood Camp and Conference Center
Wilmington, OH
937-382-3535
www.campkirkwood.net
Setting: gently rolling wooded hills of southern Ohio
Lodging: dorm and RV
Special features: walking trails, lakefront activities, fishing, hay rides

Our Lady of the Pines Retreat Center*
Fremont, OH
419-332-6522
www.pinesretreat.org
Setting: parklike grounds
Lodging: motel
Special features: three hermitages available for use, quiet prayer areas, paved walkways, grotto, labyrinth, pool

Woodland Altars
Peebles, OH
937-588-4111
www.woodlandaltars.com
Setting: wooded
Lodging: dorm and motel
Special features: challenge course, hiking trails, waterfront activities, pool

OKLAHOMA

Camp Loughridge
Tulsa, OK
918-446-4194
www.camploughridge.org
Setting: 186 acres of hilly, wooded terrain with three lakes just minutes from Tulsa
Lodging: dorm
Special features: canoeing, fishing, hiking trails, challenge course, aquatics center

Central Christian Camp and Conference Center
Guthrie, OK
405-282-2811
www.centralchristiancamp.org
Setting: wooded with ponds
Lodging: dorm
Special features: pool, hiking trails

Cross Point Camp
Kingston, OK
580-564-2505
http://www.okumcministries.org/camps/crosspoint.html
Setting: overlooks Lake Texoma
Lodging: dorm, motel, also RV area
Special features: lakefront activities, challenge course, climbing wall

Minnetonka Christian Camp
Clayton, OK
918-569-7856
www.minnetonkacamp.com
Setting: in the Kiamichi Mountains adjacent to two lakes
Lodging: dorm, motel, also RV area
Special features: paintball, fishing, nature trails, ropes course, challenge course

New Life Ranch
Colcord, OK
918-422-5506
www.newliferanch.com
Setting: in the Ozark foothills with a creek
Lodging: dorm and motel
Special features: riding arena, ropes course, nature trails, gym, prayer chapel

OREGON

Buckhorn Springs
Ashland, OR
541-488-2200
www.buckhornsprings.org
Setting: within the boundaries of Cascade Siskiyou National Monument
Lodging: motel
Special features: parklike grounds, vegetarian meals

Camp Arrah Wanna
Welches, OR
503-622-3189
www.camparrahwanna.org
Setting: 132 acres of forest bounded by the Salmon River and the Wildwood Recreation Area
Lodging: dorm and motel
Special features: zip line, indoor gym, mini golf, ropes course

Alton L Collins Retreat Center
Eagle Creek, OR
503-637-6411
www.collinsretreatcenter.org
Setting: a red cedar forest with streams
Lodging: motel
Special features: hiking trails, meditation hut

Menucha Retreat and Conference Center*
Corbett, OR
503-695-2243
www.menucha.org
Setting: in the Columbia River Gorge
Lodging: dorm and motel
Special features: hiking trails, pool

Shalom Prayer Center Retreats*
Mt. Angel, OR
503-845-6773
www.benedictine-srs.org/retreats.html
Setting: parklike grounds in a suburban area
Lodging: motel
Special features: spiritual direction available

Twin Rocks Friends Camp
Rockaway Beach, OR
503-355-2284
www.twinrocks.org
Setting: 120 wooded acres one block from the Pacific Ocean
Lodging: dorm and motel
Special features: access to Pacific Ocean beach, mini golf, swimming, fishing, gym

PENNSYLVANIA

Camp Blue Diamond
Petersburg, PA
814-667-2355
www.campbluediamond.org
Setting: 238 wooded acres within the Rothrock State Forest
Lodging: dorm, motel, also RV area
Special features: lake with sand beach, hiking trails, initiatives course

Camp Judson
North Springfield, PA
814-922-3834
www.campjudson.com
Setting: on Lake Erie
Lodging: dorm, motel and RV
Special features: hiking, sailing, equestrian programs, climbing tower, zip line

Camp Lohikan in the Pocono Mountains
Lake Como, PA
908-470-9317
www.lohikan.com
Setting: Pocono Mountains area
Lodging: dorm and motel
Special features: ropes course, challenge course, pool, waterfront activities

Camp Susque
Trout Run, PA
570-998-2151
www.susque.org
Setting: bordered by state forests and Lycoming Creek
Lodging: dorm
Special features: observatory, ropes course, pool, hiking trails

Crestfield
Slippery Rock, PA
724-794-4022
www.crestfield.net
Setting: 226 acres of fields and woods along Slippery Rock Creek
Lodging: dorm and motel
Special features: ropes course, climbing wall, canoeing

Franciscan Spirit and Life Center
Pittsburgh, PA
412-881-9207
www.osfprov.org/FSLC.htm
Setting: parklike grounds
Lodging: motel
Special features: spiritual direction and massage therapy available

RHODE ISLAND

Alton Jones Camp
West Greenwich, RI
401-397-3304
www.altonjonescamp.com
Setting: 100 acres in the Nettie Marie Jones Nature Preserve
Lodging: dorm
Special features: waterfront activities on Lake Eisenhower, hiking trails, ropes course

Camp Fuller
Wakefield, RI
401-783-5359
www.ymcagreaterprovidence.org/home/tabid/644/Default.aspx
Setting: on Point Judith Salt Pond
Lodging: dorm
Special features: waterfront activities, climbing wall, ropes course

Canonicus Camp and Conference Center
Exeter, RI
401-294-6318
www.canonicus.org
Setting: wooded with a lake
Lodging: dorm and motel
Special features: hiking trails, ropes course, waterfront activities

Episcopal Conference Center
Pascoag, RI
401-568-4055
www.episcopalri.org
Setting: wooded with lake
Lodging: dorm and motel
Special features: beach, waterfront activities, walking paths, labyrinth

Our Lady of Peace Spiritual Life Center
Narragansett, RI
401-783-2871
www.intap.net/~evanpro/OLP.htm
Setting: 40-acre estate
Lodging: motel
Special features: four hermitages available, Contemplative Arts Center

SOUTH CAROLINA

Asbury Hills Camp and Retreat Center
Cleveland, SC
864-458-2071
www.asburyhills.org
Setting: wooded mountain area
Lodging: dorm and motel
Special features: creek hiking, pool, canoeing, ropes course, mountain chapel

Camp Gravatt
Aiken, SC
803-648-1817
www.bishopgravatt.org
Setting: wooded with lake
Lodging: dorm and motel
Special features: waterfront activities, challenge course

Nosoca Pines Ranch
Liberty Hill, SC
803-273-8200
www.nosoca.org
Setting: on Lake Wateree
Lodging: dorm, motel, also RV area
Special features: climbing wall, waterfront activities, trail rides, pool

St. Christopher Camp and Conference Center*
John's Island, SC
843-768-0429
www.stchristopher.org
Setting: 300 acres on Atlantic coast
Lodging: dorm and motel
Special features: Atlantic Ocean beach, hiking through maritime marshlands and forest, gym, boating

SOUTH DAKOTA

Byron Bible Camp
Huron, SD
605-352-7267
www.byronbiblecamp.com
Setting: in the James River Valley
Lodging: dorm, also RV area
Special features: waterfront activities, canoeing, obstacle course, zip line, river path

Camp Judson
Keystone, SD
605-574-2314
www.campjudson.org
Setting: 160 acres of mountain terrain bordering the Black Hills
Lodging: dorm
Special features: trout fishing, hiking, near ski areas

Camp Lakodia
Madison, SD
800-538-9881
www.camplakodia.org
Setting: wooded with lake
Lodging: dorm and motel
Special features: waterfront activities, canoeing, hiking trails, fishing, close to golf

Kinship Mountain Ministries
Deadwood, SD
605-578-9965
www.kampkinship.org
Setting: 100 acres of forest in the Black Hills
Lodging: dorm and motel
Special features: hiking trails, canoeing, climbing wall, zip line

NeSoDak
Waubay, SD
605-947-4440
www.lutheransoutdoors.org/nesodak/about.htm
Setting: on peninsula of Lake Enemy Swim
Lodging: dorm
Special features: canoeing, sand volleyball, cross-country skiing

Outlaw Ranch
Custer, SD
605-673-4040
www.lutheransoutdoors.org/outlaw/retreat.htm
Setting: in southern Black Hills
Lodging: dorm
Special features: horseback riding available, canoeing on Lake Bismarck, close to Mt. Rushmore and Custer State Park

TENNESSEE

Buffalo Mountain Camp and Retreat
Jonesborough, TN
423-753-6678
www.buffalomountaincamp.org
Setting: in the mountains
Lodging: dorm and motel
Special features: hiking trails, waterfront activities, pond fishing, pool

John Knox Center
Ten Mile, TN
865-376-2236
www.johnknoxcenter.org
Setting: on Watts Bar Lake
Lodging: dorm
Special features: waterfront activities, ropes course, challenge course

NaCoMe
Pleasantville, TN
931-729-9723
www.nacome.org
Setting: in Sulphur Creek Valley
Lodging: dorm
Special features: hiking trails, canoeing, service project opportunities available

Penuel Ridge Retreat Center*
Ashland City, TN
615-792-3734
www.penuelridge.org
Setting: 120 acres of woods and meadows with a lake
Lodging: motel
Special features: straw bale chapel, silent retreats, two hermitages available, hiking trails

Scarritt-Bennett Center
Nashville, TN
615-340-7500
www.scarrittbennett.org
Setting: parklike grounds in urban area
Lodging: motel
Special features: labyrinth, walking distance to Music Row and Vanderbilt University

TEXAS

Briarwood Retreat Center
Argyle, TX
940-455-7002
www.briarwoodretreat.org
Setting: woods and fields
Lodging: dorm and motel
Special features: hiking trails, pool, challenge course

Camp Allen Conference and Retreat Center
Navasota, TX
936-825-7175
www.campallen.org
Setting: 950 acres in piney woods
Lodging: dorm and motel
Special features: chuckwagon trail rides, equestrian center, challenge course, massage therapy available

Lake Brownwood Christian Retreat
Brownwood, TX
325-784-5133
www.lbcr.org
Setting: on Lake Brownwood
Lodging: dorm
Special features: pool, waterfront activities, climbing wall, zip line, service project opportunities

Mo-Ranch Camps and Outdoor Ed*
Hunt, TX
830-238-4455
www.moranch.com
Setting: Texas hill country on the Guadalupe River
Lodging: dorm and motel
Special features: river swimming, trail rides, pool, ropes course, prayer tank, labyrinth

Riverbend Retreat Center
Glen Rose, TX
254-897-4011
www.riverbendretreat.org
Setting: on Brazos River
Lodging: dorm and motel
Special features: challenge course, pool, fishing, gym

UTAH

Camp UTABA
Liberty, UT
801-745-3570
www.camputaba.org
Setting: in the Wasatch Mountains with river frontage
Lodging: dorm
Special features: fishing, hiking trails, sledding

Big Canyon Ranch
Wanship, UT
435-640-5628
www.bigcanyon.org
Setting: 1,500 acres of high country meadows, wetlands, and canyons
Lodging: dorm (new in summer 2008)
Special features: new camp with numerous planned recreational opportunities, contact for current options, close to Park City ski resorts

Abbey of the Holy Trinity Retreat House
Huntsville, UT
801-745-3784
http://www.holytrinityabbey.org/retreat_house.html
Setting: on an 1,800-acre farm
Lodging: motel
Special features: Catholic retreat facility for men only

Wind Walker Guest Ranch*
Spring City, UT
435-462-0282
www.windwalker.org
Setting: dude ranch
Lodging: motel
Special features: trail rides, fishing, pool, team building activities, labyrinth, massage therapy available

VERMONT

Bethany Birches Camp
Plymouth, VT
802-672-5220
www.vtchildrenscamp.com
Setting: in the mountains with a pond
Lodging: dorm
Special features: hiking trails, near skiing

Bishop Booth Conference Center*
Burlington, VT
802-658-6233
www.dioceseofvermont.org/Orgs/BishopBooth.html
Setting: on the shores of Lake Champlain
Lodging: dorm
Special features: walking trails, waterfront activities

Gove Hill
Thetford Center, VT
802-785-4000
www.ghsm.org/govehill
Setting: 187-acre estate with views of the Green and White Mountains
Lodging: dorm
Special features: hiking trails, fishing, boating

Monastery of the Immaculate Heart of Mary*
Westfield, VT
802-744-6525
www.ihmwestfield.com
Setting: wooded
Lodging: motel
Special features: accommodations for women only, silent retreats

St. Joseph's Dwelling Place*
Ludlow, VT
802-228-4952
www.stjosephdp.com
Setting: quiet countryside
Lodging: motel
Special features: spiritual direction and massage therapy available

Weston Priory*
Weston, VT
802-824-5409
www.westonpriory.org
Setting: quiet countryside
Lodging: motel
Special features: groups prepare own meals

VIRGINIA

Camp Bethel
Fincastle, VA
540-992-2940
www.campbethelvirginia.org
Setting: in the Blue Ridge foothills
Lodging: dorm, also RV area
Special features: ropes course, challenge course, hiking trails, adjacent to Jefferson National Forest

Camp Hanover
Mechanicsville, VA
804-779-2811
www.camphanover.org
Setting: wooded
Lodging: dorm
Special features: adventure course, climbing wall, waterfront activities, pool

Makemie Woods
Barhamsville, VA
800-566-1496
www.makwoods.org
Setting: 275 wooded acres with a reservoir
Lodging: dorm, also RV area
Special features: hiking trails, boating, fishing, pool, labyrinth

Meadowkirk
Middleburg, VA
540-687-5565
www.meadowkirk.org
Setting: peaceful countryside
Lodging: motel
Special features: gardens, labyrinth, walking trails, challenge course

The Pilgrimage
202-387-6615
www.thepilgrimage.org
Setting: urban
Lodging: dorm
Special features: in the heart of Washington, DC, service project opportunities available

Roslyn Center*
Richmond, VA
800-477-6296
www.roslyncenter.org
Setting: on the James River
Lodging: motel
Special features: Stations of the Cross nature trail, pond, fitness center

WASHINGTON

Camp Arnold at Timberlake
Eatonville, WA
253-847-2511
www.tsacamparnold.org
Setting: a view of Mt. Ranier
Lodging: dorm
Special features: hiking trails, canoeing, pool, gym, challenge course

Camp Burton
Vashon Island, WA
206-463-2512
www.campburton.com
Setting: quiet, rural neighborhood with saltwater beach
Lodging: dorm
Special features: hiking, Frisbee golf, beachcombing

Huston Camp and Conference Center
Gold Bar, WA
360-793-0441
www.huston.org
Setting: on Wallace River
Lodging: dorm
Special features: hiking trails, challenge course, pool, near Wallace Falls State Park

Lakeview Retreat
Auburn, WA
888-778-CAMP
www.lakeviewretreat.org
Setting: on Five Mile Lake
Lodging: dorm
Special features: sand volleyball, waterfront activities, climbing wall

Lazy F Camp and Retreat Center
Ellensburg, WA
509-962-2780
www.lazyfcamp.org
Setting: in Manastash Canyon in Cascade Mountain foothills
Lodging: dorm, also RV area
Special features: challenge course, creek walking, snow tubing, hiking, fishing

Ocean Park Retreat Center and Camp
Ocean Park, WA
360-665-4367
www.opretreat.org
Setting: 80 acres on Long Beach Peninsula
Lodging: dorm
Special features: ocean beach, climbing wall, canoeing, hiking trails

WEST VIRGINIA

Alpine Ministries
Bradley, WV
304-877-6427
www.alpineministries.com
Setting: in the Appalachian foothills
Lodging: dorm and motel
Special features: gym, pool, climbing wall, beach, zip line, ropes course

Peterkin Camp and Conference Center
Romney, WV
304-822-4519
www.peterkin.org
Setting: 1,400 acres of woods and streams
Lodging: dorm
Special features: hiking trails, fishing, nature trail, pool

Rolling Ridge Study Retreat Community*
Harpers Ferry, WV
304-724-6653
www.rollingridge.net
Setting: on the slopes of the Blue Ridge Mountains above the Shenandoah River
Lodging: motel
Special features: hiking trails, spiritual direction available

Sandscrest Conference and Retreat Center
Wheeling, WV
304-277-3022
www.sandscrest.com
Setting: on a hilltop estate encompassing 250 acres
Lodging: dorm and motel
Special features: close to Wheeling yet quiet country atmosphere

West Virginia Institute for Spirituality*
Charleston, WV
304-345-0926
www.WVInstituteforspirituality.org
Setting: in town location near the banks of the Kanawha River
Lodging: motel
Special features: spiritual direction and massage therapy available

WISCONSIN

Camp Anokijig
Plymouth, WI
800-741-6931
www.anokijig.com
Setting: in Kettle Moraine Forest on Little Elkhart Lake
Lodging: dorm
Special features: waterfront activities, trail rides, island exploring, ropes course

Covenant Harbor
Lake Geneva, WI
262-248-3600
www.covenantharbor.org
Setting: on the shores of Lake Geneva
Lodging: dorm and motel
Special features: waterfront activities, challenge course, climbing tower, gym, near golf

Green Lake Conference Center
Green Lake, WI
920-294-3323
www.glcc.org
Setting: wooded lakefront
Lodging: dorm, hotel, cabin, campsite
Special Features: hiking trails, boat and bike rentals, rec center, fitness room, ropes course, shopping, fishing

Lake Lucerne Camp and Retreat
Neshkoro, WI
920-293-4488
www.wisconsinumc.org/lakelucerne
Setting: wooded with lake
Lodging: dorm
Special features: waterfront activities, ropes course, challenge course, hiking trails, labyrinth

Lutherdale Bible Camp
Elkhorn, WI
262-742-2352
www.lutherdale.org
Setting: in the woods on the shores of Lauderdale Lakes
Lodging: dorm
Special features: canoeing, swimming, climbing tower, challenge course

Silver Birch Ranch
White Lake, WI
715-484-2742
www.silverbirchranch.org
Setting: on the edge of the Nicolet National Forest
Lodging: dorm
Special features: beach, waterfront activities, trail rides, hiking trails, snow tubing

WYOMING

Camp Living Water
Merna, WY
307-734-1398
Setting: 90 miles south of Jackson, WY
Lodging: dorm
Special features: pool, rifle range, archery, teepees and theme housing

Camp Wyoba
Casper, WY
307-234-3088
www.wyoba.org
Setting: on Casper Mountain
Lodging: dorm
Special features: hiking, outdoor recreation fields, near North Platte River

Ring Lake Ranch*
Dubois, WY
888-458-5253
www.ringlake.org
Setting: in the Wind River Mountains
Lodging: motel
Special features: trail rides, fishing, hiking trails, just east of Yellowstone and Grand Tetons National Parks

Thomas the Apostle Center*
Cody, WY
307-587-4400
www.thomap.org
Setting: mountain view
Lodging: dorm and motel
Special features: hiking trails, labyrinth

United Methodist Circle J Ranch
Ten Sleep, WY
307-366-2241
www.circlejchristiancamp.org
Setting: 200 acres of woods, meadows, and canyons in the Big Horn Mountains
Lodging: dorm
Special features: trout fishing, hiking trails, near downhill skiing, 15 miles from Meadowlark Lake